GINTY'S GHOST

Ginty Paul, c. 1970.

For Aileen, Andrea, Ben, Bert, Boris, Britta, Claire, Cyrille, Duncan, Dylan, Etienne, Gabe, Hannah, Henry, Katherine, Katrina, Kelsey, Leslie, Mark, Max, Mike, Monika, Nathaniel, Ron, Sarah, Steffi, Stephanie, Sven, Wendy, Yvonne, and everyone who helped build my house at Ginty Creek.

CONTENTS

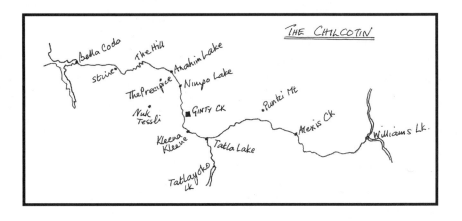

THE CHILCOTIN

Bella Coola
The Hill
Stuie
Anahim Lake
The Precipice
Nimpo Lake
Nuk Tessli
GINTY CK
Punzi Mt
Kleena Kleene
Tatla Lake
Alexis CK
Williams Lk.
Tatlayoko Lk

CHAPTER 1

GINTY CREEK

"So you bought Ginty Paul's place," said Louise Moxon with a funny little smile on her face as she filled my van at Grandma's Corner Service in Anahim Lake. News travels fast in the sparsely populated West Chilcotin.

"Did you know Ginty?" I asked.

"Oh we knew Ginty! She and her dad. They was really rich, you know. They had them candle-bras all over the place. But they lived in this tiny little shack with all their goats and chickens. We was invited in to tea once. The floor was covered in goat poop and the chickens walked around on the table pecking at whatever food was on there. So we said no.

"I've survived Fred Ingerbritsen's coffee but I didn't think I could survive chicken-shit tea."

I have a picture in my head of a woman on the heavy side, swathed in a mud-coloured coat tied at the waist with a piece of binder twine. Short, frizzy hair in that indeterminate stage between brown and grey capped a heavy, unsmiling face. Our time together was brief so my memory of her may not be very accurate. She can't have been too far into her sixties and she knew she was dying then. She was trying to find a home for a dog. I had been looking for one and a mutual friend had put us in touch, but by the time we connected I had already got what I needed so could not help her. Over the next twenty years I all but forgot about her, although her name cropped up once in a while, always infused with the aura of A Character. I had no idea, on that long-ago summer's day, that she was disbanding a large menagerie of goats, chickens, pigs, cows and horses as well as trying to farm out several dogs. I never in my wildest dreams imagined that I would eventually take over the property that she had shaped with her philosophies, eccentricities and hopes.

Extract from the Last Will and Testament of Nedra Jane Paul, who died in 1990 at the age of seventy.

```
To deliver my sapphire and two (2) diamond rings
to M——, sister of Rear Admiral C—— of Ottawa,
Ontario, for her own use absolutely;

    To deliver to J—— of Victoria, BC, Mrs. Long's
dishes, presently in his possession, for his own use
absolutely; I declare my intention that if a Northern
University comes into existence in the Province of
British Columbia that the dishes be given to the uni-
versity to be known as the Videt Long Collection

    To transfer my property at Kleena Kleene, British
Columbia, known and described as Lot A, Plan B6828,
District Lot 488, Range 3, containing 43 acres more
or less, and District Lot 1688, Range 3, containing
40 acres more or less, to the Department of Indian
and Northern Affairs, Government of Canada, and I
declare that it is my intention that the said prop-
erty be used and developed as a nature park for the
```

benefit of the Indian Bands situated in the West
Chilcotin area of British Columbia;

Ginty had, it seemed, a very strong and opinionated personality. Although she had white friends outside the area, notably Hilda and Phil Thomas of Vancouver to whom she wrote most of the letters whose extracts appear in this book, in the Chilcotin she appeared to dislike all white people on principle and just as unreservedly loved anyone who was aboriginal. Her two other properties (she owned real estate on Hornby Island off the west coast of Canada, as well as acreage near Williams Lake) were willed to individuals, but she had a special wish for her Chilcotin dream. During the 1980s, the Alkali Lake First Nations band south of Williams Lake received a lot of publicity documenting their efforts to go dry. Ginty wanted to create a haven for those needing to recover from addiction. Her failing health got in the way of her plans and she left the property to the Department of Indian and Northern Affairs. The people at Alkali Lake were not even aware of their rights to this property until they got a bill for taxes. They felt it was too far away for them to make much use of, and a rancher who lived across the river from Ginty bought it from them. He ripped down the cabins, which he maintained were in a very poor state, and used the place as an overspill for his cows.

I have lived in the West Chilcotin for over thirty years, most of the time far from neighbours or a road. I built all my own cabins, some of them without any help at all. Access to these was by a two- to four-day hike or a twenty-minute flight in a small chartered float plane. In 1988, I started the Nuk Tessli Alpine Experience, a fly-in, high-altitude ecotourism resort. I have written a number of books about these adventures so will leave them out of this story.

A wonderful life, but it was very much a hand-to-mouth

existence, and over the years I had accumulated Stuff. I was desperate for an outside place to put it in. It would have been ridiculous to fly all my possessions into the wilderness and back out again when I needed them. Town clothes, unsold artwork, large ceramics, countless books, twenty years' worth of income tax receipts. I also needed a place to stay between visits outside to earn money—tree planting and lecture tours mostly—and going back home into the mountains. The weather and ice conditions were not always suitable for travel either in the air or on land. I might have to wait weeks in winter, for instance, before a local pilot could be found who would put skis on his plane. Even if I could make the journey on foot—and I sometimes did, often encountering terrible conditions at that time of year—I still needed the plane to fly in my supplies.

My first outside billet was at a resort at Nimpo Lake, not far from the charter air company's base. Then I acquired a ramshackle cabin a few kilometres away. The landlady was welcoming and the rent was very cheap, but I did not like being there—it was too close to neighbours whose philosophies were money, playing in the wilderness with machines, and maintaining the TV tower. They kept yard lights on at night to scare away the dark. I hated the whine of snow machines on the frozen lake in winter.

In 2006 my mother died and I inherited some money. Now I was rich. Well, not that rich, but compared to a long life of scrambling to make ends meet I had a fortune. There was nothing else I wanted to spend it on except property. (And maybe a vehicle newer than my twenty-year-old Suburban.) A friend phoned me. Did I know Ginty Paul's place was for sale?

I was only marginally interested. I wasn't even all that sure where it was except that it was not where I wanted to be. I had my heart set on the Tatlayoko Valley (pronounced Tat-li-ko to those in the know). The road to it stretches forty kilometres south of Tatla Lake in the central Chilcotin, down into the mountains, ending at Tatlayoko Lake (Tat-li-ko Lake). Good friends already lived down there; the scenery was fabulous, and because of the low elevation the climate was kind—it would be possible to grow my own food, something I had never been able to do at Nuk Tessli. I visited several properties for sale down there, but figured I might as well check out Ginty's before I made a decision.

Ken Jansen and his wife, Leslie Lamb, had lived on their forty hectares across the river from Ginty for as long as I had been in the Chilcotin. They were selling out so they could retire to Saskatchewan. I had known Leslie slightly for a very long time, as one does in this vast and little-populated area, but had never met Ken or been to their home. Their ranch had been nicely developed into hayfields and boasted an octagonal log house that Ken and Leslie had built, but even if it had appealed to me, which it didn't (surrounded by mountains and backing onto a wild river, with no view of either), I could never have afforded it. Ginty's place was mostly swamp and a wetland haven for birds, which suited my naturalist temperament. A disadvantage was that it had no habitable dwelling; the advantage was that it fell within my price range.

It was a lovely sunny day in June when Ken and I drove the soft silt road through the scrubby lodgepole pine forest that covers most of this land. Although the properties were next door to each other, there was no easy way to get across the river. Four-legged animals could ford it when the water was low, but for us it was a ten-kilometre drive around. "This was originally the telegraph road," Ken told me as we turned off Highway 20. "Mr. Paul, Ginty's father, was a telegraph operator for many years. He lived at the old Puntzi air base. This place was surveyed a long time ago but no one took it up until he came along. It's actually not a bad little place." (Ken, I reminded myself, was trying to sell it.)

The property comprised two titles. We went to the upper one first. Ginty had acquired it solely for the water rights so she could use the creek that ran through it to irrigate the lower place. We could not drive to it directly, but a bush road took us past a partially overgrown clearing where a small sawmill had once operated—a couple of almost invisible piles of rotten bark were the only signs of it now—and from there it was a short walk to the ankle-snagging strands of a fallen barbed wire fence. Pushing through the lodgepole pines, soopollalie bushes and windfalls, we came to a large pond. It was surrounded by wetlands of scrubby willows, tussocky sedges and dwarf birch. There was a beaver house in the middle of the pond, like the pupil in the shining iris of an eye. The pond looked perfectly natural but I was to find out later that it was completely man-, or rather woman-, made. Beyond was a mature stand of trees on a small mound, and backing that was a view of the granitic folds of the Coast Range, quite thickly covered with June snow. They were fronted by an old, dark volcanic core that stuck out sideways. "They call that one Finger Peak," said Ken, grinning.

We backtracked, took another fork in the road and came to a thin pole gate whose hinge post sat in an old truck-wheel hub. The gate had been made well and still swung easily. It was fastened with a logging chain looped over the end post of a sturdy Russell fence that ran from either side. The farm road had been softened by a thin growth of grass in the middle, and it now travelled through a stand of strong, young conifers maybe twenty years old. It was only later that I realized Ginty must have logged the hell out of the place at one time. Rotten stumps, logs and brush piles were all still lying there, mercifully hidden under the new growth. There had been no attempt to push the piles together and burn them. Ginty must have figured that she was going to grow grass but, even with the great network of irrigation ditches she had constructed, these silty dunes were far too dry. The place must have looked a terrible mess when it was first logged. Aesthetics, it appeared, were not Ginty's thing.

The farm road ended among a scattering of old barns and corrals. Rail fences drooped; other fences had been constructed with slabs, offcuts from the sawmill presumably, placed vertically and interwoven with telegraph wire. The telegraph line had originally gone right through the property and there were kilometres of this wire spider-webbing all over the place. Most of the supporting posts for these fences had rotted and the woven panels flopped first one way and then the other. The tired-looking buildings were silvered with age on the shady side and oxidized to a rich burnt sienna where they faced the sun.

The road was suddenly joined by hydro poles and wires that accompanied us to just past the last barn. They had marched across a field from a junction on Ken's side of the river. There were six poles all told on Ginty's property; they marked the very end of the power line from Williams Lake, 250 kilometres away. I used to know the people who lived at Halfway Ranch, a few kilometres east. They complained that they could use only one appliance at a time—plug in the kettle and the toaster at the same time and the system would blow. Ginty's power must have been very minimal. Presumably the service is better now; Ken was a carpenter as well as a rancher and he had a good shop with lots of power tools. A phone line was strung underneath the hydro wire. Both services on my side of the river had long been disconnected.

Past the last barn was a building unlike anything else on the place. It was quite the ugliest structure I have ever seen. It was a massive box, sheathed in thin, bottom-grade plywood, three stories high with a single sloping steel roof. The walls were dotted with poky window holes. "This was going to be the lodge for the Alkali Lake Band," Ken explained. "Ginty was building it as a place to help the people on their path to sobriety. She never got it finished."

Inside, it was even more amazing. There was a full concrete basement, now cluttered with garbage and filth. The outer walls, inside the sheath of plywood, and the floor, had been made of rough-cut two-by-threes (a very odd size) nailed side by side to form a solid unshakable mass. There were literally tons of timber—and nails—in that building. The structure had been divided into several rooms with all the framing in place but with no coverings on the studwork so it looked like a forest of vertical two-by-fours. However, almost all of it was useless. The building itself was far too big and ugly for me to want to try and live in it, and in any case it had no view. I couldn't even consider walling off a section and camping in there while I built a cabin. This was because of the smell. Even before we stepped inside, the aroma was overpowering. Packrats. Bushy-tailed woodrats, if you want to be scientific. The floor was black with droppings, most of them so dry they rolled like ball bearings beneath our boots. Many of the walls had been insulated with yellow fibreglass between the plywood and the two-by-threes, and oh what a mess that was where it had been ripped down and soiled. A huge pile of opened but unused batts was covered with excrement like black snow. Massive nests—two metres across and built of plastic pieces, paper garbage and more fibreglass—were perched on bits of strapping that had been laid over ceiling joists, waiting for boards that had never been placed.

The name "packrat" refers to the predilection of these creatures to hoard small shiny things such as nails, spoons, trinkets—anything they can carry. Who knows what treasures were hidden in these piles? It would be an interesting experiment to take the nests apart, although one would need a hazard suit as protection from the fibreglass and the filth. Most of the smell did not come from the floor or the nests, however. All the overhead timbers were stained with dark, gluey-looking secretions. Some of this was urine, but a lot was the discharge from the males' scent glands. These organs are situated on the animals' stomachs and are used to delineate territories. The building must have been a godsend to the packrats: big enough for several individuals, lots of shelving for nests, and with a good, solid roof. It was a veritable "Packrat Palace."

Ken and I might have been wrinkling our noses but my two dogs, Raffi and Bucky (both SPCA specials), thought it was heaven. They were climbing the walls with excitement. There were glimpses of wild whiskers, beady eyes and furry tails as the resident animals leapt to safer hiding places. "I didn't know what to do with it," said Ken. "We cleared up all kinds of junk when we

The Packrat Palace.

took over. We fetched truckloads to the dump. But this . . ." He shrugged helplessly. There was enough good, sound timber in the building to erect a whole terrace of houses but, even if it had been worthwhile to attempt to free the timbers from the hidden embrace of those thousands of nails, it would have been impossible to get rid of the smell.

We walked back toward the vehicle and then squeezed past a warped slab gate onto a silty mound. Ken, good salesman that he was, had left the best until last. Sound swelled, and suddenly the river was below us. Pregnant with runoff, it rushed blue and sparkling over stones between wide gravel bars. Above the fringe of cottonwoods and aspens, rich in their new summer green, were the shining snow-capped mountains.

I already had a personal history with this river. It had its headwaters not far from my mountain resort, Nuk Tessli, and it ended its short and tumultuous ride a few kilometres downstream from where we stood. There, it emptied into the Klinaklini River (for some reason, the river and the almost non-existent settlement of Kleena Kleene have ended up with different spellings), which plunged past Finger Peak and down a wild gorge to the coast. I had camped by the headquarters of the river one summer, by a dramatically placed small lake near a glacier, and on another occasion had been diverted down it by a blizzard when I was trying to snowshoe from Nuk Tessli to Nimpo Lake in November. This wild piece of water seemed like an old friend.

I got permission from Ken to camp overnight on the knoll overlooking the river. We went back to his house so that I could pick up my vehicle. I had a small frisson of excitement as I pulled the logging chain off the gatepost. Would this place actually be mine? The idea of owning land was a new one for me. I had never possessed anything at all worth money before.

I did some more exploring: I ripped my pant leg on a fallen barbed wire fence and I found a humungous rhubarb patch in the terraced remains of what must have been an extensive garden below the Packrat Palace. The glorious weather persisted, a little breezy, a little cool, but lots of sun. The river sang and the aspens rattled and chattered their leafy summer conversations. In the evening the wind died, the mountains grew soft and grey against a lemon sky, and the morning sun painted them a deep pink.

My brother in England was handling my mother's estate. I sent him an email: How soon can you send the money?

CHAPTER 2

THE INSIDE-OUT HOUSE

(It should be noted that the older First Nations people often do not discriminate between the pronouns "he" and "she." Elaine lives across the river, across a field, and across the road from Ginty's place.)

I was born Bella Coola. I been here looong time: fifty years. Used to be a big trail across the river from here. Used to go all the time to hunt and trap. His [Ginty's] *dad was there loooooong time alone. Went to visit him lots. He had no animals, only dogs. When Ginty came he* [Ginty] *got lots goats, chickens and pigs. Old Paul went up that mountain. Walked all way there and back in one day. Didn't have no gun or nothing. He put something up there. A stick or something.*

Old Paul he don't ride a horse much. During war time he built a cabin way back in the bush. I was riding horse way over there, hunting. Saw small cabin with small logs this big. [Holds her hands round an imaginary fifteen-centimetre log.] *Reeeally low, too. It falling down. I get off horse and look at it. Old jar of matches inside. Not been there very long*

*the way it looked. I was wondering who lived there. But it
was Old Paul. Made it in 1942.*

—Elaine Dester

*Her father was a charming man. He had this real English
accent. I was working at the weather office in Williams Lake
when I was seventeen and he would phone the weather in
from Puntzi every day. Us girls would all go gaga over his
voice.*

—Libby Abbott

Two days after I camped on the knoll above the river, I broke my leg. I had been away from my ecotourism resort for two weeks, not only looking for property, but also shopping for the next three months in the mountains. When that chore was out of the way I treated myself by staying with friends for a couple of nights before heading back home. All the time I had been travelling, my dogs were chained or lead-walked as they could not be trusted with livestock or cats. My friend's place had a newly planted garden and cows nearby so the dogs were still restricted and by this stage feeling somewhat antsy. Early on what was supposed to be my last morning there, I kept them on the lead until I was away from the house. Most of the isolated valley in which my friends lived was a ranch. At the edge of the hayfields, well out of sight of the cows, I let the most reliable dog loose. He tore around in ecstatic circles. At the precise moment that I was suspended in mid-air while hopping over an irrigation ditch, the dog cannoned into my leg. I was able to walk back to the house, but after I had sat down for an hour or two, I couldn't move.

It was a three-and-a-half-hour drive down to the nearest X-ray machine at Bella Coola. A bit of bone was chipped off the inside of the top end of my tibia. It wasn't a serious break as far as broken legs go, but I would have to be on crutches for three months. Three months! How on earth was I going to run an ecotourism hiking business? Fortunately it was a couple of weeks before haying would start, so the caretaker on the ranch, who had been up at Nuk Tessli before, could come into the mountains with me right away. I was also able to get some excellent help later in the form of a young man for a guide, and a bunch of wwoofers.

Wwoof stands for Willing Workers On Organic Farms. It is one of several world-wide organizations putting (mostly, but not all) young people in touch with hosts who require strong backs and energy but cannot pay a wage. The hosts are expected to feed and house their charges and provide them with a learning experience. I have had these doughty volunteers for several years now; the odd one doesn't work out for me but most have been wonderful. I had a total of eleven throughout the summer at Nuk Tessli. They helped clean and guide and bring in a year's supply of firewood. When I was ready to leave the mountains close to the end of September, I was able to persuade the last two to return to Ginty Creek with me. Max and Steffi, both from Germany although they had never met before they came to Nuk Tessli, were able to spare me five more days.

Since I had last seen Ginty's property, the summer had burgeoned and blossomed and gone. The green grass of June, never lush, had bleached to pale straw. The deciduous trees flanking the river were speckled with gold. The stream was a shadow of its June self, and it now chattered in sparkling, sky-blue threads between wide gravel bars.

There was no habitable building on the property and I needed a place to live in a hurry. Over the years I had built four cabins in the mountains, largely single-handedly, with materials extracted from the bush. With no road or heavy machinery to bring the logs home, they had to be dragged with ropes and a come-along; many of the boards and two-by-fours were made excruciatingly slowly with a chainsaw lumber mill and packed to the site one by one, by canoe, toboggan and backpack, and in my arms. Each building had taken two years to complete. It wasn't the construction that took the time, but finding, preparing and hauling the components.

Here, I did not have the luxury of time. In six weeks I would have to leave for a two-month book tour to promote my latest publication, *Wildfire in the Wilderness*. By the time that was over, it would be the middle of December. Winter with its short days, snow and cold would be in full force. I had to have a usable shelter before the book tour started.

I wanted eventually to live on the upper property, but with no road access I would have to shelve that idea for the present. I chose a building site overlooking the river, beside the knoll on which I had camped. I remembered the winds of summer, and decided to use a site a little lower, where I would have shelter from a belt of trees. As with all my cabin locations, the orientation to the sun was paramount. I am an early riser and love to watch the light come into the world. A dwelling warmed by morning sun needs much less firewood, too.

Also, I liked the view better than from the knoll. Finger Peak and its companions were buried in trees, but I could look down-river to more distant peaks in the south. A small flood plain below my chosen site showed evidence of the river's annual flood aggression in the form of slippages along the bank, but I figured it would take a while to get eaten away, and the base of a silt mound to one side, probably an old esker, would protect me for a number of years from the worst of the water's force. Anyway, who knows, the river might not stay in its current channels—it had a reputation of moving about the valley.

I made arrangements with a local B&B to rent a cabin cheaply from them for the next three months. It was still quite hot during the day but already freezing hard at nights. We would have no running water—the plumbing had already been cut off for the winter—and we would have to find our own wood for the cookstove and heater, but the cabin was cheap. The commuting time to the cabin—about half an hour each way—was frustrating, but Kleena Kleene is a very scattered community and there was simply no closer building available.

I was no longer on crutches but still wore a leg brace. It meant I was not as mobile as I would prefer and I had to lift heavy items with care. Climbing ladders proved to be quite difficult, as my balance seemed to have been affected. I needed to make really good use of Max and Steffi's short time with me.

First we organized the site. It looked quite flat until we made a level out of the kind of tubing you get for siphoning beer and wine and found that a lot of dirt had to be moved. We had filled the level with water, and the next morning it was frozen stiff. We had to lie it on a bank in the sun and let it thaw before we could use it again. Every evening after that we hung it in a tree to drain. It was a nuisance as we didn't have an easy way of filling it. We measured angles and diagonals and eventually decided where the corners should go.

The very morning after we had cleared the sod, the newly exposed silvery silt was completely covered with a printed lace network of little hand-like paw prints. Packrats! I knew that these little critters travelled, but the Packrat Palace was some distance away, out of sight, and for them to come so far and discover us so soon was amazing. And so many of them! Either there had been an army of these things galloping around, or there had been one hell of a party.

While Max and Steffi were shovelling and wheelbarrowing,

I peg-legged around the Packrat Palace and other old buildings to see if there was anything usable that I could scrounge. Buried under a pile of warped and rotting boards, which had once been a structure whose function I could only guess at, were several massive concrete blocks. In an area where rocks were hard to find, these would make great foundations. Poor Steffi. I thought she was going to collapse under her share of the weight, but those wonderful wwoofers managed to wriggle the concrete blocks under a snake fence and heave them into the back of my old Suburban.

Back at the site, we dumped them off and fiddled around with the level and diagonals for what seemed like ages until the corners were all the same height and square. Max was good with a chainsaw and he already had cabin-building experience, which was a real bonus, so he cut down three or four trees around the site and

Steffi and Max lifting scrounged concrete blocks for the foundations.

Steffi peeled them. These would be our foundation logs. The debris piled up around us. Unlike Ginty, I would eventually clean it up, but it would have to stay there for now until I had time to deal with it.

It took four precious days to organize the foundations, set in the two-by-six joists and lay on a plywood floor. Our final day together saw the walls raised. In the bush, with no heavy machinery to lift or haul logs, it had taken me months to erect the walls of each cabin, but because I could drive to the door here, I was able to buy what was basically a shed in kit form. The walls were two-by-six tongue and groove with machine-made notches at the corners. The biggest shed the manufacturer made was twenty feet long. I asked for timbers that would give me twenty- by sixteen-foot walls. They would not be strong enough to support a roof by themselves but I could make the structure that would frame the insulation into load-bearing supports. At first I planned to use the tongue and groove as the outside walls, but when I saw them I realized they would make an attractive interior, so we built the inside of the house first. The boards, already notched, went up like a Lego set. I now had a box with no door, windows or roof. In five days, Max and Steffi had achieved miracles.

The trees were going out in a blaze of colour. We had been amazed at the red and gold against the rich deep blue of the sky. Daylight moons hung in the heavens. After Steffi and Max had gone, the weather grew cool and dull and the colours began to fade. I was now to be on my own for a couple of weeks. Lifting and climbing was still difficult, and I used the time to collect materials. What luxury to be able to drive or drag them to the site with my Suburban.

The Packrat Palace had a covered upper balcony above the entryway. On this were piles of lumber that had not been too badly soiled. Most of these were rough-cut three-by-threes. There was a considerable variation in their thickness, but they would be perfect to make the main supports along the walls. A good number were warped but I found a lot that I could use. I did not realize how hard they had grown with age until we started to put them together; my future helpers and I bent many a nail trying to drive them in. I also hunted around in the forest along the telegraph road for ceiling joists and rafters. The pine bark beetle that had so devastated the landscape further west was beginning to creep into this country, and in certain areas there were pockets of dead trees, some of them close enough to the road to be within my reach. I was finding the leg brace too cumbersome when climbing up steep banks and stepping over windfalls so I took the darn thing off and never suffered for it, but I was still frustrated at how much of an effort the simplest bit of walking seemed to take.

The pine bark beetle is long gone by the time the needles of an infected tree turn brown. During the attack the tree has tried to defend itself by oozing sap. Consequently, recently killed trees are rich with resin. Not what you really want for building purposes, but it takes several years for the timber to dry properly and I did not have the luxury of being able to wait, so I whacked down whatever I could haul to the road. I wanted three long logs for the roof but none of the rest needed to be over five metres in length. The forest was short—this is a fairly dry climate—and also much distorted by mistletoe, so it was hard to find suitable trees. Once down and dragged home, they had to be peeled. On these beetle-kills, the bark was well and truly glued on by all that resin, and peeling was a terrible job. I sat on the ground beside each log, which was propped up on firewood rounds, in the freezing, often foggy, mornings and hacked away. One log slipped: I leaned against it to support it, and there was a sudden twinge followed by a very sharp pain in my left rib cage. Certain types of movement after that were extremely painful. I was sure I had cracked a rib. Before I had the chipped knee I had never broken a bone in my life. Were my bones beginning to fall apart? It would be a three-hour drive to the nearest X-ray machine; I had no desire to waste all that time. They wouldn't do anything for a cracked rib anyway. I would have to put up with the pain. I took to wrapping my chest in duct tape, over my clothes, so that I could work.

A couple of days later, I went to fetch a trailer I had bought from a local logger. He and his wife and four kids used to live in it while they travelled around the ranches and did fencing jobs. They had been hired by Ken-across-the-river to make the snake fence that surrounded most of Ginty's property. The trailer was now north of Anahim Lake, about two hours' drive away.

Sam Whitefish hauled it for me. Generally a cheerful soul, Sam ran a garage and tow service out of Anahim Lake. He was part First Nations with a dark skin and black curly hair but he was not local. He came from Alberta I think. Sam was a rough and ready mechanic whose favourite tool was a sledgehammer, but he could fix anything and he would work any hour of the day or night if someone was stuck. Before the Suburban I now possessed, I had owned another, a white one. I had left it for Sam to sell for me while I was in the mountains for the summer. It was not insured and the brakes were dodgy. Sam lent it to someone else to drive into Williams Lake. There was a road check. The Suburban was confiscated. Sam owed me.

It was a pretty day, sharp but with a mix of sun and cloud and strong shadows over the Itchas. The Coast Range comprises granite-fold mountains, but the Chilcotin and the mountains to the north of Anahim Lake are all volcanic. Below these peaks the land is fairly flat, and the trailer was on a ranch there. Sam drove like he was on the freeway. Every bump in the rough road jerked at my sore ribs. The trailer had two flat tires, but Sam was able to borrow an air compressor from the ranch shop and pump them up. I wondered if they would survive the journey, but they still held air by the time we reached Ginty Creek. The trailer was moved onto a grassy field beside the river. "There," said Sam, unhooking it. "Now we're quits." Poor man, he was already on kidney dialysis, for which he had to drive into Williams Lake every week, and he died a year later.

The trailer had all mod cons, including a little bathroom, but there was nothing to hook the plumbing up to. It had a propane cooker—the oven and one of the burners did not work but the rest were fine—and a propane heater. The heater was useless. It needed electricity to run the fan. I had hoped to be able to use the trailer right away but our fall was much colder than usual and, without a woodstove to warm it, it would have been too uncomfortable to live in. It would be useful in the future when the climate was kinder, but for now I would have to stay in the B&B.

Accumulated building materials.

The logs hauled and peeled, I examined the fences for rails that still had life in them. The pile of building materials was growing. This rough stuff was fine for the structure, but for the ceiling and some of the interior work I wanted something nicer and contacted Cameron Linde near Williams Lake, who had supplied batches of lumber for my other cabins in the mountains. I had visited his yard when I had taken the wwoofers to the bus at Williams Lake, but I did not have a suitable vehicle to haul the lumber myself. As he had done before, Cameron very kindly drove an extra thirty kilometres out of his way into Williams Lake to pick up bales of insulation and sheets of roofing metal that I had ordered. He delivered these, and now the space around the cabin was beginning to look like a builder's yard. All of this was waiting when Dylan arrived.

Dylan was the man I had managed to acquire as a guide to fill in for me during the summer at Nuk Tessli. I had not met him before I broke my leg, but he turned out to be a real find. He'd

Dylan and myself on the roof structure.

had a bit of chainsaw experience and was generally handy, as most people growing up in the bush are; as he had a week or two to spare I was able to persuade him to come to Ginty Creek and help. At Nuk Tessli he had used the chainsaw to cut firewood but, confined by my crutches to the cabin, I had never seen him work with it. He brought a chainsaw with him, one that was bigger than mine, and when I picked it up to rip a slab off a ceiling joist I had to think again about his chainsaw expertise. Dylan's saw was so blunt I could not imagine how anyone could work with it. But that is a man for you—strength is everything. And strength was one of Dylan's great attributes. He was six foot four and could lift one of the heavy ceiling joists up into the air by himself and swing it into place. A literal human crane. One time he dropped a log while trying to manoeuvre it. "Oops," he said. "How did that happen? Must be Ginty's Ghost." And the title of this book was born.

Once the joists were on, we nailed a few boards onto them so we had something to stand on while we raised the roof logs. I was

Me hauling up my end of the ridgepole.

still finding it difficult to balance; the broken leg was to all intents and purposes recovered, but my brain patterns needed to be re-educated. I could not walk on narrow boards with the gaping hole below as I had done with every building before that—I had to shuffle on my bum. The plate logs, the ones that would go on top of the walls, were first. Then we had to build platforms at either end of the building so we could raise the ridgepole. The ropes and skids lifted the log to within the last few inches. This was the bit I had always found difficult when working alone. Dylan simply nudged the pole into place with his arms.

Next came the first lot of rafters and some of the strapping, which we placed at the river end of the building. The strapping was rescued from the Packrat Palace: it was directly under the roof and looked clean but on sunny days, in the attic of the cabin, I can still smell the aroma. It was from the river that the strongest winds would blow. Erecting the gable end and putting the first pieces of metal on would give us shelter while we worked on the rest of the roof, but there was another reason why I wanted that end of the building to be weatherproof. I wanted to hook up the internet.

There was a phone line on the property, hung underneath the two hydro cables, but it hadn't been connected for years and was going to take months to be re-established. Even if I had been able to use it, trying to do internet on it would be virtually impossible. It was too far from a major centre, and the line did not hold enough juice.

The only way to do email at that time was occasionally to go up to the house at the B&B and borrow their internet—which was on their phone line, so therefore desperately slow and not at all convenient for either the owner of the B&B or myself. The fall book tour was looming and it was important to keep in touch with the publisher and the organizers of the various venues. There was a phone in a booth on Highway 20 not far from the B&B, and some mornings would see me standing in it trying to contact people. But a lot of the folks I wanted to talk to did not get into their office until many hours after sunrise. The days were getting shorter and I wanted to work on the cabin every moment while there was light. It was nearly an hour's round trip and a big waste of time to drive to the booth in the middle of the day, especially if there was no live person at the other end of the wire.

I was familiar with satellite internet, as that was what I had used in the mountains for the last three years. The company from Williams Lake would set it up at Ginty Creek easily enough, but they came out to the Chilcotin only three or four times a year. If I wanted them on a different date, it would cost an extra $300 for travel time. The company was due to make a trip out west the day after I wanted to leave for my book tour. If I didn't get them then, I would have to pay the extra or do without until March.

Satellite internet was not going to work without a source of power. In the mountains I used a small photovoltaic system. Here, hydro poles and wires swooped close to the door—or at least, to where the door was going to be. So I phoned BC Hydro (standing in the freezing booth while listening to tapes and being put on hold . . .) the upshot of which was that they sent a man out to give me a quote. He was a caricature of bureaucracy. Podgy, officious, pedantic. There was a pole quite close to the cabin, but no, it was not grounded so could not be used. Even though the distance was not great, I would have to have another pole put in and have a certified electrician do the wiring. The man was one of those males who assume all women are stupid—I don't run into too many of those any more, but they are still around—and his attitude was that I was an idiot wasting his time. (But no matter how many idiots he talked to, he would still get paid, wouldn't he?) He snappily said he could put me in touch with a private company who would erect a pole—finding the electrician would be up to me. I knew full well that a pole would cost upward of $1,500 by the time it was installed. I wasted more precious time at the phone booth: no electrician would drive the three hours out of Williams Lake to do any work this year. If I was lucky, I might get one in April. Total costs, including the pole, hookup and electrician's time, would amount to around $6,000.

I might have paid the money, but I could not afford to wait. I wanted power now. I phoned an alternative energy supplier and enquired about his photovoltaic equipment. Sure—he could have what I needed out there in forty-eight hours. A 100-watt panel and four deep cycle batteries plus all the gizmos would cost $3,000. Such a small solar power system had its limitations—no washing machine or freezer, no plugging in the vehicle when it was cold, and no power at all if we had a long dull spell when the days were short—but I was used to that, and I planned to move up to the other property eventually. A portable solar system seemed the way to go as I would be able to move it up there with me.

It was about then that two young women arrived. Stephanie and Katherine, both Canadian, had wwoofed for me at Nuk Tessli two years previously. They had spent the intervening time teaching with the Voluntary Service Overseas in a small town called Tumu in the north of Ghana. They had finished their tour by cycling through the Sahara to Spain.

While in Tumu, they at first had to travel by bus for seven hours to reach an internet connection, but we kept in touch and I asked them if they would be interested in helping me build the cabin and maybe dogsitting for me while I went on the book tour. "Sounds great!" Katherine wrote back enthusiastically. "It's plus 40°C here. We can't wait to be cold!"

It was pretty chilly the morning they started work—about -15°C with a white hoarfrost covering everything. "You want a job to get you warm?" I asked. At Katherine's nod, I handed her a shovel. "We need an outhouse hole . . ."

Katherine was the tough one. Give her a task and she would go at it like a terrier with a rat. Stephanie was fine boned and less strong, but she had the skill with tools. She had helped her dad on various carpentry projects; between them the two women made a great team.

We had about ten days together before I had to leave. Dylan was still around for a few more days as well. The roof was first and we covered it as far as the edge of the living space. The porch would have to wait, but the shed kit had come complete with a heavy army tarp and this we strung over the ridge pole and plate logs, making a saggy cover where the porch was going to be. Bits of snow fell. A barrel heater stove had been installed while we were doing the roof. At least we had somewhere warm to eat

Stephanie and Katherine.

lunch, but there were still no windows in the walls and it was very dark inside.

We pulled down one of the barns. The women had stripped off the siding but I wanted the rafters and strapping for the porch. I would not be able to tackle that part of the building until spring, but snow would make collecting this material very difficult. If I had it to hand, I could start work much earlier the following year. It was worth taking the time to harvest the material now. We loosened side pieces, rigged up a come-along and winched the whole thing down. The women wrenched out the nails and hauled the lumber home.

Everything took so much longer than we expected. There were always other things we had to do. I went to Nimpo and Anahim periodically for mail and food. The fastest possible trip there and back was three hours. Because of the timing of the mail truck, which came three times a week, the post office was open only during the middle of the day so it broke badly into my working time.

We needed firewood. Not just for the cabin at the B&B, but also for at least a good portion of the winter at Ginty Creek. I bucked up a few trees and fence rails. The couple at the B&B came round for a few hours one day and helped with that. The women built a small woodshed. In the concrete basement of the Packrat Palace were a couple of pieces of half-rotten plywood we could use for a roof.

Then, keeping my fingers crossed, I cut a hole for the window overlooking the river. I have always had the feeling, when I slice through a cabin wall with a chainsaw, that the whole building will fall apart. But of course it never does. Light poured in. So did the wind. The view was of snow-encrusted gravel bars with the thin dark thread of the river between them, the distant mountains now solidly white behind them. The sky was dull; the cottonwoods stretched naked bony fingers against it.

The cabin at the B&B was not much warmer. Up long before anyone else, as is my habit, I would light the fire in the cookstove and huddle beside it, feet in the open oven, while I ate, kneaded bread dough and read. Hours later, when the others got up, the kitchen would be warm. We would leave for work in the half-light. By the time we returned at dusk, water would be frozen on the counter.

Bay windows are monstrously fiddly things. They take an enormous amount of time. It is not the size of a cabin that dictates how long building it takes, but the number of corners. Bay windows have four more—and there are all those funny angles to deal with as well. I ended up miscalculating a window size and had to adapt in a hurry. All kinds of other bits went wrong—Ginty's Ghost was beside us all the way. There is, however, something very special

Trying out the bed in the bay window.

about sitting or sleeping surrounded by glass and in such close proximity to the outside world; this would be the second time I would go through all these headaches, but the rewards would be worth it.

The guy who was supposed to be providing the solar power equipment was delayed. "It will be another week," he insisted as I stood on a lump of ice on the floor of the phone booth, wondering where he had got to. I told him that it was imperative we have it by the time the internet guys came but I could hear the shrugging shoulders over the phone. He had another job in the area that was much more important (i.e., worth more money) than mine. He was not going to make two trips. When he eventually did deliver it, he had no time to install it. He left scant instructions. Dylan was supposed to be gone by then but he stayed the extra day to help and we figured it out between us.

The women were starting the wall insulation, putting it between the three-by-three uprights on the outside of the building. First vapour barrier, then formaldehyde-free rockwool followed by an outer covering of tarpaper and hardware cloth (which is not a cloth at all, but a fine wire mesh used on pet cages). This last would keep the critters out until the siding from the barn could be put on.

The satellite internet guys arrived three days earlier than they originally planned, and only a single day after the power system had been installed. Talk about timing. But oh, how wonderful to have the internet. I had possessed it for only three years in the mountains, but now I could not imagine life without it.

Both of the satellite internet guys were huge—well over 150 kilograms each. I was fascinated by the stomach of the one fixing the dish onto the gable end of the cabin. His shirt and jacket had pulled away from his pants; looking up at him as he stood on the ladder I got a great view of an enormous bare belly bulging over

The office.

his waistband. The man who had flown into Nuk Tessli to install the satellite internet there was overweight, too. "What's with you guys?" I asked. "Is it a prerequisite for the job?" "Yes," they replied. "It's an Accident Compensation thing. Keeps us from getting blown off the ladder."

Two days to go before I had to leave for the book tour. I cut a hole and installed another window. On my last day I built a door. I constructed the same homemade wooden sliding bolt I had used on my other cabins in the mountains but for some reason the darn thing just would not work. Things stuck and split, and the more frantic I got, the more problems occurred. I cobbled it together after a fashion as the light was beginning to go. It would have to do. The two women would now be on their own. As I left in the dark the following morning, snow was falling steadily; I drove through unploughed roads twenty centimetres deep for almost the whole way to Williams Lake.

CHAPTER 3

STEPHANIE AND 'KATHERINE'S STORY

K K Feb. 15

I've really enjoyed my farming so far. Kind of handy
to have some land and an income of sorts. From now on
I hope to spend a fair amount developing this place.
Had about a mile of irrigation/drainage ditches dug
plus water line, pumps etc. into the cabin. I won't
be able to turn on the cold tap until I get the place
wired--but a cold tap and a drain will be a marvel-
lous luxury . . .

 . . . On the way home last year I got two New
Hampshire hens, Eglet and Molty. Right now Blue Egg,
the rooster, and these two are eating the dog food under the kitchen table. If I don't watch it they get at
my houseplants, so I cut off bits of oxalys and throw
them on the floor. My white hen was a rooster so we
ate him for Christmas . . .

Molty is at the bottom of the pecking order. Eglet
is next and Black Ida bosses the works. No one pecks
her. They ignore Blue Egg. . . . I keep a large putty

knife for cleaning up the squidges they deposit on
the floor. In cold weather, if they drink water they
have diarrhea, but snow keeps the squidges squidge-
like . . .

—Extracts from a letter
from Ginty to Hilda Thomas

*I was just a little girl when we visited here. Me and my sister
and my Mum. Ginty brought us into the house for tea, and
the goats ran in and stole the cookies off the table! When we
left, Mr. Paul gave us a pretty little bantam rooster that used
to sleep right on his pillow. I remember being absolutely fascinated that anyone would have chickens sleeping in his bed.*

—Hattie Thompson

You get, they say, what you wish for. And Katherine must
have had a guardian angel looking after her because her im-
passioned plea from the unbearable heat of Ghana was answered.
In spades.

I had worked the two women into the ground, and after I left
for the book tour they planned to spend a well-earned day recover-
ing. But a life of ease was not to be. Two days after the twenty-
centimetre snowfall I had encountered en route to Williams Lake,
the sky dumped another fifty centimetres. This was more than the
area received most winters. It was not unknown to have so much
snow that early in the year, but it was not common and it caught
everyone on the hop. The heavy wet nature of it meant that pickup
trucks and tractors could not make a lot of headway, and people
with longer driveways had to stand in line waiting for bigger machines to come and plough them out. The four kilometres of ex-
telegraph road between Ginty Creek and the highway was in an
odd position. Being on crown land, it was owned by the Queen

(and her minion, the BC government), but it was not classed as a public road. Nor was it a private one: no one, therefore, had the responsibility to maintain it. Except me—which meant that if I wanted it ploughed I was going to have to be the one who paid for it. I preferred not to have it done right away; if another heavy fall happened before I returned, I would have to fork out all over again.

Stephanie and Katherine were not averse to a nice bit of winter. They had brought cross-country skis with them and thought it would be fun to get to the cabin that way. They first laboriously hand-dug a track so that their car could reach the B&B's ploughed driveway, enabling them to drive round to the telegraph road. The entrance to this had been ploughed—it was where the road maintenance machines and school bus turned around. They parked their car, loaded a little toboggan with supplies, and happily strode off. While driving on it, the road had seemed more or less flat, but skiing through soft, knee-deep unbroken snow revealed all the ups and downs, made much harder by their backpacks and the dead weight of the toboggan behind them.

Two days later, Puntzi Mountain, the nearest weather station, recorded -37°C. The B&B insisted that at their place it was -43°C. Again, this was not completely unknown in early November, but certainly unusual. The cabin's wall insulation was only half done; huge gaps remained around the poorly crafted bay window, and drafts whistled through the hurriedly cobbled door. Originally, the two women's plan had been to drive back and forth to the B&B and move in at a leisurely pace. Even when they realized that skiing was the only option, they still imagined fairly frequent trips, but in that temperature, no one was going anywhere. When it warmed after a day or two, they went back to the B&B to round up the remains of their possessions and food. Plan B was to leave this stored in their car and collect it periodically from there. A lot of the bulk staples had been brought over before I left— bags of dog food, salt, and flour and rice in metal garbage cans, but the boxes of organic root vegetables had been left behind as the women had thought they would be more protected from freezing in the B&B. These were now rock hard—Popsicle carrots (with fetching little ice crystals sprouting all over), potatoes like river stones, and cannonball turnips.

The two women split wood and finished the wall insulation. A trickle of river was still flowing close to the bank, and every day they tramped down there and hauled water. I had already been using Raffi and Bucky to help carry that—putting a four-litre jug in each side of their backpacks—and now Katherine hooked Raffi up to the toboggan. That was a pretty steep haul!

The river water could not be safely drunk without being boiled (only three houses and a couple of hundred cows lived upstream but the river ran through logging blocks and wherever there is a road, human excrement will follow). The alternative was to melt snow, which they certainly had plenty of, but that took extra firewood.

Another job the two women tackled was the outhouse. We had organized the foundations before I left, but the hole still lay unprotected and they built a shelter around it. "Make it tall enough for Dylan," I told them as I went out the door. Consequently it is an immense height, although Dylan in fact has never been back to try it out.

At the beginning of December, Nelson Williams came from Anahim with his grader and ploughed the road. He gave me a good deal on the price because he did another long road not too far away at the same time. I arrived home on the 12th. Already more snow had fallen after the plough had been and the van I had bought while on the book tour was very low to the ground. It was all-wheel-drive and had proved itself magnificently on the ice and slush of the coast roads (they were having a horrific winter down there: many venues had been very badly attended as no one was driving anywhere). However, I had yet to use the van on snow over ten centimetres deep and there must have been well over fifteen centimetres of it on the telegraph road. Due to the cold, it had the texture of ball bearings. I launched the van with bated breath. It slithered all over the place, but I made it.

The short day was darkening; the cabin, with its black, tarpaper walls and sagging tarp porch roof, looked gloomy. Spare bales of insulation were stacked under the tarp and the women had arranged these to make kennels for the dogs. The snow heaved up by the plough was lumpy and untidy and dirty around the door; flakes of bark and wood chips radiated out from the chopping block. Typical back door in a winter cabin but never very attractive.

Inside, despite the two windows, it was quite dark. There was

The cabin at the beginning of winter.

barely room to move. As well as supplies in cardboard boxes, all the tools and timber, and the finishing materials for the ceiling, interior work and floor were stacked there. I had brought a lot of groceries with me—sacks of flour, rice, more dog food, and several boxes of vegetables, and we had to find a place for them somehow. Stephanie and Katherine gallantly vacated the bed in the bay window and crammed themselves into a narrow space on the freezing floor. They were gone before daylight the next morning. They had behaved far beyond the call of wwoofer duty. They had looked after my dogs and made life a great deal easier for me while I travelled on the book tour; they had prepared a liveable shelter for me while I was away; they had stored all the tools and supplies where I could find them without having to dig through snowbanks, and all this in conditions far worse than any of us had expected. If their departure seemed somewhat precipitous, I could hardly find it in my heart to blame them.

CHAPTER 4

CHRISTMAS IN THE PRECIPICE

She couldn't get on with anyone. She had men over there all the time doing work. Mostly useless stuff. No, I don't know anything about the new building. Didn't even know it was there. I haven't been over there for years.

—Jan Petrie

Yes I built that big square building. Me and my son and two young guys from Anahim. Oh, must have been at least twenty years ago now. More, I guess. I had a ranch at Anahim at that time. The construction [of the Packrat Palace] was all Ginty's idea. I just did what I was told and kept my mouth shut. The lumber came from a sawmill down in Tatlayoko. All odd sizes and none of it was true. I'd never have built anything that way.

Stories? Well, she had this big boar pig. It was huge. She called it Boris. It must have been two and half feet tall. I couldn't begin to guess how much it weighed. When Ginty went away, one of the boys had to feed this pig. They didn't like that as it was so big and they were scared of it. One day

Ginty came up and she was very excited. She'd found Boris eating a young goat that she called Brownie. I guess that was the end of Boris!

—Lloyd Norton

Depression is not something I have had to deal with much in my life but the start of that winter was a bad time for me. I had been struggling with increasing aches and pains, and while down at the coast I had been diagnosed with fibromyalgia and food sensitivities: in retrospect I realized that was the reason I had broken my leg. My body had been growing more and more inflexible. It was also why I was having such a hard time getting my energy level back up again.

And now I was faced with carpentry work I did not want to do (and have never enjoyed) and I had to live in an exhausting mess while doing it. This was certainly nothing new—I had moved into all of my other cabins before they were finished, and had slept and cooked and eaten among building supplies and debris, but I really did not want to go through all that again.

The weather did not help. Gloom predominated, and the small solar power system was not being properly recharged. The satellite internet took priority over my limited power supply and after a few days I no longer dared use the electric light. The long winter nights were now enlivened by two candle flames, their small circles of light barely penetrating the cluttered dark. The property was littered with glass insulators from the telegraph line; I had collected the ones I had stumbled over in the fall and now commandeered a couple of them for candle holders. The feeble gleams from the flames were enhanced somewhat by two mirror tiles hinged with duct tape and propped into a V behind them. I had nothing suitable to place this ensemble on, and I had to screw my body sideways to read. The poor light might not have been so bad if I had known where everything was, but nothing could be found without moving half a dozen other items. I had a dynamo flashlight, but it no longer held a charge and I had to keep turning the handle to get any light. I would wind my way to the outhouse and back in the dark.

Water was stored in a twenty-litre bucket. Katherine and Stephanie had left me a two-day supply but when I went down to the river it was to find that the small hole they had been keeping open had frozen over. It was too shallow just there to break into again, and too dangerous to go further out into the river. So now I had to resort to melting snow. Not such a big deal—there was certainly plenty of it—but the daily act of flattening shovelfuls into a large bowl and placing the snow on the stove was just another nuisance chore. For drinking and bathing, a bowl a day was enough, but for rinsing clothes I needed a lot more.

I could hear traffic on the highway. Sporadic for the most part and rare at night, it still bothered me. My stretch of the telegraph road might be four kilometres long, but in fact it ran more or less parallel to Highway 20 and the nearest point was only a kilometre away. Even though there was the river, a field, a swamp and belts of trees in between us, when the wind was south or southwest, which was a good deal of the time, it could sound as though trucks were driving right through my living room. Silence is one of the great joys of wilderness dwelling. At Nuk Tessli I was used to a total absence of man-made sounds other than my own for months on end. I am in my fifth winter at Ginty Creek as I write this, and the noise from the highway is something that I have never learned to ignore.

And then there were neighbours. Ginty Creek was quite private, but it didn't give me the great feeling of freedom that I was used to in the mountains. The road (when it was ploughed) allowed me access to a library and the possibility of a little social life in the winter—which I was certainly not averse to—but it also meant I could see the neighbour's power lines and, now that the leaves were gone, a barn roof. The mumble of Ken's tractor would float across the river when he fed his cows; his dogs barked.

But all these things were not the real reason that I felt so down. I was coming to terms with the fact that I could not continue with the lifestyle I had enjoyed for the last thirty years. The food sensitivities and fibromyalgia were a wake-up call. My body was sending me messages that I could no longer expect immortality. It was a bitter pill to swallow, but I was going to have to learn to compromise. It was not something that I was very good at doing.

Book tours are a very necessary part of being an author; they are a fabulous ego trip, a great time to make new friends and catch up with old ones, and they are absolutely and mind-numbingly exhausting. The only thing that keeps me going for several weeks on the road is knowing that the tours will end. I crashed for the first day back at the cabin, but knew I would go insane if I did not do something with this muddle around me. When I had owned the Suburban, I had commissioned a local welder to make a dog barrier for it out of the kind of grid that is used for industrial steps. I had rescued it before I traded the Suburban for the van; I now wired the barrier horizontally next to the heater stove, providing a table-like extension. This gave me a counter of sorts to work on, and a place to stack and wash dirty dishes. That was one pile of stuff I could now remove from the floor. The following day I drove to Nimpo to pick up several weeks' worth of mail. Nearby was a friend's cabin where I had temporary storage space. Without this, I don't know what I would have done. The storage was in an attic over a garage set behind a log house. The owner was away and the driveway had not been ploughed. Well over sixty centimetres of snow lay on the ground. The gate was half buried and frozen shut. All the unwanted stuff from the slide-show tour—boxes of unsold books and artwork, booth displays, stands and lights, city clothes—had to be lifted over the chest-high pile of snow left by the grader at the edge of the road, hoisted over the gate, and dragged by snowshoes and toboggan to the garage. The stairs to the attic were strong and well made but had been heavily varnished: when there was the slightest trace of snow on my boots they were as slick as glare ice, but at least I could get another small part of the mess out from under my feet.

I had excuses, at first, to put off the dreaded carpentry work. A lot of the mail needed attention. I made a crude shelf on the east side of the cabin and organized the smaller containers of food. The shelf was only knee high and the food was still in cardboard boxes, but it was a little easier to find.

Finally, I could procrastinate no longer. Just before the shortest day, I started on the ceiling. Stephanie and Katherine had framed and insulated it, and stapled on the vapour barrier. All I had to do was place the narrow tongue and groove boards that Cameron Linde had brought in the fall. The women had stacked them on the west side of the cabin. It made sense, therefore, to start fitting boards on the east side but to do that I would have to move the cartons of food. I could not put them on the lumber pile as I would need access to that; the only space left was the bed.

Standing on the floor, in boots, I could just reach the ceiling. Standing on the kitchen steps, I was too close to swing the hammer properly. So I alternated between stretching at full height and trying to nail awkwardly upward. The biggest nuisance was moving the boards from the pile on the far side of the room to where I was working. The chimney was in the way. To get the boards past it I had to open the door, lift up a bundle of lumber, back outside far enough to swing the ends past the stove then walk back in, put the boards down and shut the door. That first day I put up fifteen boards—only another ninety to go.

On the shortest day, it rained. The ceiling over the bay window dripped onto my bed. Then the satellite internet didn't work—this sometimes happens in heavy cloud cover but there have been a couple of times where it was a technical fault. When the installers came to set up the satellite dish, it was on one of their scheduled trips out west; to get a technician out here now would probably take weeks. I had no phone to see if anyone else had the same problem. I would just have to wait and try again. I could always drive around to Ken's phone if necessary. The following day, the internet was working again. And the ceiling has never once leaked since. Ginty's Ghost just making sure I don't forget her, no doubt. On Christmas Eve I put the last boards on the ceiling. My neck felt as though I had been painting the roof of the Sistine Chapel, but the worst of the jobs was done.

I was invited to the Precipice for Christmas. Dave and Rosemary Neads have woven a thread through my life for a long time now. Living about sixty kilometres north of Nuk Tessli, in a unique sheltered and isolated valley suspended between the Chilcotin plateau and the coast, they are my nearest neighbours in that direction when I live in the mountains. Here, they are not a great deal further away but I can reach them in two hours by road. As long as their thirty-kilometre driveway is not blocked by snow. Our similar lifestyles and aspirations have brought us together even though we may meet only two or three times a year. Long before I acquired satellite internet, Rosemary would handle email and both internet and phone bookings for my mountain business.

The Precipice (named after the extensive basalt organ-pipe rimrock) used to be one of the main meeting places for trails between the coast and the interior. One of these routes was originally touted as a prospective road to Bella Coola but a canyon at the bottom end, where the river tumbles into the Atnarko within what is now the Tweedsmuir Provincial Park, was deemed too much of a barrier. Because the main horse trail went along there at the time, however, it was through the Precipice that the telegraph line had been built. So now the Neads and I, linked for years by the common bond of wilderness living, are also joined by a special little bit of history.

Most winters, the road to the Precipice is snowed in—Dave will, unbelievably, skidoo out and then drive hours or days to ecology and land-use meetings, where he offers his services as a consultant. Sometimes he has done this as often as once a week. This year the Neads had relied on the luxury of having the road ploughed after the big dump of snow in the fall; however, I certainly was not going to risk driving my daisy-cutting van down there; as with Ginty Creek, there had already been other falls of snow since the plough had gone through. Dave said I would have an open road as far as their turnoff—he would meet me there in his Suburban.

Before I could leave, I had to devise a way to store the produce I had brought from my journey outside. (Local stores have a very poor selection of vegetables and certainly nothing organic, so I do as much shopping as I can in Williams Lake and beyond.) The weather was fairly mild—about -15°C at night and -5°C in the day—but it could easily get a lot colder and I would be away for two or three days. Without the stove on, the cabin would most likely freeze inside. I broke open a couple of bales of rockwool batts and lined two walls of a corner two layers deep. Two-by-fours framed more batts to make a floor. The coolers and boxes of produce were placed in this shelter, the remaining two walls were constructed of more rockwool layers tied on with string, and the whole lot was roofed with more batts and the feather duvet from my bed. The water bucket, which was still half full, was lifted onto the ex-dog-barrier-cum-counter. It would be less cold off the floor and with luck I would not to have to melt snow right away when I got home.

Rosemary wanted cream and a few other items from the store. I was surprised to find that McClean's Trading in Anahim would be open on Christmas Day. I thought this was extreme altruism on their part until I saw the other people waiting. Happy guys in their best clothes, mostly from the large reserve that surrounds Anahim Lake, waiting for the liquor store to open. "Happy Christmas!" they roared at me, and ran over to shake my hand. They were already having a good time. When the store opened, it did a boisterous trade.

I had been in touch with Rosemary only by email at this point and I wanted to phone her to let her know I was at Anahim and to find out how Dave was making out on their road. He had chained up all round and had apparently set off shortly before I called. He was expecting to take about forty-five minutes to reach our meeting point; I could be there in half an hour. I had just given the phone back to the storekeeper, John, when it rang again. "For you," he shouted over the busy din. Rosemary told me Dave had just called her on their satellite phone and the Suburban was overheating drastically. He might have to turn back. There had been only a few fresh centimetres of snow down in the valley but he had found a lot more halfway up to the top. She told me to wait and she would call me back. A few minutes later the phone went again. "McClean's Trading," said John. "For you!" he bawled and thrust the phone over. "He's going to take a chance and continue but slowly," Rosemary informed me. "Wait there a bit longer and we'll see how he does." Another pause and the phone burred again. "Chris Czajkowski answering service," John snapped, getting just a tiny bit annoyed. But of course this time it was a bewildered customer wanting to know the store hours on this special day.

Dave made it and I met him at what the Neads call "The Carpark." This is where they leave their vehicle when they snowmobile in and out. We would now drop about 700 metres in altitude. We had a roller-coaster ride down, slewing from side to side and slithering around the steep, narrow bends, but eventually we were driving up to their house and Rosemary's smiling welcome. She is a wonderful cook and caters beautifully. A family of friends, and the caretaker from the ranch that fills up most of the space in the Precipice Valley, came to dinner. It was a great way to visit friends so rarely seen.

December 27 dawned clear with the sun bright against the rim of the valley. It was the first cloudless weather we had had for a long time. The downside was that the temperature had dropped to -25°C. It would be colder up top; I wondered if my van would start. Dave knew he would never get the Suburban up the hill again. We would have to go out by Ski-Doo. If it wasn't for my two dogs, I would simply have ridden behind Dave, but the dogs would not be able to keep up with the machines. I would have to sit in a sled clutching Raffi; the caretaker from the ranch would drive another Ski-Doo and haul a dog crate tied to a skimmer for Bucky. This was the way I had been taken in and out of the Precipice for Christmases in the past. I knew full well that it was going to be an extremely uncomfortable ride.

We arranged that I would sit facing backwards. That way churned snow and gas fumes would not be thrown directly into my face as had happened before. Dave tried to build a solid back; we padded it with my backpack and laid a foamy on the bottom of the sled. I was dressed in multiple layers including a borrowed snowmobile suit and felt like the Pillsbury Doughboy. Dave gave me a rope to hold in one multiple-gloved mitt. The other end of the rope was tied to his waist. If I was thrown out of the sled, he would feel the pull and stop. Raffi was jammed half between and half over my legs.

Before we even crossed the ranch meadows, I had occasion to pull the rope. I was fine, but the caretaker's skimmer had flipped and the dog crate had broken open. Bucky had not been very keen to get into the crate in the first place and he was the kind of dog who never came when he was called. To all our amazement, he not only stayed close by but was easy to catch and hopped right back into the crate as if it was fun.

Me on the skimmer about to leave the Precipice, Dave Neads on the right.

Despite the padding, my body was slammed repeatedly onto the unyielding earth at what seemed, at ground level, to be great speed. Fumes from the machine choked me; blowing snow obscured my vision. At first Raffi struggled but then he huddled down. At least he kept my legs warm; the rest of me rapidly iced over. I had taken my glasses off—they would have been useless— and fuzzily, through slitted eyes and a blizzard of snow, I could see the caretaker's lean face, bearded with ice, hunched over his Ski-Doo headlamp. Bucky's crate crashed from side to side in the ruts behind him. When we stopped, the snow covering my upper body cracked like an eggshell as I stepped stiffly out of the sled like some primeval monster reborn.

I had difficulty getting into the van, for the doors were frozen shut, but it started with no problem. Low golden sun was pouring into the cabin when I reached it, and it felt remarkably warm. There were a couple of centimetres of ice on the water in the bucket. None of the produce had been frozen.

CHAPTER 5

THE BIG SNOW

She was a funny woman [always cheerful and laughing]. *I laugh with her. I walked across one time. "I got some news for you," she said. "What news?" "My bedroom is now delivery room," she tol' me. "All animals go in there to have babies."*
—Elaine Dester

The goats did fairly well. The buck I got last year is related to so many of my does he will be used on his non-relatives and then get turned into feed for the mutts and chooks. I had two singles, one quads, three triplets and three twins. The quads are three does and a buck. They are all so comical and all characters. The buck . . . father of the quads . . . came from the local judge--C.C. Barnett. Locally the buck is called "Judge, you stinker."

The neighbour hauls our mail and groceries etc. My truck is visible but unmoveable; besides we're snowed in . . .

—Extract from a letter
from Ginty to Hilda Thomas

We would bring Ginty's mail from the Kleena Kleene post office. Ginty accused us of damaging it. She told the post man to initial any tears on the envelopes. At that time you could cross the river on a logjam. People with good balance could walk. People like me had to crawl.

—Leslie Lamb

I t would not take a lot more snow to block the telegraph road again and I wanted to ask Ken and Leslie if I could leave my vehicle parked across the river in their yard. Ken would keep his road open with his tractor. Rather than drive around, I thought I would try and cross the river on skis. It was pretty much frozen over although very lumpy and bumpy. It shouldn't be that deep even if I did fall in, but the current was swift and there would likely be ice along the bottom. If I broke through, there would be a good chance that I would lose my footing.

The dogs had been visiting back and forth across the ice. There was a snow-covered lump of something on a gravel bar—probably a bit of fallen bank—and this was completely yellow. My dogs would go and pee on it; then Ken's dogs would come and pee on the other side. A well-packed trail of paw prints crossed the river nearby. When I approached, I could hear water gurgling below but it seemed to be as good a place as any and I shuffled across. I floundered through a belt of cottonwoods and alders, followed moose tracks to a low place in the fence, then trudged through the field to Ken and Leslie's house. "Sure," Ken said. "No problem leaving the van here. Ginty used to put her vehicle in our yard in the winter. She had her mail delivered here when they used to drop it off at the end of our driveway."

I retraced my tracks and just as the tip of my skis touched the spot where water ran below the ice, there was a crack and a long hiss, and a whole section of river caved in. That had happened to me once before near Nuk Tessli. There, I had been on snow-shoes; I had crossed the river with some concern but no problem, had gone to a nearby trap cabin where I was going to spend the night, then came back with a billycan to fetch water. The minute my snowshoes had touched the edge of the river, even though all my weight was still on the shore, in crashed the ice. There, I could avoid crossing the river again. Here the only alternative was an eight-kilometre walk. With my heart in my mouth I chose a different spot and crept over. Perhaps the river would be safer later in the winter, but leaving my van at Ken and Leslie's was not going to be an option at this time.

The new year had been ushered in by rain. The sky cleared for the night of January 3 and the full moon was profoundly brilliant, shining on my face through the bay window and making the snowy landscape glow with ethereal light. For a day or two we had blinding sunshine but it was very mild and the snow was glazed in the morning and wet and sticky by the afternoon. More snow fell. I thought I had better see if I could still drive the telegraph road. Thirty centimetres of snow had fallen on it since it had been ploughed, almost half of that since I had last driven on it. I threw an axe, shovel, rope, come-along, toboggan and snow-shoes into the van just in case. Once again the vehicle amazed me. It slithered and slewed and bottomed out the whole distance but kept clawing its way along. And it didn't even have chains or winter tires. But on January 8 it snowed another five centimetres. I doubted I would be able to drive the road again.

About two-thirds of the way along the telegraph road is a Y-shaped junction. A further four kilometres along the other branch is a property owned by a man who lives in the Bella Coola Valley. The cabin on this property burned down but he still runs horses there and likes to visit once or twice in winter to bring bales of hay. His road had never been ploughed at all and Rosemary, in our email correspondence, told me that Neil Griffith was going to plough him out and we could share the cost as far as the Y. This seemed an attractive proposition.

I had met Edgar a couple of times on the telegraph road. He was a shortish man, around my age, who wore his straggling grey-ing hair shoulder length and sported thickly knitted handspun sweaters and hats somewhat the worst for wear. He had a strong US accent. It was not in his nature to make friends, but I rarely saw him and he smiled at me as much as he scowled. Rumours abounded about him, the most common of which was that he was actually very wealthy, was the black sheep of the family, and that when his family company in Silicon Valley required a signature on a document they flew up in a helicopter to get him to sign it. I took all this with a grain of salt: I was once told that when I first came into the country to start Nuk Tessli, some locals (men of course) decided that as I was a single female, I was building the remote resort in the mountains to have wilderness sex orgies. Anyone who is a little different . . . and yet everyone who lives on the Chilcotin develops individualistic traits. Whether they are odd because the country has shaped them or gravitate here be-cause they were misfits elsewhere is a moot point.

Rosemary kept in touch with Neil by phone and passed the information to me by email. She first told me to expect Neil on January 10 but his Cat broke down. This was fortuitous, because later that day it started to snow in earnest and it continued for twenty-four hours. Everything was drowned in snow. My van was a white mound with two black wing mirrors sticking out like ears.

Through the kitchen window the wall of snow that had dumped off the roof had nearly joined the eaves. I took the tape measure to the chopping block, which had been bare before this latest dump started. The tape recorded another fifty fresh centimetres.

The van and the cabin in the Big Snow.

Belly-deep moose track.

I slogged outside on skis and snowshoes. The total pack would have been chest high if I could have stood on the ground. This was more than triple the usual fall for the area. Moose were plentiful; their belly-deep tracks ploughed ditches through the snow. They could step over the fences without knocking snow off the top rails. The little trailer by the river was half buried. That night, the sky cleared and the temperature bombed to -36°C.

I was put to the bottom of the ploughing list. First Neil had to dig himself out. Then there was a score of people whose pickups and tractors could make no headway in this; they had to wait until a bigger machine was available. There was so much work to do but the snow was so beautiful I allowed myself some time off to explore. I broke ski trails to the south and the north, finding myself both times on high bluffs with gorgeous views of the mountains and the wild, snow-clogged river below. I skied to the upper place. The creek through the ponds and fields was roaring within its cocoon of ice. It was officially called after Ginty but using her real name, Nedra. I know that is how she was christened because there was an abandoned credit card in the Packrat Palace. Nedra Jane Paul. No one can tell me why she was called Ginty.

During this time, Ken and Leslie emailed me an invitation for lunch. They had a buyer for their place and were preparing to leave; there would not be many more chances for me to get details of their relationship with Ginty. I was still waiting to be ploughed out, so the only way I was going to get there was by crossing the river again. The ice would likely be a little more stable by now. Still, it was with great trepidation that I shuffled my way across. The new deep snow was soft and fluffy. On the far side, in the bush, even with skis on, it was thigh deep. Latching onto a convenient moose track, I found the best way to cross Ken's fence—

like the moose I could step over easily. I did not have to take off the skis.

When I first bought the place, Ken and Leslie had given me documents pertaining to the land. The first was the initial survey, whose scale was twenty chains to one inch. The part I now inhabited, the triangle fronted by the river, had once been the northeast corner of a quarter section whose opposite corner was buried in the lake on the far side of the highway from me, but when I looked at the document I was confused. There was the river, although its course had changed a bit, and two branches were indicated instead of one, and there was the lake, but the highway in between did not seem to be marked. Then I saw the date below the backward-sloping copperplate signature of the surveyor in the bottom right corner: "Dec 1909." Highway 20 did not exist in this part of the Chilcotin then. It was not completed until 1953, although the section past the lake would have been driveable (more or less) by the 1930s. A finely dotted line wavered up from the south corner of the map and ended in the middle of the plan. The line was labelled Chilcotin Trail. A later hand had added crude dashes further west and written Approximate Bella Coola Highway and added an arrow at the top: "Bella Coola Approx 100 MI," and at the bottom: "Williams Lake Approx 165 MI."

The second dated document was part of the Land Act.

GEORGE VI, by the Grace of God, of Great Britain,
Ireland, and the British Dominions
beyond the Seas, KING, Defender of the Faith
On all to whom these presents shall come, Greeting:
Know ye that We do by these presents, for Us, Our
heirs and successors, in consideration of the sum of <u>Three
hundred and twenty</u> Dollars to Us paid, give and grant
unto

<u>BATICE* DESTER, his</u> heirs and assigns

All that Parcel of Lot of Land situated in <u>COAST</u> District, said to contain <u>One hundred and sixty</u> acres, more or less, and more particularly described . . . and numbered <u>North East Quarter of Lot Five hundred and fifty-eight (558), Range Three (3)</u> . . . hereby granted, with their appurtenances, unto the said <u>BATICE DESTER, his</u> heirs and assigns for ever: . . .

It was signed on

this Eighth day of November, in the year of our Lord One thousand nine hundred and Forty Nine and in the Thirteenth year of Our Reign.

The map accompanying this piece of paper showed only the west branch of the river, which is now no more than a slough, thanks to the heaps of gravel that have been bulldozed to block it off. (This, of course, is why the river is eating into my property.) Adrian Paul took over the tract north of the river on March 1, 1951. For whatever reason, it is his daughter's name that appeared on the deed. In 1959, Ginty signed another land agreement, this time with "Elizabeth the Second, in the sixth year of her Reign, for the adjoining Lot One Thousand Six Hundred and Eighty-Eight (1688), said to contain Forty acres more or less, in consideration of the sum of Sixty dollars." She wanted this property solely for the water rights. Even then it was cheap. It was probably considered useless to anyone else. Surrounding both properties were "Vacant Crown Lands."

---

* Although the name "Batice" is on the official document, most people knew him as Batiste.

Part of the original deed to Ginty Creek.

This was a notice in the *Victoria Colonist* of November 21, 1919:

> Lt WAB Paul, together w/wife and infant child returned to Victoria from Eng. He left here w/30th Bn 1915, served in Fra and was given a commission in Imperial Forces. WIA twice, the 2nd time, in 1917, he was taken POW and it was not until 1918 that he was repatriated. Mrs. Paul, formerly Miss RA Thomas of Victoria, went overseas to

offer her services as VAD, and served at St Thomas Hosp, London.

The infant child was most likely Ginty's brother. Ginty herself was born in Victoria, probably in 1920. Like so many pensioned ex-service men, Mr. Paul became a chicken farmer. This was on Vancouver Island near Comox.

Ten years later, the government asked those who did not need their army pension to forgo it. Adrian was well enough off and did so; he sold his farm, left his wife and children in Victoria, and came north along the coast as a surveyor. He worked inland from Bella Coola first (there was no road to the interior then) but eventually came up to the Chilcotin. He built a rough cabin in the bush somewhere, but then moved to the stone pump house, which is now one of the few remaining buildings at Puntzi Mountain Air Base. He phoned the weather in every day but also got a job as a linesman for the telegraph line.

Puntzi had been built in 1953 for the US Air Force as a radar site to track invading aircraft. It was turned over to the Canadian Air Force in the early 1960s, then closed a few years later. There is not much left of it now, but the long runway is used for fighter aircraft practice for a few weeks each year, and for water bombers if they are needed during the fire season. The weather station has been maintained, although all the data are recorded automatically now. Puntzi is a high, bleak place, with little protection from the north, and has on more than one occasion reported the coldest temperature in Canada.

Although Ginty Creek had been surveyed in 1906, no one had lived there until Adrian arrived. Ginty would come up for visits during her school vacations. After she became a teacher, she mostly lived where she worked, which was all over BC. She was never in one place for more than a year or two. Adrian was already an old man when Ginty inherited money and came to stay. "That wasn't too long before we arrived," said Ken. "When we were looking for property I stayed the night in a cabin that was on the knoll next to where you have built. That was in 1976. The cabin had been built by some awfully English friends of Ginty's. It was in a disgusting mess when we took over the place in the early '90s, missing half the roof, full of junk, and riddled with packrats. So we pulled it down and hauled everything to the dump.

"Ginty and her father were living in a tarpaper shack when I stayed there. There was no Packrat Palace then. The cabin was tinier than yours but had three rooms—an entryway, a living room and kitchen, and a bedroom. When Ginty moved in full time she got the bedroom and Adrian slept on a cot in the kitchen. On one occasion I went over for lunch. Some people arrived and Ginty and her father went outside to talk to them. While I was sitting there, a goat ran in and slurped the dregs in all the teacups.

"They planned to build a bigger cabin and got hold of Batiste and his son Mack Dester to do it. They were both pretty good builders. A lot of their structures are still standing. The new house of Ginty's was supposed to be two stories—a basement and a log upper floor—but in the morning Adrian would tell them one thing and in the afternoon Ginty would say something else so the Desters quit. When Adrian died, Ginty destroyed what there was of that building and found someone else to build the wannabe lodge."

"We started our own house in 1977," Leslie told me. "I was also a teacher by then. While we were building, we had relatives come and help us. Ginty crossed the river on the logjam and told us I was not feeding everyone properly. She went back and brought us a chicken. Only problem was, it was still alive. Just what I needed, having to pluck and gut a chicken when I was so busy.

"It was not long before we were in Ginty's bad books," Leslie added. "I asked a neighbour why she thought that would be. She said Ginty was like that with everyone. 'You were getting the brunt of it because you were the closest,' she said."

"Email me when you get home," Leslie admonished as I set off back across the river. Should I use the same crossing or would it collapse? I decided to try a different route and got over without mishap, but it was too nerve-wracking for me to continue doing it. Either the winters used to be colder or Ginty was built of sterner stuff than me. Leaving my vehicle in Ken and Leslie's yard was not going to be an option as far as I was concerned.

Rosemary emailed me and told me to expect Neil, the man with the snowplough, to come on January 16. It was -22°C. I warmed up the motor of the van so I could move it easily when he came. I waited all day. On the morning of the 17th I thought I heard voices and a car door slam, but nothing happened so I figured it must have been people on the highway. It was -25°C. I switched on the van again for a while. And then it came. A huge, beat-up old Cat that had once been a colour I had heard a farmer describe very aptly as "calf-shit yellow." The big blade on front pushed a mountain of snow. I once spent a summer in Cambridge Bay in Canada's central Arctic. At the end of August the icebreaker came, forging a way for the barge bringing the community's supplies for the year. That's what it felt like when Neil's ponderous behemoth hove into view.

It had taken him six hours to reach the Y the day before. Edgar had followed him but Neil had been unable to go further. Edgar had spent the night in his truck at the Y. "Why didn't he come here?" I asked. Neil shrugged. Edgar was like that.

Slowly the yard was cleared and I dug out the van and moved it. Neil came in for coffee. He was a squat, strong man with icicles in his beard. The Cat had an open cab with no weather protection. His handshake was icy and, once indoors, his face turned such a vivid red I was alarmed for his health.

By early afternoon I could drive out between the walls of snow to the post office and store. I had not picked up mail since before Christmas and I had been reduced, for several days, to reading by the light of a single candle. For some years friends have been sending me *The Globe and Mail*'s cryptic crosswords. The print is small and I was having a hard time reading the clues. At Nimpo and Anahim I stripped the stores of their emergency candle supply.

It was dark when I returned. Neil's flatdeck was parked at the turnoff from the highway and I hoped I would not meet him on the telegraph road as there would be no room to pass. As I slowed to turn, I was surprised to see someone materialize out of the darkness. Neil flagged me down. "You can't get through," he said. "But how do I get home?" I wailed. "Just temporary," he explained. "I ran out of fuel about a kilometre in. A friend's bringing some. Should only be about fifteen minutes." We stood outside in the cold and waited. Neil's cigarette glowed red in the dark.

A pickup arrived and the two men disappeared. They seemed to be gone a long time. Eventually an alien light began to pick out the trees, and the machine lumbered into view like a yellow-eyed dinosaur. Neil still hadn't got all the way to Edgar's. He would finish the job the following day; presumably Edgar was spending another night in his truck. By the time I reached my cabin, it was snowing again.

CHAPTER 6

GETTING ORGANIZED

She was our teacher at Kleena Kleene when I was in grade one. I would have been five or six—I was born in '59 so that makes it about 1964. There were only four families in the school—must have been about twelve kids altogether. I had four brothers and four sisters but they were not all in school then, only my older sister Rhonda and I were. My cousins were there and a couple of white families. She only taught for a year as they wanted to open the school and couldn't find a teacher. At least, that's what she told us.

Her dad was a quiet person. He was always interested in watching my brothers and cousins when they were building or mechanicking. The boys were always full of energy and getting into mischief so Old Paul gave them some projects to do. He showed them how to build bird houses.

Ginty was very good friends with our family. Grampa [Batiste Dester] had a ranch next door. He was a trapper and a grizzly-hunting outfitter as well as a rancher. He had a lot of clients from the US and some of them were celebrities. One was Johnny Cash! Mum and us girls would ride to the camps. Mum would make bannock and we would clean the

*camps afterward. Sometimes Ginty rode with us. She had a
horse called Country.*

*Everything was done on horses those days. Instead of
having a driveway in front of your house to park a car, you
had to have a place to tie your horse. Ginty would take us
places in her truck. She'd take Mum to the store or into
Williams Lake sometimes. She'd take me and my sister on
day trips to places like Tatlayoko. It was our gateway to the
world.*

—Karen Dester

The thermometer on a post outside my door registered
-18°C on the morning that I cut a hole in the wall to fit in
another window. There were the usual fiddles and hassles, but the
job went reasonably smoothly and during the night I was pleased
to see an extra hint of light in the room. Without street lights to
distort one's vision, a rural night is never truly dark, especially
when the snow lies on the ground. At sunrise, parallelograms of
sunlight flooded across the floor; this was where my kitchen was
going to be.

But before the kitchen could happen, I needed to finish that
part of the floor. I had got a deal on some laminate flooring; it
was sitting under a pile of boxes and equipment at one end of the
room, so once again here was a case of moving everything around
to clear both the floor and the working space. The laminate had
been the end of a run and I could see, after I installed it, why it
had been sitting in the store. I like light interiors and the flooring was nice and pale, but it showed every scrap of dirt. Laminate
flooring is too plastic-looking for me to want to live with on a
long-term basis (I was concerned about possible formaldehyde
gassing-off although I learned later that newer floors exude a lot
less than used to be the case) but speed and cheapness were of the

essence here, and for this cabin it would do. I had never installed the stuff before. The instructions talked about having a dead level subfloor—mine was of particle board screwed onto machine-cut joists. It was bound to be level, wasn't it? I soon discovered that there was a vast difference between dead level and what we had cobbled together. In places, the long, narrow tiles popped together like they were supposed to; mostly I had to cajole and wrestle and curse and swear to get them to fit.

I did only a narrow strip of the floor at first. Before I moved the mountain of stuff again, I was going to build a kitchen counter under the newly installed window. Now I was really getting somewhere. Shelves above the counter framed the window, but the storage area I would eventually put below the counter to house the pots and pans was deferred because that space would now be taken up by the lumber pile and other building materials while I worked on the rest of the interior. So once again I was backing out of the cabin with armfuls of lumber, do-si-do-ing round the chimney, and waltzing back into the room.

The stove area was next. At Nuk Tessli I had built two stone ovens, one outside and one in the living space. Both were primarily for baking bread but the indoor one was supposed to double as a heater. In that regard, it was overkill. I was, however, very impressed with the incredible heating quality of hot rock.

The kindest thing that one could say about the existing stove in this cabin was that it had character. It was incredibly ugly. Years ago I had acquired two cast-iron ends that had been designed to sandwich a forty-four-gallon drum laid horizontally between them. The front end boasted a hinged door above which were embossed CORD WOOD and COAST FDRY CO LTD. On the door were the words VANCOUVER BC. Two ornate cast-iron legs raised the round disc off the floor. The rear end contained a hole for the chimney. It had been much butchered so was not attractive any more, but it was functional. Three long external bolts fastened everything together. I used this stove for quite a while at Nuk Tessli. The drum eventually burned out. Nothing daunted, I went to my favourite building supply store—the local dump—to see what I could scrounge. I found a smaller drum, which, I was told, had probably been a fuel tank for a truck. I already had a section of a top of a cookstove complete with removable lids.

I presented these various objects to a welder who apparently had some experience of making stoves but when I picked up his creation I was appalled. Instead of the nice compact heater I had envisioned, the welder had spawned a monster sporting all sorts of extra slabs of crudely welded cast iron more than a centimetre thick. The three sections of stove were all so heavy I could not lift them unaided. Fortunately Dylan was with me when the stove arrived. The cabin had no windows then, and we fumbled around in the half dark putting it together. There is something very special about lighting the first fire in a new building, even if the structure is very rudimentary. We celebrated by toasting our lunch with a fork made from a chunk of telegraph wire beaten off a fallen fence with a stone. All the ills of the stove had yet to reveal themselves, however. When adding the slabs of cast iron, the welder had actually cut through the drum in several places. Gleams of light flickered everywhere in the cabin's gloom. Most were in hard-to-get-at spots: it was necessary to wait for the stove to cool before reaching into the sooty interior with ripped slivers of aluminum foil and jabbing them into the holes with a screwdriver.

When Katherine and Stephanie were with me in the fall, we had driven along Highway 20 to where broken bluffs snugged up against the road and we'd collected rocks. These were going to be a heat sink, and while I was away Katherine had built walls on either side of the ugly drum. She did a beautiful job, but unfortunately these had to come down so I could lay the floor and my reconstruction was not as attractive. Like so much in this cabin, however, it was not going to be permanent; it would do for now.

A month after the shortest day, when the days were getting noticeably longer, I had the interior of the cabin to a stage where I could live with it. A second counter and a shelf over the solar power storage batteries constituted an office, and a fourth and final window had been installed in the west wall. A section the width of a double bed had been partitioned off at the end of the cabin near the door. The upper part of this area would indeed be used as a spare bed; below was a permanent produce store with thickly insulated floor and walls. Now when I went away in winter I could safely leave my food without having to worry about it. Two tables against the walls supported things like water jugs, and all kinds of junk could be pushed out of sight underneath. I would

The interior of the cabin after I got it more organized.

still have to live with a pile of lumber and building supplies along the east side of the room, leaving me a very narrow path between the door and the bed, but that was a minor irritation. I now had a well-lit, orderly interior.

I went to the storage space above the garage at Nimpo and fished out a bit of artwork to grace my new walls. One painting was a triptych, the first I had ever done. It is based on a view from a high point along the hike into Nuk Tessli that I especially love at the beginning of summer when the foreground is a mass of early flowers, mountain marsh marigolds and globe flowers for the most part.

Behind, in the centre, is the snow-streaked pyramid of Wilderness Mountain. To the right is a hint of the land dropping down toward the cabins, the way I would be going, and to the left of Wilderness Mountain is another high valley. The peaks behind are even snowier. This area comprises the headwaters of my river. I have always liked this painting and never tried to sell it. When I created it I had no idea that it would have such a special link to my future home.

The painting of the headwaters of my river.

CHAPTER 7

A PHONE!

. . . phone me collect at Kleena Kleene 3C. Phone
Williams Lake. KK phones are all toll stations. Make
the call station to station.

—Extract from a letter
from Ginty to Hilda Thomas

*She used to accuse Ken of climbing the poles with leg irons
and "stealing" calls so he could speak to his relatives in
Saskatchewan. She maintained she could tell he was doing
this because she could hear double clicks on the line.*

—Leslie Lamb

*The phone was a forty-party line and Ginty was an inveter-
ate rubbernecker. I had five brothers and sisters; our father
was the local doctor. We kids used the phone a lot. We knew
she was there and would always say "Hullo Ginty" at the
beginning of our calls and "Goodbye Ginty" at the end. One
time my Mum said, "Get off the phone, Ginty," and Ginty
replied, "I'm not on the phone!" All calls went through the
operator at that time and Ginty complained to her and said*

we were rude and should not be allowed to use the phone. "But how do they know I am listening?" she asked the oper- ator. We knew because we could hear the chickens clucking in the background.

—Joanne Kirby

I had a road and the internet—now I wanted a phone. The nearest cell phone tower to Ginty Creek is over three hours' drive away so that was never an option. A satellite phone would be expensive to run, and radiophones were pretty much obsolete. Early in the new year, I made enquiries about reinstating Ginty's old phone. I went through the rigmarole on the Telus website and on January 10 received a reply from someone signed Todd wanting "the exact address." I replied by describing in detail how to go through Kleena Kleene and where to turn off. This was right after the fifty-centimetre dump of snow; I told Todd that we would have to wait for the road to be ploughed. I had never owned a phone before; I was naive enough to think that the installer might come at once.

The next person who corresponded with me was a Karen, and I gave her more details. She wanted me to phone the call cen- tre. I emailed back that I was presently snowed in and could not get to a phone. (A little white lie but I did not want to cross the river again.) I gave her the lot number and the name of the previ- ous subscriber. I also told her the number and name of Ken and Leslie—mine would be the next phone down the line. Ginty's old number, I informed her, was 3C.

After that came a Steve who informed me that he required a house number. You've got to be kidding! I sent him the informa- tion that I had sent everyone else and he replied asking me to "call the call centre for this inquiry due to the difficulty of the address. Please have the exact info with you. We do need to set something up ASAP for the spring and [our] lists are getting full." But, Steve, I can't call the call centre because . . .

"What on earth," I emailed Rosemary, "is my house number?"

Then my inverter blew. This meant no power and therefore no internet. Fortunately, the road had been ploughed by this time. I drove around to the phone in the booth at Kleena Kleene to tell the Neads. The floor of the booth was a concave sheet of ice. I had to straddle it to be able to use the phone. The Neads run an impressive amount of appliances with their photovoltaic system. Dave told me to call the man near 100 Mile, from whom I got the inverter in the first place. He was undeniably an expert on solar systems but I always felt he did not know how to talk to a complete ignoramus like me, so it was with some misgivings that I phoned his number. There was no answer. I didn't particularly want to make another forty-minute drive again that night, so I called Rosemary and asked her to wave her magic wand as she has done so often for me in the past. When I drove to the phone the next day she told me she had contacted the solar power guru and I was to send the inverter to him. What was more, Dave was going into Williams Lake in the next couple of days and could take it along and put it on the bus, which would save me the freight truck charges on the Chilcotin. However, Dave's plans changed and I decided I would have to go into Williams Lake myself. It was mild and I hoped to return the same day but I threw my sleeping bag into the van and packed all the perishable food in the storage area just in case.

I left at around 4:30 a.m. For the first two hours the highway was good and totally empty of any sign of life except two moose who fled across the road and pounded uphill through belly-deep snow as if it was a flat field. They were pinned against the steep white slope in the sharp cone of light from the van's headlights. As I drew close to Alexis Creek there was a faint bluish tinge of approaching daylight. There was a smokiness to the light and I realized it had recently snowed and the road was very slick. I slowed to round a bend, and without really seeing anything I became aware that there was something in the road in front of me. I was enveloped by falling snowflakes at the same time that I registered the horses. Some were arranged on the banks beside the road, but a white one was actually lying down in the centre of it. I was lucky that I had been going so slowly.

In Williams Lake, I put the inverter on the bus to 100 Mile, phoned the solar power man and left a message, phoned Telus and got nowhere, phoned Rosemary to inform her what was happening, loaded up a pile of veggies, and arrived home two hours after dark. On the way back I stopped at the phone booth at KK. Rosemary had some news. She had contacted the Regional District and after a considerable search had found, to my utter amazement, that I did indeed have a house number. It had 5 figures and was officially located on "Chilcotin Highway." Apparently everyone is issued with one for emergency purposes (although I was never given one in the mountains).

It was up to Rosemary now. I was at the phone booth most days, contacting both Rosemary and occasionally the solar power man. The repair was not serious and it was on warranty but the technician charged $100 to drive the inverter from his place to the bus (a distance of about twenty-five kilometres) and I also had to pay the bus freight to Williams Lake. Dave's delayed trip to town meant that he could at least pick up the inverter and save me the Chilcotin freight charge, and I arranged to be with a neighbour on the highway when he was due to drive through. However, he banged at the wrong cabin door, found no one home, and took the inverter with him, so I had to make the two-hour round trip to Anahim to pick it up. Coordinating people and objects in a place like this is never easy.

I now had power again and could at least use the electric light at night. Trouble was, now the internet wouldn't work. This periodically occurs when the satellite wobbles out of range or the cloud cover is too thick, but usually if you try again in a few hours it will be fine. This time it was completely dead. Back to the KK phone booth. I called the internet installers. They made a couple of suggestions and I went back to the cabin and tried them to no avail. Another drive back to the phone booth. The installers said it might be the transmitter. So I dismantled the arm off the dish and sent it in by freight truck. That was a Friday and on Monday they confirmed the transmitter was indeed dead and informed me that the ubiquitous "they" did not make this kind of satellite dish and arm any more. So six months after the original installation I had to buy a whole new set of equipment. Fortunately the installers were scheduled to come out onto the Chilcotin the following week and would try and fit me in. Which they did. Two and a half weeks and a considerable expenditure later, I was finally back online.

In the middle of all this we had a terrible thaw. In spring, thaws are one thing: the sun shines, birds sing, buds swell. In winter they mean uncomfortable humidity, heavy gloom, violent wind, and rain oscillating with periods of frost so the world becomes a skating rink. I had no idea that my flat-seeming yard sloped so much. I would hack at the trails to the woodshed and the outhouse with the splitting maul but by the next day they would be glare ice again. Ashes from the stove would have provided a non-slip surface but when the ice disappeared they would have made a terrible mess. My crampons were up in the mountains and slip-on spikes were not available in the local stores. I had one very unpleasant fall that gave me a lot of pain for weeks. The green tarp that had provided a minuscule and not very effective porch all winter was now sagging alarmingly with the weight of all that wet snow. I shovelled it off as best I could, hacking a bit at a time until another layer thawed. When it was finally relieved of its monumental load, it was lifted and worried by the wind, clapping like gunshots when the wild gusts blew. The snow level dropped thirty centimetres. The pack was now waist deep.

Rosemary drove to the coast and rolled their Yukon on glare ice. She was trapped, but fortunately a couple of guys cutting firewood nearby, who just happened to switch their chainsaws off, heard her honking the horn and they rescued her. Despite a lot of damage, the Yukon was driveable but a tow truck was needed to get it out of there. The accident was close to the Redstone reserve. Someone went and phoned, and the wives of the firewood cutters made a big bonfire by the side of the road to keep Rosemary warm while she waited for the tow. Rosemary christened my "guest bedroom" on her way back to the Precipice. She brought me veggies and two pots of spring bulbs. On the occasions when the sun shone, the light poured through the petals of the crocuses as they perched on the kitchen windowsill—what a treat.

I was running out of firewood. I knew in the fall that I would not have enough to last the winter but there were a number of beetle-killed trees close to the telegraph road that I figured I would be able to get when I needed them. I did not want ones too recently dead as they would be sappy inside and loaded with pitch from their efforts to fight the beetle—a perfect recipe for creosoting chimneys. I loaded snowshoes, chainsaw, gas, tools and toboggan into the wheelbarrow and walked up the road. I had learned from experience that it was better to pack down snow the day before around the trees to be fallen; that made both the footing safer and pulling the firewood on the toboggan much easier. I falled and limbed and bucked and dragged and stamped fresh trails for most of two weeks, and then brought the van along the road and carried the wood to the cabin. Poor van. Its papers showed it had been a city dweller for the first five years of its life. Now it was forced to buck axle-deep snow and have its innards buried in bits of bark and dog hair. But it performed like a trooper.

I was now in touch with a Kevin at Telus and things were looking much more promising. Rosemary had been badgering the technicians who serviced their own remote phone and a message had been passed to a Jim Shetler. I knew Jim slightly. I had met him when he had been setting off on horseback to check on a friend's line. He was close to retiring. He knew everything there was to know about the remote phones in the area. He even remembered Ginty's wind-the-handle contraption.

Kevin was the service manager for the Customer Solutions Delivery of the Cariboo/Chilcotin. "I believe we have found your place on one of the old plant maps. Has there ever been a telephone service at that location?" (Obviously none of the previous information had been passed on.) "I show a pole line with a telephone cable on it crossing the river headed approximately where you are. If this service is still there, then there would be a small metal box on the cable about twelve inches by six inches that has the number 221 stencilled on it." There was a box all right, way over on the last pole by the Packrat Palace. I could not see the number from down below.

The Packrat Palace would be a good three hundred metres distant. I figured it would make more sense to use a closer pole. I cut a clear way through a small grove of trees (mentally groaning at the extra mess to clean up in the spring), but when Jim came on March 8, he said that the line from that pole would sag too close to the ground where the land rose. I had wondered about that and had left a suitable tree to hook the line onto. I had collected several glass insulators from the old telegraph line and thought they would be ideal, but Jim said this would not work as the tree was not grounded. If I ran the line from that direction I would need to pay for an extra pole and the cost of installing another box. That, of course, would not only cost money, it would take months. "The easiest thing for me to do," Jim explained, "is to put a phone box on the last post where the connection already is. You get Dave Neads' old wire from when he had his own extension in the Precipice. They don't need it now they have a microwave tower in there. You could run the wire along this fence."

Jim strapped on a thick leather belt and wicked-looking leg hooks and shinnied up the pole. I'd never seen anyone do that before. He checked the metal box but there was no dial tone. "It's probably nothing serious," he said. "It has likely been disconnected where the line to the ranch splits off across the river." Right now, getting to that point was not going to be easy. The river was no longer safe to even attempt to cross. It was also a long way from the ranch's driveway and there was no trail of any kind to it from that side either. Ken and Leslie had left; the new owners were supposed to have moved in but I had not seen or heard any sign of life.

Jim said he would be back the next day and he'd see what he could do. He had no snowshoes with him and I told him I would see if I could break trail for him on the ranch side of the river and I would leave my snowshoes in a barn beside their driveway. That afternoon

Jim hooking up the phone.

I drove around to where the line angled off the highway and as it looked as though I could go in from there I thought I would try that route first. It was hot and the snow was thigh deep and totally rotten. I floundered for a while, then came to a slough. I picked a way between the wet patches and overflow but was turned back by the old channel of the river. It was filled with half-frozen water and looked too rotten to risk. It would be necessary to go back to the highway and break trail through the ranch meadows after all.

It was a good excuse to be nosy and introduce myself to the new owners. I was lucky to catch them home; they had spent most of their first week going back and forth to Williams Lake to ferry supplies. He was from France but had lived in Canada for twenty years; she was fresh out of England. She was the daughter of an innkeeper and had grown up in a pub. Chilcotin life would be very different and I wondered how well she would adapt. They planned to run sheep—the man had been a shepherd—and open a B&B.

The sun was setting by the time I finished the visit so I didn't break any more trail but left my snowshoes in the barn as planned. Jim did not go to the ranch the following day, however. Instead he drove to the cabin and said he would not have time to finish the job right now. Telus had given him other, more urgent work. My phone would have to wait for his next trip to the area in about ten days' time.

I forget where I was when he did turn up. I came home midafternoon to find that someone had driven in on the road. The spring thaw was happening big time and the van wallowed in the churned-up mud and slush created by Jim's truck. A ripped piece of cardboard box was jammed between the cabin door and its frame. On it, in ballpoint capitals, was the message:

IT IS WORKING AT THE POLE
OPEN BOX WITH FLAT SCREWDRIVER
PLUG YOUR PHONE INTO THE JACK PLUG
Jim

The pole was in a sunny spot and the snow had shrunk to knee depth there. I plugged in an old phone Ken had given me. Of course I called Rosemary first. It felt silly to be standing in knee-deep snow by the pole in the hot sunshine having a conversation. I had nothing to put the phone onto and its wires were not long enough for it to lie on the snow. I had to hold it in one hand and the receiver in the other. If I needed to write something I was going to have to acquire another pair of hands. In the Packrat Palace was a table complete with the remains of a filthy oil cloth that had been nailed on with carpet tacks. It was glueily brown with pack-rat secretions. I dragged it out, cleaned the top off as best I could with snow, and voila! I had an office.

For years, Dave and Rosemary had maintained a kilometre-long phone extension in their valley. At first they had used speaker wire stapled to a fence but later invested in some very expensive line that could lie on the ground. Now that the microwave dish had been installed on the Precipice rim, the speaker wire was sitting there unused, but when I contacted Dave and told him what Jim had said, he replied that it was not in good shape. In any case, it would not be available until their road was open—probably late May. "You could always have an extra loud bell," he said.

The new couple across the river were still going back and forth to town a lot and I drove over and asked them if they could pick up some speaker wire for me. So on Saturday, March 24 I dragged a ladder to the pole and strung the wire over an old gateway and along a sagging Russell fence to the cabin. "It's got to be eight feet off the ground," Jim had told me. In places I tied a spare rail vertically to the fence to prop up the line. The following morning I enjoyed the luxurious sensation of sitting awash in the sunshine pouring through the bay window, talking on the phone. A phone was something I had never had in the mountains, and having one right by my hand seemed almost more miraculous than being hooked to the satellite internet. Ginty Creek was now thoroughly connected to the world.

CHAPTER 8

SPRING

He [Adrian Paul] *was quite the birder. He even argued with Roger Tory Peterson about the marks on some bird's head. Some sparrow I think.*

—Ken Jansen

Her father, Mr. Paul, I really enjoyed him. He was quiet. He had this dresser set full of little drawers and inside were all these birds' eggs he had collected. He would show them to me and talk about them.

—Rhonda Nygaard

There's a funny story about Mr. Paul. Well it's not really funny, but you have to laugh.

W— B— had a bad asthma attack at the bridge by your turnoff, and Mr. Paul found him. Mr. Paul was—what do you call them?—an ornithologist. He spotted all kinds of rare birds. Anyway, one day we get this phone call and it's Mr. Paul. He's all excited about this bird he's seen—I dunno, a yellow-bellied fluffy-headed something. He's telling us all about it. How it sang and how close it was to him. Then he

says: "Oh by the way, could you please phone the RCMP and
tell them there's a dead man at the bridge and you should
have seen the way this bird flew this way and that . . ." Well
we laughed for a long time over that. He must have been
about eighty-eight at the time.

—Louise Moxon

Spring. Nedra Creek roared over the snow from the upper property, its waters flashing and sparkling blue in the sunlight, and plunged into a widening hole in the river. Chunks of ice began to collapse in the river itself and the water began to rise. Suddenly there were silvery buttons on the early species of willows—I swear they had not been there the day before. Cottonwood buds started to swell and form the sticky outer coat that smells so divine after a spring rain. I brought twigs of both species into the cabin and sat them in canning jars on a sunny windowsill beside trays of sunflower and quinoa sprouts.

The first spring migrants came through; as in the mountains, the herald was a junco. I scrounged up a bit of board, rimmed it with offcuts of one-by-threes, and nailed it to a post stuck into the snow just outside the bay window. Now I had a bird feeder; within days, upward of thirty juncos were scrapping and posturing. I loved the way that two would face off and, with little twittering noises, would try to stand taller than their opponent. Redwing blackbirds were next, flashing their wonderful red shoulder patches, then other species of blackbirds, song sparrows and pine siskins. As soon as the south-facing slopes lost their snow, robins sang. Varied thrushes, red-tailed hawks, purple finches, gold-crowned and white-crowned sparrows, song sparrows—the list was exciting, with new birds arriving every day. Many of these species I had never seen before, as the ecology here was quite different from that in the mountains. Red-naped sapsuckers. Red-headed woodpecker. Evening grosbeak. Woodpeckers beat tattoos on dead branches, flickers cackled, ruffed grouse drummed on fallen logs, snipe made their ghostly winnowing over the ponds in the upper property. Northern harriers swooped the open spaces. Rough-winged swallows, yellow-rumped warblers. Once, flying overhead with pterodactyl silhouette and a croak fresh from the swamps of Siluria, a sandhill crane. Dick Cannings has stated that the Chilcotin is the bird world's best-kept secret, and here I had my own private wetland—as well as a patch of open grassland, and the river, and the bluffs, and the forest. All these eco-niches encouraged different species. How glad I was that I had not taken any of the other properties I had looked at, as none of them had anything like the diversity of this landscape. Many species I could not identify. Their observation was going to provide me with years of joy.

The wildflowers, on the whole, were disappointing. Mostly introduced species, they were sparse on the ground—nothing like the fabulous alpine abundance I had come to accept as my backyard in the mountains. A few early purple violets peeped shyly along a bank, and dandelions made forests of yellow suns where the ground had more recently been disturbed. The terraces of Ginty's garden were still evident below the Packrat Palace, and in the rhubarb patch, convoluted brain clusters of new leaves started to push through the blackened sprawl of last season's plants. There were several comfrey plants, too, but I couldn't see much else that had survived until I crossed the roaring creek on a weathered, wobbly plank and found a lawn-sized plot of chives. Dandelion leaf and chive salad was on the menu for quite a while.

The road took a long time to dry up. The end closest to the cabin received more sun and it rotted out first; just when this was more or less usable again, the part closest to the highway disintegrated.

If I wanted to go to the post office and store I would leave early in the morning when the road was still frozen, but the post office was open from eleven 'til two and the mail truck came around noon so the road was generally pretty bad when I returned. Other occasional visitors to both myself and Edgar's property were not so mindful of the damage being done and they churned back and forth in the afternoons, leaving a legacy of ruts and bogholes. The road would no longer be the dusty and little-used bush trail that I had travelled over the first time I saw Ginty Creek.

The road was still in pretty bad shape when the first wwoofers arrived in mid-April. Claire and Ron lived in Nanaimo and they had driven up in their town car. They were so appalled at the state of the road they parked near the end and walked the four kilometres to the cabin. I assured them we would be able to retrieve the vehicle in the morning. They were to sleep in the little trailer; I hoped it would be warm enough for them. There was no means of heating it. The sun blasted on it during the day so it was not too bad in the evening but it was still freezing hard at night and the mornings were frigid.

Claire and Ron were a little different from most wwoofers in that they were my age. They had no less energy than the younger ones, however. Ron was a handy carpenter, which was a great bonus, and Claire was a cleanup whirlwind. I had inherited a large area of decayed wood and other garbage around the cabin that had never been moved in the fall—there had been no time then—and this was now emerging from the snow. It became apparent that there had once been three outhouses among the debris; they must have serviced the cabin on the knoll that Ken had stayed in. But why three?

Before Ron and Claire came, I had been chipping away at the ice around the door area where the porch was going to be. I would chop a bit, then wait for it to thaw, then chop again. Eventually the foundations appeared. The previous fall, I had propped scrounged logs and poles and heavy boards against a nearby fence so that they could easily be found in the spring. Now I could use them to frame the porch walls and put rafters across for a ceiling. When Ron and Claire came, we nailed on the boards for an upper floor, stripped off the old green tarp and set up rafters and strapping. The remaining pieces of roofing had been stored in the attic; these were now retrieved and we managed to put all but the last two on before my helpers left. When it was too windy to work on the porch, we built a bigger woodshed, and cut and hauled more wood. One day we trudged through the crisp, patchy snow to the upper property and I started to fall trees where my house would eventually be.

Claire and Ron were fun. Claire had been brought up in francophone Manitoba and she had a strong French Canadian

Ron and Claire.

accent. She had problems pronouncing the "th" sound. We played Scrabble and one day she used a three-lettered word that I did not recognize. "It's in t'e Scrabble dictionary," she said. "It's a tree-tooted slot." I did not want to be impolite but I could not help myself and burst out laughing. She was trying to say a three-toothed sloth!

Now it was May. Bits of snow kept falling. I had set up a hand pump to make it easier to get water from the river, but half the time the pipe was frozen. I started making a road to the new building site. I had marked it with flagging tape while the snow was still thick on the ground. It angled off the bush trail that had once serviced the sawmill. There was a wet area partway along that would need a culvert before a vehicle could be taken over it. I did not mind cutting the scrubby, sometimes dead, pines so much, but it was sad to bring down the aspens. They were so beautiful in the fall and now they were beginning to sport a mist of green. I also worked on the access to the building site from the lower end. It was far too wet to put a road in from that direction but I made a wheelbarrow trail so I could carry tools up that way. I built a stile to cross the snake fence that Ken had put up for his cows.

In the middle of the month I went to Williams Lake to pick up a huge pile of supplies, much of it for the mountain business, and three more wwoofers. Boris and Sven were both from Belgium, although they had not met before they arrived at the bus station in Williams Lake. Sven was in his early twenties, Boris only nineteen. Monika was from Switzerland and was a little older. She would be arriving at the airport in the early evening. I jammed them and all their gear into the van somehow—a lot of stuff was tied onto the roof. Monika would have the trailer and the boys would have to sleep in tents.

Wwoofers are supposed to work half days. I tell them that as long as they work half the time, that is fine. They can slave for a week and take a week off—they will still get fed. The deal with these three was that they would work hard for me at Ginty Creek (with a few breaks) and then come into the mountains for a two-week vacation. It was not to work out quite that way.

They were incredible workers. We filled the woodshed ready for next winter and finished the porch roof, and the boys built a barrier in the attic to make two rooms, fitting windows scrounged from the Packrat Palace in either end. I continued to fall trees to complete the road to the upper place, then they cleared everything off the right-of-way, peeling any log that was remotely straight (Monika was an incredible peeler) and piling the rest for future firewood. I cut down a lot more trees on the site, and now I had a view of the mountains. I also had an enormous mess of brush and stumps and logs. It was brutal work, but the weather warmed and soon it felt like summer. We had one gloriously hot bug-free day. On the next, they hatched.

From left: Boris, Sven and Monika opening the new road.

We went down the famous cliff-hanging switchbacks known as The Hill to Bella Coola. Friends own a property at Stuie at the upper end of the valley. They were not home but were happy for us to stay overnight. The house used to be my outside base when I lived in the bush near Lonesome Lake, and I spent a winter there once. The scenery is spectacular. The coastal forest in spring is weeks ahead of the Chilcotin and I always love to visit, especially at this time of year. The winter gloom and rain is something else, however. I would not be able to live there full time.

We went to see the bears. In fall, they are to be found along the river, eating the spawning salmon. In spring, they camp out on the roadside. Down in the valley we spotted a number of black bears, singly and in groups, wallowing in the lush green grass and dandelions, but our best sighting was back up on the Chilcotin not far from the top of The Hill. Way ahead of us, a car coming the

The young grizzly boar beside the road.

other way had stopped. Nearby was a dark mound that appeared to be moving. I slowed down so as not to scare the animal away and ruin the other car occupants' chances for photos. I needn't have worried. The other car left and we parked right beside a magnificent young grizzly male with a pale stripe across his shoulders who could not have cared less about us. I warned the wwoofers to stay in the vehicle both for safety reasons and also not to crowd the bear unnecessarily. Stay in the vehicle they did—just. Everyone was hanging out of every door and window as far as they could to take pictures. The bear eyed us once or twice but ate calmly. We were so close that when I zoomed my camera all I got in the frame was part of his head.

At the end of May all the local ranchers turn their cows out onto the open range. At first the animals crowd the roadside, as that is where the grazing is. Driving becomes a nightmare because the calves have not yet learned to keep out of the way. Sometimes they are on one side of the highway and their mother is on the other, and at the last minute they panic and run across. One ranch makes a two-day cattle drive from Kleena Kleene to Anahim Lake. The highway becomes paved with a mess of sloppy fresh cowpoop.

The rancher at the Precipice, where Dave and Rosemary live, drives his cows up the side of the valley to an area beyond the basalt rim. He makes a party of it; half the countryside attends and there is a barbecue and lots of homemade music. I see people I haven't seen since the last cattle drive party a year before. I would class most of them as neighbours even if they do live sixty kilometres or more away.

I arranged to take the wwoofers down to the Precipice with me. Because of the excessive snowfall the road was barely thawed. About halfway down, the rancher had bogged his truck and we had to park above it; Dave met us and ferried us into the valley with his Suburban. The river down there had broken its banks in a couple of places and washed away the farm roads. There was water everywhere. We stayed an extra day or two, and while I visited with Rosemary we put the wwoofers to work helping to prepare Rosemary's extensive vegetable garden.

It had been excessively hot for over ten days before that weekend. Temperatures had reached 28°C. Everyone was worried about flooding due to the exceptionally heavy snowfall. Then, while we were in the Precipice, it poured with rain. We returned to Ginty Creek to find that my river, previously several separate skeins flowing around a number of gravel islands, was now wall-to-wall water. Brown and roaring, it was lapping the tops of the banks.

More chunks of land had fallen into the river, including a large

The spring flood.

piece very close to the trailer. A corner of the snake fence now hung over the water unsupported. A group of mature cottonwoods on a point that jutted into the river had been a prominent part of the view from the bay window of the cabin. Three of these trees now lay in the water, their newly leafed-out branches half drowned in the boiling flow and their roots catching all manner of floating debris. That evening, in the half-light, a cow moose walked into the river just past the new logjam. I was sure she would be swept away, but no, she calmly waded from one side to the other, the water piling up against her flanks. Moose are such disjointed-looking beasts, but so supremely adapted to their environment.

During my twenty years in the mountains, the ice has gone out from the lake at Nuk Tessli between May 17 and June 4. I like to get in there as soon as the lake is open: it is so wonderful to watch the land explode from the grip of winter. Because of the heavy snow, I expected breakup to be later rather than sooner this year. A pilot had flown over on June 3 and reported a lot of open spaces in the ice; the owner of the float plane base figured we would probably be able to go in on the 6th. As we drove to the float plane base there was not a single square centimetre of the van that was not occupied. The two boys, one of whom was very tall, were crammed into less than a single seat space in the back (they shared a seat belt and I hoped we would not meet any cops); Monika had several items piled between her legs and on her lap. I sent the wwoofers off in a smaller plane so they could have a flight-seeing tour as a thank you for all the work they had done. Fortunately it took a long time for me to load the Beaver with the dogs and freight, and I also had to wait for a pilot to return from another job. We were just taxiing out when the smaller plane returned. The wwoofers were still inside it. They had not been able to land because the lake at Nuk Tessli was still frozen.

This was obviously going to be a record year for the ice, and it would in fact be another week before we could fly in.

Which meant we had to return to Ginty Creek.

We left some of the freight in the hangar at the float plane base so that we could drive back in greater comfort and safety. The river had peaked and was already dropping. I had been observing unfamiliar mounds under the roiling brown water; now these emerged as new piles of flood debris, either lumps of bank or piles of logs, some of these newly swept away from where they had grown and still bearing leafed-out branches. As I watched the brown swirls and riffles, it seemed as though the main channel might have changed, and sure enough, as the water dropped, a whole new landscape was revealed. Instead of curling around the closer bank, the main stream now rushed by on the far side of the river.

One day I went to the river to rinse clothes and heard a strange cry. I thought it might be a bird I did not know and crept cautiously through the thick alders along the bank. On the far side of the river, on an emerging patch of gravel, was a newborn moose. The cord was still hanging from its belly. I ran back to fetch the wwoofers, but warned them to be very careful as cow moose can be very dangerous when they have young calves. Of the mother, however, there was no sign. At first, when the calf saw us, it tried to cross the river. It waded in, was nearly swept away, and scrambled out again. I had come across this kind of thing once before when two mule-deer fawns had temporarily lost their mother. They had run to my side; presumably they are programmed to attach themselves to something tall. When the mother called them they were gone.

The moose calf's little cry was a bit like the baaa of a sheep, but without the quaver. "We've got to do something," said the wwoofers, but the baby was on the far side of the water and we certainly

The baby moose.

could not cross. I went back to the cabin and emailed anyone who might be interested in trying to rear it: we could not take it on as we expected to be going into the mountains in a couple of days. I phoned the wildlife service but got an answering machine (there is only one warden for half the Chilcotin.) The wwoofers ran back up from the river. They were wildly excited because the calf had actually swum across and one of the boys had touched it, but it had gone back into the water before he could catch it. It had been swept quite a way downstream before it had been able to scramble out.

The day drew on and the sun went down. Monika's trailer was right opposite where the calf was still bawling, bawling. I was in bed and it was dark when the wwoofers came up. "We've got to do something," they begged again. "I suppose we could drive around to the ranch and see if we can get to it on that side of the river," I said. "What are you going to catch it with?" It appeared that they thought it would simply lead like a dog. I had dealt with enough cattle in my life to know that, newborn or not, the baby moose would probably kick like a mule. I phoned the ranch. They had irrigation pipes over the field so we would have to walk from their driveway. We found a flashlight, a sack (to put over the animal's head to try and calm it) and some rope. Sven grabbed a quarter-full jug of milk. "How are you going to give it that?" I asked. "It will want to suck. You won't be able to pour it down its throat." "I've got a condom," said Sven. "Would that work?" There, I thought, is a wwoofer who is prepared for everything.

We drove round to the ranch, walked across the field and climbed the fence. We would have to fight our way through a swampy thicket of cottonwoods and alders. We thrashed to the gravel bar where we had seen the calf. Except for the gurgle and chatter of the river, there was silence. We hunted up and down for a half-hour or so. Not a sound. That moose calf had been bawling for nine hours. What had happened to make it stop during the thirty minutes it had taken us to drive around to the ranch and walk across the field? Did it fall into the river and drown? Did something eat it? Did its mother come back for it? We returned to our side of the river and to silence. It was a mystery we would never be able to solve.

CHAPTER 9

GIN AND TONIC, VODKA AND LIME

July 10, '80

. . . I wrote to Rafe Mair--my views on Health care. He wrote a really nice letter back and said he'd taken the liberty of having copies made and sent to the various officials in his ministry. One thing I said was that as long as ailments are money-makers for MDs people will ail. I suggested having a Preventative Medicine Assn, and let the others belong to the exploiting ailments gang. I really tried to write nicely--and did. . . . When we had an MD here he told a v. good nurse not to go around getting people to live in a more healthful way--she quit. All his prescriptions etc. were to keep people ailing or worse--what a racket. I think Rafe Mair is a good type. He did well in his previous job.

—Extract from a letter
from Ginty to Hilda Thomas

*We delivered hay to Ginty. One time George went over there
and there was no one around. Then he heard a quiet "help."
She was in a building and something heavy had fallen across
the door. She'd been there overnight, anyway.*

*She had a war with O— K—. His cows got in. It was
her responsibility to fix the fence, but she made such a stink
about the cows, he would buy two or three bales from us
every year and dump them off at her place. He would drive
in there, throw the hay out, and drive away again without
ever saying a word.*

—Lynne Rettberg

O n a sunny afternoon in the middle of February, I thought
I heard a car door clunk; sure enough someone had arrived. My two "fierce" SPCA Rottweiler crosses didn't bark but
they were doing their best to beat the visitors to death with their
tails. The two men were the first people, apart from the guy who
ploughed the road, to come to my cabin that year.

When I bought Ginty Creek I knew there would not be enough
of the inheritance money to build the house of my dreams. Nor
did I want to do the actual construction itself. There had been
very few years in the last quarter of a century when I was not involved with some kind of building work or other, and I found it a
monstrous chore; it was, however, the only way I could afford to
have what I wanted.

Ginty Creek was composed of two separate titles. If I sold or
traded one of them, I could afford to have someone else build the
house. I approached a couple of builders I knew, but that didn't go
anywhere. Then I met a local man who said he had a friend who
might be interested. The friend had expressed a desire to have organic greenhouses and a metal recycling business (at the time, all
metal waste—cars, appliances and so on—was simply piled, and

eventually buried, at the dumps). The friend's wife had a love af-fair with rivers; for her the place would be ideal.

The local man was Chilcotin born and bred, even if he did have a penchant for pretty hair and necklaces. His wife was a transplanted city girl who loved the summers but found the win-ters difficult. I will give them the initials V and L: their friends' in-itials were G and T and I immediately thought of Gin and Tonic. I have no idea why, as they are not drinkers and I never touch alcohol, but for some reason those words popped into my head. V and L, consequently, are referred to as Vodka and Lime.

"Gin" was short and wore his thinning hair pulled into a strag-gling pony tail. It was bottle-coloured black. He told me he was sixty-seven and just back from four years in Thailand. (I never did find out what he was doing there.) Before he went overseas he had apparently built houses and installed garage doors but he had sold all his tools and heavy machinery as he had not expected to come back to Canada. His wife, however, had developed too many allergies from the food to be happy there. I liked the idea of organic greenhouses and a commitment to recycle metal from the dumps. I also thought that having a mechanic next door, and someone who would help keep the road ploughed, would be a great help as I grew older.

A couple of weeks later, his wife ("Tonic") came to see the place. It was a gorgeous day with chunks of blue open water be-tween the thick ice slabs that lined the river. Tonic loved it. Gin babbled on in his Newfie accent (a touch of the blarney maybe?) about how he was buying an "escavator." At the end of March we started to work out an agreement, emailing it back and forth to iron out the details. For the deposit I wanted a truck for the bush (it had to be legal for the road but I probably would not insure it), a hole for an outhouse, a road (they would have to put in a culvert), and a basement dug for my new house. I reckoned this would be worth about $20,000 in labour and supplies. Allowing for the fact that Gin and Tonic would have to start shaping their own lives as well, I restricted my demands to having them finish the shell of the new house by the end of the second summer; by the time the snow flew in year three, I wanted every detail in place.

A pickup was presented to me in the middle of April and it worked fine except that it was fuelled by propane. If I was not going to insure it and could not therefore drive it to Nimpo Lake to gas up, a propane truck was not a lot of use to me. It would not be much good in winter either because my small solar power system did not have enough juice to operate a block heater and a propane motor will not start cold. A diesel truck was not practical for the same reason. It had to be a gas truck (as I had stipulated from the beginning). However, the propane pickup would do for the time being. The two Belgian wwoofers had a great time hauling logs and firewood with it. Nineteen-year-old Boris, who lived in downtown Brussels and did not even have a driver's licence, was in seventh heaven.

By the end of April, Gin had begun to stockpile wrecked vehicles in the meadow close to the river—he vowed he would transport them to the recycling depot when he had bought a flatdeck. Further into the bush there grew a pile of old chassis, backhoe buckets and other heavy pieces of iron and steel whose purpose I could only guess at. Not very pretty, but I told myself that it was going to be his backyard so I might as well get used to it. Compromise, I thought. Compromise. It was going to have to be my new mantra.

I was up at Nuk Tessli, my mountain resort, for three and a half months and had little time to think about Ginty Creek. I did email Gin and Tonic a little before I was due to fly out at the end of September, hoping the gas truck was ready for me. We had not yet signed the agreement; they did not reply. When I drove into the yard by the cabin, the propane truck was sitting where I had left it and its battery was dead. As soon as I could, I walked up to the upper property (the grasses tawny, the leaves beginning to turn: it was a year since I had moved in). A very battered culvert had been inserted into the marshy area along the new road and some ditching had been done on either side, but the "escavator" work was an appalling mess. I had cleared trees over a good wide swath, but the ditches wriggled all over the place and sometimes the centre of the road was barely the width of a vehicle. The underlying silt that was now exposed was pure slime when it got wet and it was almost impossible to stay out of the ditches. Vodka told me that Gin had made a payment on a long-distance truck and got a job hauling freight to earn money for his building endeavours. He had hired someone else to do the "escavating." There was no basement: Vodka explained it would be a waste of time to dig one so late in the year as it would sluff in all winter. Far better to wait until the summer when the shell could be built over the top to shelter it. That was disappointing but it seemed a reasonable enough argument so I was prepared to let it ride. Gin and Tonic had now enlisted Vodka and Lime's help. The four of them would do the work and build my house and all would share the property. I got a few warnings from one or two other local people who had known Gin before he went overseas but Vodka was well liked and seemed a decent enough guy. I was prepared to accept his word as I could very well be rubbing elbows (metaphorically speaking) with him for a very long time.

While I was still in the mountains, another wwoofer had emailed me looking for some wilderness experience. I told her I had enough help at Nuk Tessli for the summer but if she was willing I could certainly use her at the end of September at the winter place. There is no public transport on the Chilcotin and I did not think a nineteen-year-old would want to hitchhike. I had to shop as soon as I came out of the mountains anyway and so I arranged to pick her up at the bus station in town.

Since Dylan (the human crane) had worked for me, I had become friendly with his mother, Patricia. She lived near 100 Mile House, an hour south of Williams Lake, and, as the selection of organic and health food was much better there, I took to staying with Patricia on my shopping expeditions, even though it meant the extra time behind the wheel. Patricia is a keen ecologist and birder. She had visited Ginty Creek at the peak of the spring migrant season and taught me a lot.

The wwoofer had introduced herself in her email as Sarah. As she stepped off the bus my heart sank. She was tall and slim, had waist-long white-blonde hair and looked as though a puff of wind would blow her away. She was very polite, but extremely quiet: it was difficult to find anything we might have in common to talk about. It was not without misgivings that I drove her back to Ginty Creek.

Which shows how wrong first impressions can be. Sarah was not only a workaholic—she was also extremely handy with tools. What is more, she loved nothing better than to solve a problem and had really good ideas as to how to approach a piece of work. She had grown up in the Lower Mainland but a couple of years earlier her folks had moved to Vernon and she had helped her dad build their house. She adored animals. She had grown up with horses and dogs and cats and chickens and loved them all.

The cabin at Ginty Creek was full of cuddly critters after a summer's abandonment, but they were not at all welcome. Mice had overrun the living area while I had been up in the mountains and a packrat had pre-empted the upper porch. I was surprised at the mice because I had worked hard to block any hole into which my little finger could be poked. Eventually, I realized that they were coming in underneath the door. I was going to be building a new door anyway—the old one would be installed in the porch—and for the time being I laid some stuffed socks at the bottom and set a bunch of traps. One time when Sarah and I were sitting in the cabin, a mouse ran across the floor and sat by the door waiting to get out, just like a pet dog. "It's so cute!" Sarah exclaimed. Cute they might be but I didn't want to live with them. I trapped seven or eight before we got rid of them.

The packrat was a lot harder to deal with. There had been no time to build walls around the porch before I left and she (females are smaller and less stinky than males) had enjoyed unrestricted access. Tools and other items had been stored in the upper porch and these were not only littered with packrat poop, they were also buried in great piles of dried leafy vegetation, which were the packrat's winter food supply. In one spot the creature had made a nest of rockwool filched from the batts still stored around one of the dog kennels; the nest was a cup, just like a bird's nest. Her trinket cache (nails, the tops of several water jugs, shiny pieces of paper and so on) was separate from her nest. She had marked her territory well with her scent gland. This was Packrat Palace number two in the making.

I cleaned and swept, and Sarah put hardware cloth in the spaces between the rafters along the bottom edges of the roof, and blocked up any other packrat-sized hole. I set a trap with leafy greens (packrats are strict vegetarians but ignore oily things like peanut butter). Twice she managed to eat the food and set off the trap without harm. I had to get smarter. I walled the trap in with cardboard boxes so she had less choice of route for getting to the goodies. She still succeeded in extracting the bait unharmed and was by now so used to me that she was running to the trap as soon as I set it—she thought I was feeding her like a friend. Made me feel pretty bad when I got her. Poor Sarah held her hands over her ears and looked away while the packrat met her end. Sarah and I then worked hard to close in the walls and make them packrat proof. The cabin was now completely surrounded with hardware cloth. Its exterior would eventually be finished with the siding I had collected from the barn we had pulled down, but part of the deal with Gin and Tonic was that this cabin should be moved to the upper property where I would continue to use it as guest accommodation. The siding would be put on after the move, and that is when I would also line the porch. So it didn't look very pretty, but I at least had an extra shelter that would keep the worst of the weather away from the door. The coming winter was going to be a great deal more comfortable than the first.

Sarah was quite terrified of the idea of bears. She got that fear, I was to find out later, from her mother, who had experienced quite a scare when she was sleeping in a tent as a child. I told Sarah that I had not seen a sign of a bear at all that fall (they had certainly been present in the spring) but if she thought she heard them around the trailer at night she should bang a couple of pots together. "I'll just phone you," she said, holding up her cell phone, bought new especially for this trip. "There are no cell phones here!" I laughed. When I thought about it later I realized how brave she was, going down to the trailer in the dark on her own.

One consequence of this fear was that she would not go for a hike without me. I find it difficult to have to relate to people every waking hour of the day, which is why I usually accept wwoofers in batches: that way they can entertain themselves and be out of my hair on occasions. I wanted to enjoy the fall colours, which were again spectacular. Everything looks richer and brighter when I am on my own, but wherever I went, Sarah came too. I have to admit I found her one of the easiest people to get on with, so it wasn't too onerous to have her tag along. We explored the bluffs both north and south (me dragging a reluctant Sarah up the south bluffs before dawn one frosty morning to watch the sunrise) and made several forays onto the gravel bars along the river in front of the cabin. These had been out of reach when the main channel of the river had flowed on my side; now that the channel had moved, we had a large area of river-worn stones and piles of driftwood to explore.

Ironically, it was with Sarah that I had some of my best bear sightings ever. The fall colours had already passed their best on the Chilcotin when we went down the 18-percent-grade switch-backs, known as "The Hill," to Bella Coola, but at that much lower elevation they were at their finest. Where my friends live, at Stuie in the upper part of the valley, were some excellent bear-viewing points. Five species of salmon spawn in the Bella Coola River and the gourmet feast lasts for weeks. In the past I have visited often at that time of year and rarely seen another human being. This year, however, things were different. Word had got out.

I had been down there a week or so earlier with another friend. We had seen only a couple of bears (grizzlies) but people were everywhere. Cars drove up and down—they were irritating but not dangerous. They did, however, take away the precious-ness of being the only, silent observers.

Tweedsmuir Park Lodge at Stuie has run bear-viewing drift-boat trips for a number of years. One came by as we watched from the top of an esker on a trail high above the river. The water was shallow and slow and the steersman gently and calmly moved the boat along. His passengers were absolutely silent and barely moved except to carefully raise their cameras. They had only just disappeared when we heard voices upstream. There was a lot of yelling and aggressive shouting: someone must be in trouble! Soon another drift boat floated into sight. This was obviously a private craft. Two men rode in it while two others, dressed in hip waders, were slogging through the shallows alongside. This was totally illegal. All four had rifles slung over their shoulders.

The slope of the esker was almost precipitous at that point, and the river was largely hidden from us by trees. It was obvious by the men's behaviour, however, that there was a bear directly below us. The men were yelling and gesticulating, trying to get the bear to give them a more active picture. One started to throw river stones into the brush. I knew from experience that, when startled, bears often run uphill away from water. I have also seen them gallop up steep slopes as if they were racetracks. If this bear did so, we would be directly in the way. I called down to the men and asked them not to startle the bear. "Oh nothing will move this sucker," said one of the men, and he fired another rock. I was utterly appalled. Not only were they creating danger for themselves and other people, they were also abusing the bear's sense of security. The Atnarko River during the spawning season is one of the best grizzly habitats in the world. This kind of abuse would lead to the bear becoming stressed out and either failing to eat enough fish to hibernate properly or taking it out on another human and getting shot. I had no idea where the single park ranger might be. The park headquarters was at least thirty minutes' drive away and there was no guarantee anyone would be there. By the time I had walked back to my vehicle and made the drive, the men would be long gone.

When Sarah and I went down to Stuie, there were still people everywhere. Occasionally we met other quiet observers, but most drove to a viewpoint, saw nothing in two seconds, and drove on. Our timing was not good: we had managed to hit a single, two-day opening for steelhead. As we came to the end of the high trail we looked down over a fairly long stretch of water, on one side of which was a drive-in campground. Vehicles were parked among the trees and men were casting from the banks. Generators were roaring to operate the freezers in which they would store their catch. Goodness knows what the fish would taste like with all that rotten salmon in the river. Immediately below us was a man fishing on one side of the river and a grizzly fishing on the other. Both were in full view of each other but both seemed quite unperturbed by the situation. The bear wallowed happily in the water and hooked up a rotten fish. He sat on his haunches so that only the upper part of his torso was above the water. With one hand he held the fish to his jaws like a corpulent bather eating an ice cream.

Near the fisherman was a small roofed structure fashioned around the trunk of a big Douglas fir that hung over the water. It contained two stools made of battered car seats, one on either side of the tree. It had been built as a fish counting station. A wire was stretched across the river there and the counters had to click a button every time a spawning salmon passed it. The breeding season had peaked, so although there were a few sockeye, already blotched with mould, swimming in a desultory manner below us, there were no people occupying the viewing station and we had the place to ourselves. It was an excellent spot to watch the goings-on of the river.

Our grizzly meandered a little downstream, constantly going back into the water to pull out another delicacy and either eating it there or on shore. It was Sarah who spotted the adolescent black bear up a nearby cottonwood: from occasional words exchanged by two fishermen it was apparent that the grizzly had chased the black bear up there. Then one man warned his neighbour that there was a bear behind him. Right below us a magnificent black bear emerged onto the stones beside the river. He stood on a point and fished. His coat was black and thick and shiny. He had no fear of the grizzly. Finally, both bears moved off and we relocated to the campground. We were joined there by our hosts, Katie and

Dennis. Katie told us she had been at this exact picnic table having lunch the day before and, while sitting there, they had seen eight separate bears. She had been part of a group pulling noxious weeds (burdock) along the river and they had encountered sixteen bears altogether.

We walked down another trail and saw a more distant grizzly, then came back along the high trail to Katie and Dennis's house. Just before our route dropped back down to the road, a well-used track comes up from the river and crosses the esker. We were almost at the junction when we saw a sow with two year-old cubs coming up from the river toward us. They would pass within a few metres of where we stood. We absolutely froze. Seeing bears nearby from the safety of a vehicle is one thing: this was a little too close for comfort. Mum must have known we were there but she just kept plodding along. One of the cubs eyed us suspiciously but both youngsters kept beside their mother. They crossed the road and investigated a couple of wall-less shelters that are used in

Mother Grizzly with two second-year cubs.

July by First Nations people to dry fish. One of the cubs rubbed hard against the structure and they poked around, but eventually they wandered off and we could breathe again.

In the misty dawn the following morning, I walked along the road to a viewpoint I had often had good luck with before. Sure enough, there was a mum grizzly and two cubs down below on a gravel bar. It was a different family than the one we had seen the previous day; these cubs were much smaller. They must have been born that spring. Mum stared at me for a while and one of the cubs, who was sitting in the water, turned to look at me. The ruff of pale fur that framed his face was round as a moon.

CHAPTER 10

NAHANNI

I was living near Quesnel, had no wood or chainsaw or truck and had an accident. I walked to hospital. I'd broken my jaw but because I couldn't speak, they thought I was stupid and said I was okay and sent me away. Two weeks later I was back. I nearly died. Now I have a plate in my jaw. . . . And another time I had a bladder problem. Swelled up to here and they never admitted it and I nearly died again . . .

When we heard Ginty was sick and moved to Williams Lake, we came up, Mum and I, to see if we could help. Ginty had logged the property. There were logs everywhere. She had put up Anderson shelters for barns but the goats and chickens lived in the house.

She didn't want us. She could have given us something. We had nothing. She could have helped.

—Mildred Baines (daughter of Hilda Thomas)

I went over to Ginty's place one time with Yarrow. At least, I think it was Yarrow. I lived with three different women during the twenty-year period when I kept goats so can't remember who went with me. At any rate we had a nanny goat we needed to get bred and Ginty was the only one in the country who had a billy. We were a little leery engaging in such a delicate matter as animal husbandry with Ginty, because she was known to be quite eccentric and easily feuded with her neighbours, but the rendezvous turned out quite successful. Our goat got impregnated and our friendship with Ginty, such as it was, endured.

—Sage Birchwater

Although Sage Birchwater lives in Williams Lake now, he was a long-time resident of the Chilcotin who styles his career here as a "hippy trapper." He started writing anecdotes for the Williams Lake Tribune in the early 1980s, and over the years got to know a large number of people. He collected stories; one of his most notable anthologies is *Chiwid*, the life of a First Nations woman who lived outside, alone, in summer and in fifty-below weather in winter. As a young woman she had been hit over the head with a logging chain. That was when she moved outside. She recovered from her injuries but she never spoke again. In a city she would have been a bag lady, but here her ability to survive with a .22, a few fish hooks and an old horse was respected. Sage has produced a most sensitive portrait of this tragic and remarkable woman.

It was Sage who gave me the names of many of the people I have contacted regarding Ginty's history. One of these was Mildred Baines, the daughter of Hilda Thomas, to whom Ginty wrote most of the letters quoted in this book. Ginty had seemed to be very fond of Hilda and her husband so Mildred's account of how they were treated when Ginty was dying is puzzling.

I visited Mildred when I was down at the coast for that year's fall book tour. She was living in her father's house, he having passed away a few months before. It was a foul day, the rain verging on sleet—winter coastal weather does not sit easily on my soul. There was much evidence of neglect as I approached the door: crumbling concrete steps, rotten wood and peeling paint.

Inside, however, it was warm—and quite wonderful. It was an Aladdin's cave of shabby furniture, stuffed birds, stacks and stacks of boxes; ill-framed and ill-hung pictures, both paintings and photographs; two Indonesian shadow puppets, obviously old, one seriously broken; skulls, rocks, cheap plastic knick-knacks, all in a glorious jumble. I wondered if the confusion was because Mildred was packing her father's effects, but the way she slid easily along the narrow twisted passage between the piles made me think that everything had been there for a very long time.

The visit took a while. Mildred's mind was like a butterfly, flitting from one thought to another before the first had finished. She was further distracted by a woman phoning for advice (Mildred apparently designed websites), and a man from a museum who came to look at the stuffed birds. She was a heavy smoker with a hoarse smoker's voice. I sat in the tiniest kitchen I have ever seen outside a fifth wheel, breathing fumes from her cigarettes and the hot oily furnace. Above my head was a very good oil portrait of a Chilcotin resident that Mildred had painted.

In between her other chores, Mildred shared with me a number of documents, photocopying part of Ginty's will and several letters Ginty had written to Mildred's mother. She also gave me a couple of photographs—Ginty's graduation picture from Bing High School in Vancouver and another taken on the farm. This last showed a younger and less shabby Ginty than I remembered. She wore baggy men's clothes and her hair was chopped short in such as way that it stuck up in all directions. She looked happy.

Mildred was being forced out of the house. Either rent or taxes—I was unclear which—had not been paid. I heard later that she did manage to move into a clean and orderly home. I hope her last years were happier; she died in 2009.

Because I had no new book that year, the fall tour was mercifully short and I was able to return to Ginty Creek in early December. I had not found a dogsitter; because no one was staying at Ginty Creek, I had no idea how much snow had fallen there. I needed to know whether it was necessary to have the road ploughed. Gin and Tonic were down in the States hauling freight. Vodka and Lime were beyond the end of the hydro line and had a phone only when their generator was on, so were not easy to contact. It was no good asking the Neads; the Precipice Valley had a much warmer and wetter ecosystem. Even on the Chilcotin plateau, snow conditions can vary tremendously. We are all affected one way or another by the Coast Mountains hovering on our border. Valleys like the Klinaklini can puff warm air up onto the plateau from the coast where just a few kilometres away the sky is clear and the temperature is 25°C colder. One thing the Neads were able to tell me: the English/French wannabe shepherds had split up already and gone. The property had not yet been resold but a young couple with a small boy had moved in as caretakers. I took a gamble on the phone number being the same and sure enough a woman answered when I put the call through. She couldn't tell me much about the snow; she didn't have a vehicle and was tied to the house with the child (couldn't she look out the window?). She said she would ask her husband when he came back from work. The following day she told me that my road should be driveable; there was probably less than twenty centimetres of snow on it. Her husband had been travelling back and forth every day on his driveway without ploughing it.

It was a sunny mid-afternoon, with the temperature around -14°C, when I turned off the highway onto the telegraph road.

The snow depth was well over twenty centimetres. Old tracks showed that someone had driven the road at some point, probably Edgar taking hay in to his horses. I was a bit dubious about tackling it but remembered how well the van had performed the year before so decided to give it a go. The van actually made it up the steeper bits but at the highest point a short climb has a curve to it and there the vehicle foundered. I could smell something hot: I had heard of an identical van burning out its all-wheel-drive mechanism under such conditions so I took this as a sign to quit.

I was more or less halfway between Highway 20 and my cabin; that meant I was about two kilometres from home. The toboggan and snowshoes were in the van. I had put them in there before I had left for the book tour in the event that this kind of problem would arise. If it was only a question of getting myself home, it would have been no big deal. But in the van were four boxes of produce, probably weighing a hundred kilograms all told. The temperature was already -14°C; it would probably drop even more overnight. The produce would have to be taken to the cabin. I loaded a box onto the toboggan and slung a backpack with a few essentials onto my shoulders. I figured that once I reached the cabin I could phone around and see if anyone had a snowmobile to help me haul the rest of the stuff.

The snow was the texture of little ball bearings and was impossible to pack down properly, but it was wonderfully peaceful and clean trudging through the quiet forest after all the weeks of people and noise and driving. The low sun sent golden fingers through the trees. I plodded along, conserving energy; it was going to be a long haul. When I reached the Y, the vague snowed-in tracks veered off toward Edgar's place. I could see then that he had ploughed his road at some point. The snow on my branch was untouched and deeper than ever. It reached the tops of my snow pack boots. Even though it was mostly downhill from that point, I would never have got the van through it.

It took perhaps an hour to go from the van to the property boundary. I had left the gate open, tied to a tree with a piece of rope. If I had hired someone to plough the road before I got home I did not want him to have to dig the gate out. But some **** had shut it and now it was snowed in. A shovel was something I did not have with me. I pushed and shoved and managed to make a space big enough to wriggle the toboggan through. Ten minutes later I was swinging open the door of the cabin.

I lit the fire, scooped up a bowl of snow to melt and got on the phone. The people across the river were out. As usual, all I found at Vodka's place was the answering machine; I did not even know if they were home. I tried one more neighbour but there was no reply there either. There was nothing for it but to go for another load. The pretty afternoon was over; already pinkish clouds were fading in the sky. Going back to the van, I had to walk up some fairly steep hills. Even though I had a broken trail, the going was only slightly easier because of the ball-bearing texture of the snow. There was no moon. I had no headlamp so had to carry a hand-held flashlight. I hoped the battery would last. I had bought a new one but it was buried somewhere in the mound of supplies in the van.

After load number three I made myself something to eat. It was already getting late. Before setting off for the final trip I phoned Nelson Williams, the man who had ploughed the road the first time the year before. "How about tomorrow?" he said, which was really good news. But I did not dare risk leaving the fourth box of produce in the van. Out again into the cooling night, slogging up the ball-bearing hill. The more I used the trail, the worse it got, as the toboggan kept sliding off sideways and dumping its cargo. That last load was a nightmare of capsizing.

Nelson had a grader, so he wouldn't be travelling quickly from his home in Anahim. (Like many local people, he had bought the machine and hired himself out to Interior Roads. That way he could do private work as well.) He phoned me when he left Nimpo Lake. I figured he would be at the van in about an hour. I took a snow shovel and axe back up the road with me. I dug out the gate and chopped through a small tree that had fallen onto the road, although the grader could probably have pushed it out of the way. When I breasted the last rise in front of the van, Nelson was already walking toward me. "Hope you remembered the keys," he grinned. (I had not locked the van—I never do in the bush—and why I had bothered to take the keys I don't know. No one was going to get in there and steal anything.) Nelson had cleared a pullout behind the van and he towed me out backwards. I drove onto the pullout and then followed the grader to the cabin. It was fascinating how Nelson was able to wriggle that huge ungainly machine round some of the tight corners in the yard. He charged me only $200 as he was working on someone else's road nearby.

That winter I got a new dog. I had given away Bucky, one of my Rottweiler crosses, because he was a killer. Anything living that he could get his teeth into was instant toast. He had to be kept tied for most of the time at Ginty Creek because of the pets and livestock at the neighbours'. Bucky was used to water, and the river—which would give me second thoughts about crossing at any time—was no barrier to him. In the mountains there were fewer distractions and both dogs usually stayed close to the cabins. Apart from the odd mouse or packrat and, more regrettably, a few birds, they could do little harm. During the previous summer, however, we had come upon a cow moose with a pony-sized calf. The calf ran away from its mother and I could not call the dogs back. The calf plunged into the lake and tried to swim across;

close to the other side it drowned. That was the last straw; Bucky had to go. Fortunately, friends in the Lower Mainland gave him a good home.

As there had been no one to look after the place when I was gone, Raffi had come with me on the book tour. It was certainly easier both at home and on the road having just one dog, but for backpacking trips I needed two so that I would not have to carry so much. I put the word out that I was looking for another animal. I found one in, of all places, Inuvik.

It was Dylan (the human crane) who led me to the dog. He now worked out of Inuvik as a land use planner for the Gwitch'in First Nations people. He had been an avid dogsledder as a teen-ager (and had in fact been a stuntman for the movie *Eight Below*) so was delighted to find accommodation at a tourist outfit where he could drive dogs in his spare time. The place was called Arctic Chalet and they ran white huskies. I looked at the website and saw a small paragraph saying they were looking for homes for dogs who were either too old or who for one reason or another did not fit in. I contacted them and mentioned that I knew Dylan: I wondered if they had a suitable dog and if it might be shipped with Dylan on one of his journeys south.

They did indeed have an animal who might work for me. Nahanni was three years old. She had been sold as a pet when she was a pup. Two years later, the owner had moved south and been unable to take the dog with her. The Arctic Chalet had re-possessed her, but Nahanni did not like working with the other dogs. She was lazy when put into harness; she would not pull. She was good-natured with humans. They sent me a picture; she was very pretty. She could, they said, be at Williams Lake within the week. Dylan was not coming south, but Nahanni could hitch a ride on the vegetable truck.

Bill, the vegetable man, has made a remarkable niche for himself in this world. A quarter of a century ago, he bought a five-ton truck and drove sporadically to stores in the Lower Mainland to buy fresh produce to sell to northern communities on his way back home. Inuvik, a largely administrative town of some four thousand souls, has a communal greenhouse but that is of any use only in the summer. For the remaining nine months, so-called fresh produce is shipped from outfitters in Edmonton. The stores and restaurants of the Chilcotin use these very same outfitters. In order to keep the price down, most of the food is of the most tasteless and chemical-ridden varieties. It has already travelled three thousand kilometres from California and Mexico to reach Edmonton. On the Chilcotin it is trucked for yet another day: to get to Inuvik, it makes the last part of its journey by air and this makes the cost exorbitant.

Bill now owns a fifty-seven-foot refrigerated trailer and he makes the journey south every three weeks, weather and road conditions permitting. This doesn't just mean blizzards in winter (in fact they probably do not faze him at all). There is a river south of Inuvik, and this is crossed by a ferry in summer and on an ice road in winter. It is, however, undriveable during freezeup and breakup. In the south, Bill spends a few days maintaining his truck in Kamloops, then goes down to the Lower Mainland for some of the produce, and finally shops again in Kamloops on his way north. He then heads for home—pretty much non-stop as far as I can gather. When the ice road is good he can deliver right up to Tuktoyaktuk.

Bill's first trip south since freezeup was to be right after Christmas. People had been driving over the river already, but with such a big, heavy rig he wanted to be absolutely sure the ice was safe. If there were no major problems, he expected to be in Williams Lake on December 30. We would meet—where else would I pick up a husky dog?—at the Husky station. Coordinating our separate journeys was going to be crucial. Bill obviously did not want to wait for me; I had no desire to hang about Williams Lake indefinitely either. Bill had a cell phone but would drive over long stretches of highway where it would not work. Cell phones were useless on the Chilcotin: once I left the cabin I would be out of touch until I reached town. We arranged that I would call him at 8:00 a.m. on the 30th, just before I went out of the door. Poor man, I woke him up. He was at Smithers, having driven there without a break. The Dempster Highway had not given him any grief. He would have breakfast with friends at Smithers, then take four hours to reach Prince George, where he would fuel both himself and the truck, and another three hours to arrive at Williams Lake. He expected to be at the Husky station around 6:00 p.m.

I drove into town and did what shopping and business I was able to and was sitting in the Husky station an hour earlier than the designated time. I phoned Bill from a pay phone and he confirmed that he was on schedule. I could hear the drone of his truck in the background over the phone. At Williams Lake it was foggy and already almost dark. Fresh snow had fallen and now it was raining; the temperature was right around freezing. I hoped it would not be raining at home, but Williams Lake is quite a bit warmer than the Chilcotin. In the town the roads were ankle deep in brown sludge. Snippets of conversations from the truckers in the restaurant told me that a semi had overturned just south of 100 Mile and another truck was off the road at Lac La Hache. While I sat there, two ambulances wailed by with flashing lights.

Bill rolled into the yard right on time. His rig was enormous, its lights blurred by the swirling fog. The engine brakes hissed; he left the motor running as he stepped down. The passenger door was on my side of the vehicle and to my great surprise it opened and a diminutive little girl in pink down coat, white tights and pink boots climbed down. She would not have been able to reach the door from the ground, but she shut it while she perched on the axle hub and then jumped into the sludge. She was obviously perfectly at home with this routine. This was Emily, Bill's nine-year-old daughter. She liked to go with her dad when she was not at school. Her first journeys had been when she was still in diapers. She was obviously a very bright individual and an avid reader. I gave her a copy of *Lonesome: Memoirs of a Wilderness Dog* and she had read the first two chapters by the time she had finished her chicken nuggets.

Mindful of my world-travelling wwoofers, I asked Bill if he ever picked up hitchhikers. He laughed. "One trip I saw one not far south of Inuvik. When I came back a week later he was still there!" But he would not have thought to pick him up—if his daughter was travelling with him he would have no room. It is notoriously difficult to hitchhike in the north. The further you go up, the harder it is to get a ride. Despite this, he was going to take an extra passenger back to Inuvik with him. This was to be none other than ex-carpenter-wwoofer Sarah. She had said how much she would love to work with sled dogs so I had put her in touch with the Arctic Chalet. Sarah had never experienced a cold winter in her life and I wondered how she would make out, but she loved it. She arrived on January 17, the day that the sun first came back. She had to spend the whole three-day journey sitting up in the cab: the bed could not be used while driving, and on the rare occasions that they stopped, it was needed for Emily and her dad.

Nahanni had ridden down to Williams Lake in a crate in the back of the truck. She had received an occasional chance to stretch her legs but the journey had obviously been quite stressful for her. I walked her—or rather, was unceremoniously pulled—around the car park for a few minutes and then I pushed her into the van. I was staying with people in town overnight and had left my other dog, Raffi, tied up in their yard. The two animals spent the night outside on chains. I heard an occasional growl but nothing untoward. For our journey home, Raffi was confined behind the dog barrier and Nahanni was allowed in the other section of the van. I had had more business to do in Williams Lake before setting off, and it was dusk before I arrived at my turnoff.

I fed the two dogs separately—Raffi was given his dinner in his usual place in the porch but Nahanni was shut outside. However, she pushed the porch door open and there was a big fight. Raffi was quite bewildered. He always got on with everyone—people and dogs alike. He was bigger than Nahanni but was now so frightened of her he wouldn't come into the porch. There were two kennels in there; I had also put a rug down. Nahanni usurped Raffi's kennel and Raffi spent the night in the woodshed. So the following day, with great difficulty because it had been built in situ and was very heavy, I rolled Raffi's kennel out into the woodshed—and he spent the night on the rug in the porch!

Nahanni was appropriately subservient to me, rolling on her back and crouching down, but she obviously considered herself to be top dog. I thought she and Raffi might settle better if I brought them both inside but there was another big fight. After a couple of days I was able to let Nahanni off her chain and she settled down a bit, but the two dogs never became good friends.

Nahanni.

Otherwise it was a quiet winter. Only a little more snow

fell and I didn't need any more ploughing done. I worked on manuscripts and went to the Tatla Lake library once a month for the book club meeting and to collect armloads of new books to read. I had also found a good drinking water source. New people had taken over what used to be the post office-cum-restaurant in Nimpo Lake. The post office remained, but the building was now used as a Christian school and later a coffee shop was added. There was an outside tap that never froze. Every time I went for mail, the postmaster kindly allowed me to fill up my water jugs. (This saved a lot of snow-melting.) I still used the latter for bathing and laundry, although sometimes I would take the washed clothes to the post office in a bucket, and rinse them right on the street. I got some good laughs from people coming to pick up their mail.

The only other incident of note was on January 30. Once again, I couldn't get the satellite internet. I tried a few hours later and it was still out. Was the problem universal or was it my equipment on the blink once more? When in doubt, phone Dave Neads. But the phone was dead as well. This was very odd. Later that afternoon, however, it rang. It was Dave checking to see if my internet was down. We have the same system: it turned out to be a problem at the satellite end. Fortunately service was restored a few hours later. And yes, he knew that the phone line had been out. Someone had shot through the single fibre optic cable that links Anahim Lake to Williams Lake with a .22.

CHAPTER 11

BADGER

My latest acquisitions are two geese. Goosilla and
Gandergog. Aren't they eminently suitable names? . . .

The cat had kittens--their eyes are just beginning
to open. She wanted to have them in between the quilts
but I got her in a box just in time. So that is where
her three only (thank goodness) still live. Ma goes out
at night and I have to have the little things in bed
with me to keep them quiet.

This past winter the ewe had lambs in the cabin.
The first batch that never froze. I'm trading the ram
lamb for a goat in milk. He is v. cute--I call him In-
the-Pot. His Pa is Rameses the Second. I'd like to get
rid of Rameses this fall. He has a marvellously aris-
tocratic nose--only his horns grow into his eyes. In-
the-Pot has long horns already about 6--8 inches long.
The ewe lamb is Alexandra. The telephone lineman had
a son Alexander Jay the same day as the lambs arrived so Alexandra is named after him. I didn't think
it would be v. good to name the ram lamb Jay since he
was destined to go into the pot.

—Extracts from a letter from Ginty to Hilda Thomas

The first wwoofers to arrive that spring were an Austrian couple in their thirties. They had been in Canada and the States for a year; Ginty Creek was to be their last wwoofing place before they went back to Europe. They arrived at the beginning of April—about two weeks earlier than Ron and Claire had come the year before—but the much lighter snowpack meant that the ground was all but clear. The wwoofers were able to drive their van down to the trailer right away. It was still pretty chilly at night but since the previous spring I had scrounged an old tin stove from a disused trapping cabin. It was not in very good shape, but with aluminum foil stuck into the worst holes it would work well enough. It would provide some much-needed heat in the trailer. First, though, we had to make space for it. The bathroom was useless to me; we ripped it out—the tub, the toilet, the sink and cabinets—and fitted an old insulated chimney piece through the skylight. The stove was too small to stay alight for very long but it made a big difference to the comfort of the trailer.

On April 8 we went down to Bella Coola. We planned on being back the same day so we left at first light. It was snowing on the Chilcotin and we had a great sighting of a group of caribou crossing the wintry-looking road. Down in the valley, spring had sprung and it was hot. I had to go to the dentist and shop (a couple of the stores in the valley have pretty decent vegetables), and it seemed that wherever I went I ran into someone I had not seen for a long time, so it was necessary to spend time catching up on the news. All of this made for a very long day. The dogs were brought out of the van wherever possible and given drinks, but they were distressed at being cooped up and kept on a lead for so long. They were enormously relieved to be let out of the van to run along the telegraph road as we travelled the last few kilometres home. It was almost dark by the time we reached the cabin. I waited about half an hour before I fed the dogs, but I was very tired after the long day so gave them their dinner and went to bed.

The next morning Raffi seemed reluctant to get out of his kennel. I have always encouraged the dogs to chase squirrels off the bird feeder and usually just the word would be enough to send Raffi tearing around the cabin, but he walked over slowly and looked uninterested. He seemed bloated. Perhaps he needed a walk. He came with me but stayed at my heels. I phoned the vet. "Bring him in right away," they said. The vet was in Williams Lake, over three hours' drive away.

I threw together a sleeping bag and some food (my dietary sensitivities meant that I could rarely buy meals that I could eat). The Austrian couple were having a day off at the trailer. I ran down and told them the news and gave them the Neads' phone number. I had no answering machine so I couldn't leave a message for the wwoofers. I would call Dave and Rosemary, and the

My favourite picture of Raffi.

wwoofers could come up to the cabin at suppertime and phone them to find out what was happening.

The drive along Highway 20 seemed interminable. The receptionist at the vet's told me to have a seat and I waited two more hours. The prognosis: Raffi had a twisted gut. This affliction is apparently common with large dogs that have big chests, and is particularly prevalent with Rottweilers and crosses. It happens from the age of six and up (Raffi was in his seventh year) and especially with dogs that inhale their food (which Raffi did.) The excessive exercise at the end of the long, hot day and the late feeding probably contributed to the situation. The X-rays showed that, even if they operated, it was unlikely they would be able to cure him. I was going to have to have him put down. He was sitting there, on a mat, in the back area of the vet's. He looked puzzled, more than anything. And resigned. I was heartbroken.

So now I had only Nahanni. She was already showing her innate instinct to roam. The caretakers across the river were planning to leave soon, but they were still looking after four horses and two dogs that belonged to the French/English no-longer-wanna-be shepherds. The minute Nahanni was given her freedom she would go over there to visit.

Raffi had been an excellent pack dog but I had yet to try Nahanni with a backpack. The day after Raffi had been put down, I slid his pack over her head. It was empty; it was meant to get her used to the feel of it. Most dogs have no problem with packs and I would have thought that Nahanni, already experienced in harness, would have accepted it easily. She hated it. The second time I put it on her she disappeared for two days, causing me all sorts of worry, but she came back and the pack was still on her. I tied her up for a while and she put on her pathetic look. She would sit there, staring at me mournfully, with drooped ears and one paw raised. I made a lot of fuss of her and took her for walks but the minute she was let off she was gone.

Maybe she would stay at home more readily if I found her a companion. I needed another hound for the mountains in any case. Spring book-promoting travels took me to the Okanagan among other places; whenever I got to a town, I would check out the SPCA. In Salmon Arm I walked in and said, "I am looking for a large, strong dog with a good coat that doesn't bark unnecessarily and is friendly with people." The face of the woman behind the counter lit up. "Have we got the dog for you!" she exclaimed.

They called him Reno. The staff raved about what a great personality he had. He was at present on a hike with a volunteer but would be back in a few minutes. Every one of my dogs, its seems, gets a little smaller. When Reno appeared dragging his handler in I could see he was shorter than Nahanni, but he was very wide. Apart from his stocky build, he was also fat and had a very long thick coat. My first impression was of a hairy barrel with legs; he waddled like a badger. He was billed as a Rottweiler cross shepherd cross Lab cross . . .?? He was Rottweiler coloured; people since have suggested he might be more of a Belgian shepherd but I didn't care what sort of a mutt he was as long as he was suitable. First we tried him with Nahanni. The dogs seemed indifferent to each other. "How long have you had him?" I asked. "Eight months!" they replied. This was somewhat surprising for a dog with "a great personality." "He doesn't like men," they confessed. Apparently he was beaten by young guys in baseball caps. He would not attack men—he simply growled and stayed back. I could see that would not endear him to a lot of families. "All you've got to do is get the man to give him a cookie and he'll be fine," they told me. I thrust a cookie at his face. I was deliberately not being gentle as I wanted to see how he would react if a stranger did the same thing at Nuk Tessli. I discourage people from feeding the dogs but there are always some who will do it and I needed a dog who was not going to bite their fingers off. Reno took the cookie with a bored expression on his face. He ate it but you could almost see him shrug at the banality of it all.

Reno (now called Badger) was delegated to the area behind the dog barrier in the van and Nahanni rode like a queen in the front. I drove the four hours to 108 Mile House where I was going to spend the night with Patricia. In the back, Badger had thrown up: he had unfortunately been fed just before I picked him up. I hoped he was not going to have that kind of problem. I had already owned two different dogs who had been carsick. I don't drive a lot, but when I do go anywhere it is always a long journey. When

Badger.

I was unloading him, somehow Badger's collar came undone and he got away from me. Off he went around the 108 subdivision, me in fast pursuit. The faster I ran, the wider the distance between us grew. This was a potential disaster. How was I going to catch him? Would anyone be able to? With no collar on, no one would be able to identify him. There was no shelter in 100 Mile House. All strays were taken to Williams Lake. I went back to Patricia's house to see to Nahanni and fill a bucket of water from an outside tap. Water! Badger ran right up behind me and stuck his head in the bucket. He didn't blink an eye when I snapped the chain on him.

That afternoon I picked up another wwoofer from the bus station. Ben was from Australia. By now the dogs were tied in Patricia's backyard under a big fir tree. As soon as Ben walked round the house, Badger growled fearsomely and backed off. Although the SPCA had warned me of this behaviour, it was the first time I had seen it. Entreaties made no difference. Uh-oh, I thought. Is this going to work? I had bought a bag of cookies in a grocery store and gave one to Ben. He approached, good man that he was, gently but firmly. Badger stopped growling, eyed the cookie, took it in his mouth, and Ben was his best buddy after that. As Badger grew used to me and was able to spend the bulk of his time off the chain, he began to accept most men without a problem. Just once in a while he will take exception to one. He can pick a pure, dyed-in-the wool redneck a mile off.

At first, Badger's "great personality" seemed to be mostly indifference. One trait came to the fore right away, though. As far as other dogs were concerned, he was very possessive with food. I tied both dogs up to feed them. Nahanni was outside, Badger in Raffi's place in the porch. Both dogs had finished eating when I let them off but I had not picked up the dishes. Nahanni sashayed in like she owned the place—and Badger turned on her and beat her up enough to draw blood. That, I had not expected. Nahanni still considered herself the boss, but after that she never got over being frightened of Badger in enclosed spaces, including the van.

Badger was very good at finding old bones. A number of animals must have died on the place; there were goat and cow skulls, and various other bones both large and small; all were well cleaned of flesh but Badger spent hours chewing them. If Nahanni so much as looked at them, she got a warning growl.

Ben, and later Nathaniel from England, cleared up my logging mess at the new building site. The propane pickup had now been replaced with a 3/4 ton Chevy old enough to have a carburetor. There was something seriously wrong with the choke and it took a massive amount of pumping to get the motor to fire, but once it was warmed up it performed well enough. The wwoofers hauled some logs with it, but mostly they carried short lengths of trees on their shoulders and piled them, and all of the brush, in heaps scattered over the knoll. The building site was clean and orderly, and ready for Gin and Tonic and Vodka and Lime to build my house.

I took the wwoofers down to the Precipice for the cattle drive party and left them there; they would work for Dave and Rosemary and the rancher for a while. It was time for me to go into the mountains.

CHAPTER 12

ANOTHER FALL

She always had a cigarette in her mouth during bug season.
She said she never inhaled but the smoke kept the bugs away.
—Ken Jansen

One time my sister and I rode over there and Ginty had made
some homebrew. She asked us if we wanted a glass. She said
it would quench our thirst. So we did. Ginty must have been
into her third or fourth glass because the table was holding her
up. She tried to walk around and fill our glasses again but she
couldn't. My sister got up and fell over! The world was going
round so much I decided we could not ride home so we stayed
the night. The next morning when I woke up Mum [Elaine
Dester] was at the door, really worried because we hadn't
come home. Ginty apologized for giving us homebrew. She
asked Mum if she wanted a glass. Mum said Yes. My sister
and I we got up and left right away and figured we wouldn't
see Mum until the next morning. But she came home later
that day.

—Karen Dester

That year I flew out of the mountains on September 21. Replies to emails I had written to Gin and Tonic and Vodka and Lime had been sporadic and I was not entirely sure what had happened at Ginty Creek. During the summer I had been recommended two excellent Dutch wwoofers who were skilled at building. I could not use them at Nuk Tessli, but I passed them on to Vodka and Lime. More than once Lime emailed me and said how much they liked the wwoofers and what great workers they were. Each email concluded with: "We are going to start at Ginty Creek any day now."

When I came out of the bush, there was a nice new extension on Vodka and Lime's house. Nothing whatsoever had been done at my building site. The brush piles had changed from green to brown but otherwise everything was exactly as I'd left it. Gin and Tonic were still trucking in the States. Vodka had bought the "escavator." Earlier in the summer, Gin had been doing a job with it and while he was loading it onto the back of a flat deck had somehow miscalculated and the machine had rolled off. The motor was toast. Vodka was a good old Chilcotin mechanic and figured he could fix it; $10,000 and three months later, it was done. Vodka had also bought a big flatdeck so he could do some long-distance hauling as well. Trouble was, the motor had needed a lot of work. My house had been put on hold. There was now no time to build the shell of the house before the snow flew so there had been no point in digging the hole for the basement.

Vodka did at least bring in the little excavator and make me an outhouse hole, and he smoothed an area for the trailer. I was going to have to move the trailer when I traded the lower property. When we had ripped out the bathroom in the spring we had found that the plywood wall at that end was so rotten you could stick a finger through it. The old tarp that had once done duty as the cabin porch had been stretched over the trailer to try and keep the rain and snow out but obviously that had not been enough. If it was to survive another winter it needed a roof. It would go to the dump as soon as I had done with it but now I needed it as guest accommodation. It was pointless building a shelter where it now sat if I was going to part with the lower property. So we had to move it. Two tires were flat; we pumped them up with a little foot pump. Vodka towed the trailer over and popped it into its new slot with impressive expertise.

I still had not sorted out a water supply for the new place. Nedra Creek, which had looked so promising during and after the heavy-snow winter, was now just a seep. In the spring I had sent a sample to an irrigation company to be tested. The test, as far as I was concerned, was a rip-off. For $200 they informed me that the sample was full of potentially dangerous fecal organisms and should not be used for a water supply. Too much people use in the form of logging and back-country recreation upstream, I guess. Fecal organisms are in fact not too serious; they can be rendered harmless by boiling the water. I was doing this with the river water anyway. The test did not inform me whether giardia (which causes beaver fever) or any dangerous minerals such as arsenic or unhealthy levels of iron were present. Both elements are naturally present in Chilcotin waters, sometimes excessively. I would have thought that a giardia test was automatic. It is a serious problem in many water supplies. But no, that test is not included in the $200 fee as it is apparently too costly. Giardia is a large organism and it can be filtered out or, like the fecal matter, killed by boiling. The minerals were of much greater concern. To get the water test-ed for these minerals would apparently cost thousands of dollars. (A friend has since told me that they had their new well tested for arsenic and the fee was $35. Someone is making a lot of money under false pretences.)

Before he left on his trucking venture, Vodka had time to see if he could dig a hole or two for a possible shallow well. I paid him cash for this work as it had not been written into the agreement. I checked the lie of the land and the vegetation. Most of the mound was covered in pine, with kinnikinnick and soopollalie in the damper areas. None of these plants indicated water. Where the marsh began there was an instant change to scrub birch, willow and sedge. They like wet feet, but if a backhoe well was dug at that point, would it be possible to keep the spring run-off from contaminating it? I chose a couple of likely spots right next to the swamp. Vodka agreed to give them a try. He could dig three metres down with his little excavator. A few mornings later I heard the drone of his machine and walked up later to see a shovelful of dirt being lifted out of a deep hole and deposited on a nearby heap. The air was full of the scent of new dug earth and crushed soopollalie berries. For some reason there had been an extraordinary crop of those that year. As the bucket upended to dump the earth, dust rose into the air. Even three metres down, the soil was dry as a bone. It is interesting how swamps, lakes and rivers are prevented from draining away into apparently porous soils directly beside them. There is a reason that they are contained. About fifteen centimetres of water eventually seeped into the very bottom of the hole, but it was obvious that a shallow well was not going to happen there.

After much emailing on my behalf, I finally received a reply from Tonic—thank you very much, but developing my property was not going to work for them. Vodka was on the road hauling hay by then. He was putting in a lot of hours and I had to catch him in between jobs to ask him if he was still interested in the trade. He was exhausted and had a hard time getting his head around it, but he decided that, yes, he and Lime would continue with the agreement and build my house themselves. They absolutely promised to spend the whole following summer doing nothing but. "What about all Gin's wrecked cars and junk?" I said. I was particularly concerned about the pile of iron and other debris in the forest. Vodka and Lime agreed that they would move what they could in between trucking jobs. Among the debris was a forklift piled with old car batteries. That was one of the first items that Vodka took to the dump.

New owners had moved into the property across the river. I had now been at Ginty Creek for two years and these were the fourth residents of the ranch during that time. I was beginning to feel like an old-timer.

This couple lived in Alberta but had spent a lot of time on the Chilcotin; their son lived in Bella Coola. They were close to my age; she was a community nurse who was working at the moment in the clinic at Tatla Lake. He didn't seem to be doing much of anything although he occasionally disappeared back to Alberta for a week or two. They had several dogs and cats, and even though it was fall, the place was full of baby chicks, puppies and kittens. They left dog and cat food out all day so their animals could help themselves; Nahanni was in seventh heaven.

I went over to the new people to say Hi and apologize for my dog. I was hoping that, if they got nasty with her, she would not find their place so attractive. We got to chatting: the man told me their son had made a great find at the dump. He was into re-cycling (sounds great!) and had seen all these car batteries piled on a pallet; he was hoping to make a good one out of them. He had brought them home and they were stored behind the barn. I could help myself to as many as I liked.

The wwoofer I had that fall was Kelsey. She had been with me for five weeks in the mountains. A young Canadian, she had travelled widely and was an excellent cook. She had not done much building

Kelsey on the roof over the trailer.

or carpentry work before but she tackled it with aplomb. We built a roof over the trailer and a structure over the outhouse hole. Kelsey agreed to stay and dogsit while I went on my annual book tour, this time to promote *A Mountain Year*.

I was due back near the middle of December. It had often been very windy while I was at the coast. I was lucky and always missed the worst of the ferry crossings and power failures and roads blocked by fallen trees. Violent winds are usually products of unseasonably warm weather, and this had kept the snow away. My last slide show was in Upper Delta; that night heavy snow was forecast for most of BC. My hosts tried to press me to stay to wait out the weather, but I had a sleeping bag, axe, matches and food, and was not worried by falling snow. I was much more concerned at being trapped down at the coast by avalanches blocking Highway 1 in the canyon, as often happened in these conditions.

I was not the only one anxious for me to get home. Kelsey was getting a fairly severe case of cabin fever; also her dad was coming to pick her up. As he worked overseas for long stretches, with only short periods of time back in Canada, he did not have a lot of leeway. We needed to stick to our schedule. Snow or sleet fell the whole way to 100 Mile House but in fact it did not settle on the road until about fifty kilometres south of that town, so was not a problem as far as the drive north was concerned. (The canyon was, in fact, closed the following day.)

As I drove into Patricia's yard, wet snow was falling. The temperature was around freezing. I planned on leaving at 6:30 a.m. the next day as I wanted to be the first customer at a garage in Williams Lake. My van needed servicing and by getting there before 8:00 a.m. I would not have to put up with delays. The only problem was, at 6:30 a.m., the temperature was -36°C. It had dropped 36°C overnight. Slushy snow had coated the van when I had parked, and now it was frozen solid. The doors were encased in ice. I was able to thaw one of them with the frantic application of Patricia's hair drier. Driving in the dark to Williams Lake, I passed several vehicles abandoned beside the road.

Poor Kelsey. She had grown up on Cortes and Quadra Islands on the coast. She'd had a mild, almost coastal, winter at Ginty Creek up to that point: it had not even been necessary to plough the road. The storm that swept the province had brought little precipitation to Ginty Creek, but the cold on that morning—-39°C in the West Chilcotin—was a shock. It was fifteen degrees warmer when I arrived around sundown. Kelsey had baked bread, stuffed the woodbox and, with her dad, had driven into Nimpo Lake and picked up my mail and hauled several five-gallon containers of water. What a wonderful welcome home—and what a stark contrast to the previous year when I'd had to haul all that produce home with the toboggan. We barely exchanged hellos before they were out of the door. Kelsey had enjoyed her time at Ginty Creek but enough was enough. She could not wait to get to a shower.

CHAPTER 13

THE BULL

When we were at school, after she quit teaching, we would sometimes go over to Ginty's place on a field trip. She would talk about all her animals and what they ate. It was very interesting. The pigs, the turkeys, the goats. All had names and her doors were open to all of them. She even used her bedroom as a maternity room.

I loved flowers. My mum was an outdoors person, always riding in the bush and bringing home meat. She didn't grow anything. Ginty had a big garden with lots of flowers. She showed my sister and me how to start them off in tin cans. We put stones in the bottom, then the soil. My sister and me we liked this so much that Dad had to make us a garden.

Ginty would come over to Grampa's ranch and visit at least twice a week. She taught us all about English etiquette, which knives and forks to use, and how to hold them. She also taught us to say please and thank you, and how to pronounce words properly. She said we used too many shortcuts. My mum [Elaine Dester] spoke Carrier to us at home (yes, she was born in Bella Coola but raised in Ulkatcho Village, near Anahim Lake, and both her parents are Carrier), and my dad [Mack Dester] *spoke Chilcotin. They were valuable lessons that she taught us, and we carried all that away with us.*

—Karen Dester

A few days after I had first come to Ginty Creek with Max and Steffi, an ATV rolled up. The driver was the rancher who ran his cows on the range in my area. The fence was down in places so the cows had full access to my property. The telegraph road originally turned left at the Y and went to this ranch, continuing on to join Highway 20 a little west of Tatla Lake. It was no longer possible to drive through, as both the rancher and Edgar had closed the road off. The ATV could circumvent the barriers by using a network of old bush trails. Sitting behind the rancher on the ATV was his partner, Hattie. I had met Hattie years before: she remembered visiting Ginty when she was a little girl. "The hens were so tame," she said. "You could pick them up and stroke them."

The rancher was looking for his bulls. We exchanged contact information and I said I'd let him know if we saw any. That year there were none but before I left for this last book tour, a single bull had been hanging around. It was a polled Red Angus. It did not seem scared of us; neither was it threatening. It usually just stood and stared. I let the rancher know: he said he would be rounding up his livestock soon for the winter and thanks for the information. After I had left, Kelsey emailed me and said the rancher had been for his cows but the bull was still at Ginty Creek. She had phoned and left a message on his answering machine.

A couple of weeks later, Kelsey called me. She had been walking with the dogs in a thick patch of alder just below the cabin and had come upon the bull again. Only now it was dead: upside down in a ditch. And she informed me with some alarm that the dogs had been eating it. A sprinkling of snow had fallen and there were both wolf and cougar tracks around the carcass. She had called the rancher again and once more left a message on the answering machine. He never replied; I guess the bull, being dead, was now of no consequence to him.

I was not too concerned about the dogs snacking on the bull. We would not be able to prevent them from doing so unless they were permanently tied and I did not want to be bothered with that. I reckoned it would be a cheap way of giving them some treats. When I arrived home, Badger was there to greet me. He had turned into an affectionate dog—not particularly smart, but happy. His "terrific personality" had finally surfaced. Nahanni, however, was nowhere to be seen. Kelsey told me she had been gone since the morning. She did not turn up until the following day. She enjoyed being cuddled and fed, but as soon as I let her out, she was gone again. The people over the river had disposed of all their animals and were no longer leaving dog food outside so she rarely went there any more. She didn't need to with that enormous snack bar among the alders.

There was a lot of activity around that dead bull. Badger, and Nahanni if she was home, would sit on the bank by the window and look over the frozen river and short segment of meadow that lay in between the cabin and the alders. Unfortunately, although the carcass was no more than two hundred metres away, it was completely hidden by the brush. Badger would often bark and this drove me crazy. Sometimes I saw coyotes crossing the ice—the dogs would hare off in pursuit—but mostly, whatever was feeding down there was a mystery. Wolves sang often, a most haunting sound floating up the frozen river on a cold, starry night. When Badger's barking got too bad, I started shutting him in the cabin at night, and Nahanni as well if she was home.

Nahanni was not a happy dog. She was affectionate when she was around, but she had a mind of her own. She hated Badger, skirting around him if he was close, and now it was getting increasingly difficult to put her in the van. She loved to run behind it along the telegraph road but I had to resort to trickery to catch her when I wanted to drive along the highway. One day she ended up at Vodka and Lime's place several kilometres away. She ate half a bag of cat food and threw up copiously. Vodka and Lime had some kind of phone hooked up to their satellite internet. Reception was so erratic they could rarely be heard properly, and I became used to picking up my phone and being presented with either a long silence or sometimes a half word, which might be the sum total of a sentence that had come through. Usually Vodka would try again in a few minutes. I had to drive to their place a number of times to pick up the dog. In January, they left for Mexico and I wondered where she would end up next. I phoned around the neighbourhood and described her in case she turned up anywhere else.

She was often to be found down by the bull. A big spruce leaned over a bank nearby and she had made a bed for herself in the snow-free needles underneath. She was always pleased to see me. I would put the lead on her and bring her back to the house and feed her. She enjoyed whatever I gave her. I would keep her shut up for the night, but the minute the door was open she was gone. One night I tired of this. I called her and rattled the food dish—she would certainly hear it if she was down by the bull. I figured she would get hungry and soon return. She did not come that night, or the following morning. Nor did she turn up on the second night. There was a skiff of snow when I went down to the bull the next morning. Badger had been barking a lot. I had him on a lead as I wanted to see what fresh tracks there were beside the carcass. The big round tracks of wolves were there, and also the softer-edged paw print of the cougar. Small dog prints ran away from the carcass. Nahanni had been feeding, but she had not wanted to be caught.

At the very first hint of light the next morning, Badger wanted to go out. Nahanni still wasn't home. Badger immediately started barking furiously at the top of the bank. I yelled at him to shut up. He ran down the bank a short way; the next thing he was by the corner of the cabin again, barking like a maniac. I had never seen him like this before. He tore into the porch through the half-open door and barked and growled and snarled like one demented. I squeezed past him. Sitting on the snow, in the blue half-light of a winter dawn, halfway between the cabin and the outhouse, was a large cougar. I rushed inside for my camera but of course when I returned the cougar was gone. Badger was very frightened for the rest of the day. He had to be coaxed outside to pee. I had no idea where Nahanni had gone.

Badger was always bringing home bones. A couple of days later, while we were on a hike, he came triumphantly out of the bush with a treasure that looked as though it was from a fresh kill. It was encrusted with snow and Badger was not going to let me take it from him, but from what I could see of it, it was from quite a small animal. It could have been a deer. Hunters would leave carcasses around and Badger never failed to find them, but hunting season was long over. This bone was gleaming white and the marrow inside the splintered end was still a rich red. I followed Badger's tracks back but there was no evidence of a recent death. The bone must have been moved away from the kill and dropped where it lay.

Badger packed it home to add to his collection. A lump of frozen snow encrusted one end. When he grew tired of it, I rescued it and brought it inside to thaw. The fur that emerged was white. It had most likely belonged to Nahanni. Was it a wolf or a cougar that brought her to her end? I phoned the neighbours for some distance around in case I was wrong and she turned up somewhere, but no one ever replied.

I heard some months later that another Kleena Kleene resident had lost a dog to a cougar that winter. They had gone to town for the day and the dog had been taken off the porch. A blood trail led into the forest. A local guide who loved hunting cougars was summoned. He tracked it for half a day and shot it.

Ginty Creek was proving to be very hard on dogs. I was now looking for a companion for Badger. The weeks went by. It used to be easy to find unwanted large dogs. I heard of a young local one that sounded ideal but the owner had wanted to go away; he couldn't find a home in time and had shot it. Rosemary (from the Precipice) had a friend who was involved in a private rescue group. They had a "really big, hairy dog" who was less than a year old. He had been roaming the reserve at Lytton, in the Fraser Canyon. The rescuer had kept him for three months and advertised on all the local notice boards, but no one came to claim him. The rescuer had become very attached to him but already owned three dogs and could not keep any more. He was gentle and seemed to accept cats and ignore horses, although he and another dog did manage to kill a neighbour's chicken. She called him Harry.

Harry first had to be neutered and then sent down to the headquarters of the rescue organization in the Lower Mainland so the paperwork could be finished. He would be flown up to Anahim Lake on the Chilcotin. Pacific Coastal Airlines, who run a network of remote flights in BC, apparently fly "rescue" dogs for nothing as long as they do not need the plane space. The dogs do, of course, have to be crated, but the rescue organization was often donated crates and other dog equipment. The crate they shipped Harry in was a gift to me.

Just before I was due to pick Harry up, another local person had a dog flown up by the airline. This was a purebred pup, a Komondor. The pup had been bred up north but had to be flown to Vancouver as that was the only way he could reach Anahim by air. The woman arranging the flight from Vancouver had put him on board; at Anahim, despite a fairly high cloud cover, the pilot decided not to land. The pup was taken back to Vancouver. The woman who had organized his flight could not be reached for several hours. The poor pup was hungry, dehydrated and lying in his own filth by the time he was rescued. (He was flown up a few days later without incident and seemed none the worse for his experience.)

It was a sunny, spring-like day in late March when I drove to the Anahim Lake airport to pick up Harry. The plane was late—a not unusual circumstance despite the perfect weather. The airport building is simply a trailer with a weather-worn hangar behind it. I needed to go to the bathroom. The toilet was in a shabbily partitioned area that also contained a shower and a urinal. Above the toilet a crudely executed message was written in blue felt pen on the wall. "If you splatter use uronwall" [their spelling]. A series of rough arrows pointed irregularly around the shower to the urinal, where a cardboard sign was tacked: "FLUSH. Push handle down while performing. Tricky ain't it."

The nine-seater King Air arrived, and a dog crate was loaded onto the luggage cart. A label had been fixed to it: "My name is Harry. I am 2 years old. My Mom is . . ." Locals, who knew me, were looking at me with some amusement. On the Chilcotin, a dog is a dog, no matter how much he is loved. I was even more embarrassed when I fished Harry out of his crate. Not only did two large stuffed toys (beautifully hand-knitted!) come out with him but the dog was also wearing a diaper. And the "really big hairy dog" was so tiny! He was shorter than Badger and extremely slim.

Now for the big question. Would he and Badger, both neutered males, get on? I usually like to have a mix of genders, reasoning that they would be less likely to fight, but Nahanni had been at odds with both Raffi and Badger. I need not have worried. Harry and Badger were instant buddies. Badger, who had not had much exercise for quite a while as he had rarely joined Nahanni on her excursions, now played and played. Harry was a bit too independent for my liking and he was usually the instigator to go some place, and of course he soon found the bull, but everything seemed to be working out well. He was otherwise quiet and affectionate and such a pretty colour everyone was immediately taken by him. And perhaps having smaller dogs was no bad thing. They were easier to transport in either a plane or a van (and both dogs loved riding in any vehicle). In the mountains, Harry proved capable of carrying a pretty reasonable pack. The tourists adored him. He was a good addition to my life.

Harry.

CHAPTER 14

JIM AND JOE'S BARN

Jim Fell and I built a barn on Ginty's place. It must have been thirty years ago now. We were in her house only once. We stayed in that cabin on the knoll. It isn't there any more? It seemed a pretty decent cabin when we were there. It had two rooms. One was mostly used for storage and was full of books. When I asked Ginty if I could look at them, she came and locked that part of the cabin up.

She had this pig. She called it "Peggy." It might have been "Piggy" but Ginty had this strong English accent and it sounded like "Peggy" to me. She doted on this pig. She was going to eat it anyway but she was nuts about it and it ran everywhere. Ginty gave us some preservative to put on the bottoms of the barn posts to stop them rotting. The pig came up and started to lick it. Ginty panicked. "Will it die? Will it die?" she cried. Then she wanted to know if the meat would taste of creosote.

—Joe Cortese

I visited while Jim was working there. We were invited in for tea. I had three kids then, so Kary, who was the eldest, must

*have been five or six. She was amazed at the goat poop all over
the floor. We lived in a tiny rough cabin with no running water
and we kept goats, but we never had them in the house. The
thing that fascinated my daughter most, however, was on a
shelf at her eye level. It was a sealed canning jar full of pickled
mice.*

—Jeanie Fell

It was actually quite a cold winter. The temperature reached
forty below (or close to it) on four different occasions. It was
also comparatively sunny. I've never minded cold as long as the
sun shines. There was very little snow and I didn't need to have
my road ploughed at all. Snowploughs still cruised up and down
the highway though, even at night. I could recognize the particular timbre of their motors. There is a point, as they turn a corner
at the top of a hill, where their headlights shine through the bay
window into the cabin. Try as I might, when I am driving this
same stretch of highway, I can see nothing of my dwelling—only
bush and the dunes both north and south. I was aghast at first
to hear that the ploughs continued to drive up and down when
there had been no fresh snow, but it is a safety thing. In this land
of no cell phones, scattered habitations and potentially dangerous
winter conditions, the road maintenance service patrols every
four hours. Between the telegraph road and Nimpo a small cabin
stands beside the road. The roof has long gone—it had probably
been made of sod—but the walls are still straight and true. It was
built by Batiste Dester. It was commissioned as a shelter for road
emergencies. This was when it took days to drive to Anahim from
Williams Lake. If your vehicle died between Kleena Kleene and
Nimpo Lake in the winter, it was an awful long walk to anywhere.

Because there was so little snow I was able to wade through
it quite easily and burn most of the brush piles on the building

site. I did not want ash pits all over the place so spent a lot of time dragging branches quite a distance. I had some humungous fires. I had fallen several more trees before I left on the book tour, and these were now also limbed and bucked up. It was surprising how many of the bottom branches were solidly frozen to the ground— and how long it took before they could be removed.

One day while working up there, I heard the distant putter of a snowmobile from near the house across the river. Next thing there was a blood-curdling scream. It sounded like a chainsaw about to burn itself out (been there; done that) but much louder. The distance would be at least a kilometre but it cut through my eardrums like a knife. Periodically the sound dropped to a normal snowmobile whine. Then this horrific howl would happen again.

A few days later I was in the cabin enjoying lunch after an invigorating snowshoe trip in gorgeous sunshine. It was a Sunday; soon various snowmobiles fired up across the river and the riders started to zoom round and round the fields. Interspersed with the normal whines was this sudden excessive scream. The machines came to within a hundred metres of the cabin but even when they were at the far end of the property the screaming pierced my brain. The noise, apparently, was deliberate. It came from a racing machine that had been specially tuned. I sat in the cabin with ear protectors on and tears streaming down my face. Was this now to be my destiny? Having these hideous machines destroying every beautiful winter weekend? Later I was talking to the woman of the house on the phone. She didn't like the noise, either, she said, but her grandson liked to play with it. It was her husband, however, who owned it.

Fortunately, it did not happen as often as I had feared, probably because the snow conditions were so poor; they must have been riding on bare dirt much of the time. Then I learned that these people had been finding homes for their dogs and cats because they were going away. They loved the property but were having a problem finding the money for it. She had found a nursing job in Cape Dorset. They would be leaving shortly and be gone two, maybe three years. They would have no caretakers. Their kids might be up once in a while but the scream machine was to be stored with another neighbour across the road. In the meantime, though, I was to have a respite from it. By the time the couple came back, I would be in my new house. I would still be able to hear it, but it would be that much further away.

It is hard for me to explain to most people why I don't like living within sight or earshot of neighbours. It is difficult to describe the freedom of spirit that I experience when I cannot see or hear another living soul. I enjoy people when I choose to socialize, but in between I need space. I don't know why; but without doses of this kind of solitude I cannot be myself.

One day I was trudging along the riverbank, enjoying the delicious emptiness on the other side. The new owners were actually quite pleasant people. She was certainly a conscientious nurse; he was easygoing and friendly. If only they weren't so noisy with their snowmobiles, barking dogs, and guns. Yes, recreational shooting was another pastime; at one point the grandchildren were actually firing across the river at a silt cliff on my property. At least the owners put a stop to that. My dogs and I walked up there all the time. The youngsters of course thought that all "wilderness" was simply a big playground for them to abuse as they wished.

I tried to imagine what it would be like when Vodka and Lime moved in. They would cut off my access to the river. It would be a while; they had all sorts of other plans they wanted to complete first. By then, perhaps, I would be more inured to the idea of having neighbours. I told myself that it would be good to have a mechanic next door, and someone who would feed my dogs on occasion and help plough the road. Compromise, compromise. Everyone else seems to be able to do it, why not me?

At the beginning of April, Vodka phoned from Vancouver. They were en route back north from Mexico and expected to be home in a week or so. The low snow cover meant that the bush roads were already opening up. I was pleased to see Vodka and Lime planning on an early start in the Chilcotin. They would be in good time to build my house. "Oh we won't start that right away," said Vodka. "I have some trucking to do. And the excavator is at Edgar's. I'll be doing some work up there with it first. It is too awkward to take it back and forth. We probably won't start on your place until August." My heart sank. Did they really think they could begin a house with a full basement in August and have it ready for me to move in before the snow flew? And do all the things they wanted to do with their own place? Was there any real guarantee that the excavator would continue to work? If his truck broke down would he have to attend to that first? They had never built a basement before: Would they be able to do the concrete work properly? I put the phone down and went down to stand beside the river. It was so peaceful having nobody close by. No machinery, no dogs.

And I suddenly thought: Why am I doing this? I would be crazy to trade or sell this place. But what about money? How would I be able to pay for a new house? I would not be able to make enough as a writer; that income paid the bills and that was about it. The mountain business had never made any money at all. It barely paid for itself. I had always run it in a very low-key way as I could not have handled a major tourist business. I don't have that kind of temperament. It had given me a fabulous place to live and write about but the fibromyalgia and lack of available planes on skis made it difficult to go there in winter. I was now there only in the summer and these months were full of people. I spent all my energies catering to them and had no time to visit many of my favourite places any more, or to enjoy the place alone. Nuk Tessli was no longer the same. I would not be able to keep the mountain business indefinitely, and I was finding it difficult to operate in two different locations. I don't know why it took so long to come to that conclusion, but it was Nuk Tessli that I would have to sell, not the other title at Ginty Creek.

When I told Vodka and Lime my decision after they arrived home about ten days later, they were livid. "We've even spent a lot of money on this fantastic building program for the computer," they raged, but I no longer knew how much to believe them. Their record was hardly one I could rely on. They now told me they had never liked Gin and I could not blame them for introducing him. We bitched back and forth like that for a while and I agreed to pay them $1,500 for the work they had done trucking stuff to the dump and moving the trailer: they had also taken the steel roof off one of the barns for their extension (without consulting me first) so I figured they were well compensated. Letting people down is not something I am happy doing, but having made that decision I felt as though a great weight had been lifted from my shoulders.

So it looked as though I was going to have to do my own building again. I had no idea when I would be able to complete the house. Putting Nuk Tessli up for sale was one thing. It did not mean that it would be sold in any great hurry. Half the properties on the Chilcotin had For Sale signs at the ends of their driveways; some had been sitting there for years. And Nuk Tessli was not the kind of place most people would be looking for.

There was enough money left from my inheritance to build a basement. I hunted around the property to see if there were any other building materials that I could scrounge. One of the barns was by far the most promising. It was the best made of all the standing buildings and the lumber in it was of good quality. This was the one from which Vodka had removed the steel roofing the previous summer. He was welcome to it: I didn't want shiny metal on my buildings and would have had to take it off anyway. I found my ladder and a claw hammer half hidden in the long grass beside the barn. They must have borrowed them and left them there. I had not missed the hammer yet but had been wondering where the ladder had got to.

All of Ginty's barns had feeding areas below and large hay storage spaces above. They had been designed to house goats and the bottom storeys were too low for a human to stand up in. The floor of the barn I wanted to demolish was covered in dried cow poop so presumably Ken had fed his cows in there. The manure would be great for a garden if I ever managed to get one started, but for now it was the upper part of the building that interested me.

It had been built by Jim Fell and Joe Cortese, husbands of Jeanie Fell, the librarian at Tatla Lake, and Deborah Kannegiesser, whom I had also met at the library book club. When speaking to Jim on the phone it was obvious that at least two log buildings that had been on the property thirty years before had disappeared, and the Packrat Palace had not existed then. One warm, slightly hazy spring morning, the four of them came for a visit.

Unlike a lot of the lumber on the place, the material for the barn had come from a sawmill out of the area. Joe had brought a trailer load with him, and this explained its superior quality. Jim remembers that Ginty had just come back from a visit in Fiji. One time she brought to their cabin a brown powder that she made into a tea. It was supposed to produce some kind of effect. It seemed to Jim that Ginty looked at them intently while they drank it but Jim can't remember feeling anything special. Joe has no recollection of the incident at all.

We trailed over to the Packrat Palace. Few artifacts of interest had been left anywhere on the property, but in a closed-in porch there was an old trunk and a sagging cardboard carton full of much-chewed books and magazines. I had already rescued quite a few volumes—*The Thirty-nine Steps*, a Maigret, a book of haiku, George Orwell's *Keep the Aspidistra Flying*—and I thought I'd found all the good ones, but Deborah started fishing and found all sorts of treasures. First there was a much faded colour photograph of a tall white woman in a white skirt, accompanied by a Fijian woman and several children. A large leaf hid the white woman's head and there was no indication if it was Ginty or if it was she who had taken the photograph. With it was a curled and stained sepia postcard of an outrigger canoe in full sail. No date, but the canoe was obviously genuine and not something set up for a tourist picture. Then there was a damp-warped hardcover book entitled *Life of John Churchill, Duke of Marlborough, with portrait, maps and plans.* This John Churchill had been born in 1650. The "new edition" of the book had been published in 1904. The book had W.A.B. Paul's name inscribed in it, and it must have been a prized possession because several lines on every page were underscored with pencil. It looked to be monstrously dull to me—mostly battle tactics as far as I could see. Several mouldy *Nature* magazines, to which Mr. Paul occasionally contributed, were of more interest but they were published in such an academic way that they were only slightly more attractive. More intriguing was a volume of *Working Instructions WIRELESS SET (CANADIAN) No. 19 Mark 111* published by the National Defence (no date), containing strict printed orders that "the information given in this document is not to be communicated either directly, or indirectly, to the

Press or to any person not holding an official position in His Majesty's Service."

The real gems were a couple of items that Ginty had made. A scrapbook with a red cover bearing a drawing in black ink of a collage of classical architecture boasted the label:

History of Fine Arts
Nedra Jane Paul
January 19, 1954
Book 1

Inside were magazine pictures supplemented by a penned text in Ginty's large, clear handwriting. The pen used was thick-nibbed, the kind you dipped in ink. A word would fade out, and the following one would start thick and darker until the pen ran out again. Whether she had made this book for herself or her students was unclear. She had selected some very wide-ranging and interesting art pieces. The text was poorly written.

Finally, there was a Public Schools Drawing Book, made in England by Reeves and Sons, Ltd., London. Only a few of the yellowing pages had been used. The drawings had been made with a hard, fine pencil. Two small sketches were of the same man, who had a somewhat nondescript face—he looked too young to have been her father unless she had done the drawings at a much earlier date. There was a stiff and awkward portrait of a young boy sitting on the floor. Four larger drawings were of the face of a woman who could only have been Ginty herself. Self-portraits are always revealing. The face was strong and long, the nose slightly hooked. The eyes were calm.

When I had pulled the first barn down with Stephanie and Katherine, it had taken maybe half an hour. Jim and Joe's barn

Self-portrait of Ginty Paul.

took me five days. The siding had been taken off by wwoofers two years before. Now I ripped the diagonals off the sides and attached the come-along to a tree on a nearby slope. I cranked it so tight I thought the rope might break, but there was not so much as a creak from the barn's timbers. The rope was very difficult to loosen. I went into the building to cut off more supports. I was scared that the whole thing would come crashing down onto my head, but I climbed out unscathed and when I ratcheted up the come-along again, the barn still wouldn't budge. Every day I cut more supports. At first I used the chainsaw but in the end I had to perch on top of a ladder that was sitting on a steeply sloping bank. If either the ladder or the building gave way I did not want to be falling with a working chainsaw in my hands, so I hacked away with a handsaw. The remains of the bull were close by and the aroma often wafted over. It was bear season already and sometimes the dogs barked as if something was there. At one point I went to see how the carcass was disintegrating. It had been a slow job because the greater part of the bull had been wedged in the ditch and this had taken a long time to thaw. The ice must have finally loosened its grip, however, because the carcass was now in pieces and pulled up onto a patch of grass. There was little left except the heavy bones and ragged chunks of stiffened, red-haired hide.

Finally the barn came down. I had disconnected the home-made phone extension while I worked as I was worried that the barn might hit it, so that had to be put together again. Now all I had to do was pry apart the useful timber, ferry it over to the building site and start to build my house.

CHAPTER 15

THE BASEMENT

I used to live at Porcupine Meadows. That's right across the highway from Ginty's but there's not much left of the place now. I used to visit Larry Lovering, the artist, when he was alive. He had his tea leaves told a number of times by Ginty.

Ginty was a very welcoming person. The house was unbelievably cluttered. There wasn't even enough room to put a cup down; you had to hold it. One time I didn't drink all my tea—guess I wasn't thirsty or something. But Ginty told me to drink a bit more then she read the leaves. She didn't tell me how she knew what the tea leaves said but she forecast a bad time with lots of tears. I don't want to go into the details but she was amazingly accurate.

—Sandi Giovanelli

So once again I was faced with the overwhelming chore of building a house. This was to be my sixth. Some I had constructed with logs, others were frame. The first four had been off road; there had been no way to drive heavy machinery to the site so a large portion of those buildings was made from materials gleaned from the surrounding forest. For the first and last of them, I had been lucky to have had help with the heavy lifting and, in the case of number four, some of the construction, but the middle two cabins I had erected completely alone. The fifth building was the cabin I now inhabited. I had received a great deal of help with that one, but the biggest saving in time was because of the road. Materials could therefore be dragged or delivered to the door.

I had lived in all these buildings for various periods of time and had sorted out the design of the living space to my satisfaction, given the limits of the topography, my physical strength, and money. The only changes in the layout of the last three cabins were minor ones. I knew exactly how I wanted to orient the building for the views and how I wanted the light to fall in a room (I am an early morning person and love to face the hint of dawn coming into the sky). I was also happy with the placement of the stove, and how it and both sleeping and seating areas could be located in relation to the door (the latter being the most likely cause of drafts). I had sorted out the width and height of the counters (but had never yet ironed out all the bumps regarding storage space: there was never enough!).

However, I had never built anything below ground before. It was time I had a warmer floor, and a cool space so that vegetables would keep better in summer and not freeze if I went away in the winter. And, if I could ever figure out a water supply, I wanted plumbing. For this absolutely last dwelling I would ever make, I was going to have a basement.

I had heard good things about polystyrene insulated basements. The ads made it sound as easy as building Lego. A man in Nimpo Lake had put one together and I went to look at it. The blocks were dirty white with the texture of fluffy white foam. They were hollow, like breeze blocks, and cement was poured into them. Conventional concrete basements needed heavy

plywood framing that would have to be removed once the concrete had set. Any insulation would have to be added later. These
blocks stayed in place and provided insulation at the same time.
They did not appear to be a lot more expensive than conventional basements. I was worried about their chemical properties
but polystyrene, I learned, does not emit formaldehyde, con-
trary to my fears.

I started to draw plans for a basement on a scrap of paper
but then realized I should have measured the blocks while I
was in Nimpo to see exactly how big to make it. I googled the
blocks and several sites came up, but none told me how big the
L-shaped corner pieces were. I phoned a builders' supply store
in Williams Lake. A lot of business has to be done by phone
on the Chilcotin; very few business people, even in Williams
Lake, use the internet. I asked about the size of the corner
block. "You'll have to speak to Brian," said the woman. "He gets
in at eleven: I'll get him to call you right away." I phoned again
at 11:20. Repeated the question. "Hang on," said the woman,
and clunked the phone down. I wait. And wait. A man picks the
phone up: "Is anyone there? Who do you wish to speak to?"
"Brian." "Maybe I can help you." I repeated the question. "You'll
have to ask Brian that." Clunk. I wait. Another man. "How can I
help you?" "I need to speak to Brian." "I am Brian." "What size
are the polystyrene corner blocks?" "Haven't the faintest idea!"
"Don't you have specifications somewhere?" "Probably. But I'd
have to look them up. You just have to tell us what size your
basement is going to be and we'll order the blocks." Trouble is, I
didn't know what size the basement was going to be until I knew
the size of the blocks. This was the first indication I had that
working with materials and skills outside my experience was
not going to be as straightforward as I had hoped.

Brian did tell me that they did not sell a lot of these things and I might like to try True North Ventures at 150 Mile House. This company was owned by Bev and Ward Haskins; they were a family business and proved to be excellent to deal with. Bev was the office person. She was not only efficient—she also used the internet! I emailed her a plan and she got back to me with a quote within hours. It appeared, however, that the blocks were not all I would need. There was rebar and anchor bolts and a plate and plastic ties, tape, a foam gun with two cartridges of foam, a damp course, and some kind of waterproofing for the outside of the basement. I would also need a network of framing to support the bocks while the concrete was poured. It was obviously not quite as easy as the people selling the stuff online had made out. A few days later I drove into town and paid a deposit for the blocks. I ordered plywood for the floor and some long two-by-eights for the plates. I picked up the smaller bits and pieces: "How far apart should the anchor bolts be?" I asked the woman behind the counter in the builders' supply store. She shrugged her shoulders; fortunately—very fortunately—a building contractor was standing next to me and he supplied the answer: "Seven feet." It seemed like an odd measurement but I went with it and calculated how many I needed. I had to buy nuts and washers for them, too.

It was by now the middle of April. The large pond had lost its ice and the small one was half open. Tiny tips of green were showing among the winter-faded sedges in the marshes. It was time to contact local excavator operators. There were two of them. Some people recommended one, some the other. I was trying to get both of them to come by and give me a quote. The digging contractor whom I thought I would go with suggested it was a good idea to hire a carpenter to put the basement together. If it was not done right, the concrete might burst the blocks during pouring. I asked him if he knew of anyone and he recommended a man south of Tatla Lake. However, this carpenter reckoned the job would be too small for him to want to bother to come all that way (over an hour's commute), and he told me to get hold of Mike Witt. Mike lived only twenty minutes down the road. He drove into the yard a few days later. Average height, late thirties, round face, cowboy hat and wraparound shades that reflected the world in deep ultramarine. He seemed a pleasant person, he was an experienced carpenter and he had done one of these types of basements before. "You'll need all sorts of extra two-by-fours and two-by-sixes for the supports and also a scaffolding to stand on when we pour." I pointed at the pile of lumber salvaged from the barn. "We'll have to do the footings first, let them set up, then build the walls on top." I mentioned the digging contractor who, in a roundabout way, had led me to him. "Well I prefer to use the other one, Len Lamothe. I do a lot of work with him. His best driver is a good buddy of mine. He charges more per hour than the other man but he has a much bigger Cat so works faster." So I phoned Len. "Should be able to get there by next week," he said. He didn't come and I phoned again. "I'm just waiting for parts," he said. (Where have I heard that before?) "Besides," he continued, "I was digging with my small excavator the other day, trying to get stumps out, and the ground was still frozen." The knoll where I wanted to build had been naked of snow and blasted by the sun for weeks so I did not think there would be much problem there. "Should be ready by the end of the month," he assured me.

On May 4, a pickup truck drove into the yard beside the cabin. A couple of spotted, short-haired hounds moved restlessly in the back. A lean man wearing a cowboy hat and with a red bandana tied around his neck climbed out. He was a slimmer version, but he reminded me of pictures I'd seen of Tom Mix. "The excavator is here," he said in a soft voice. "It's being unloaded at the turnoff to your house site." No warning, no phone call, they just arrived.

The driver was Henry. He would have to walk the Cat to the site as the road was still squishy in places and, until Henry had re-worked it, there was nowhere for Len's big rig to turn around. The machine clanked along with a massive squeal of tracks. Mike was already there (they had obviously phoned him). I had marked the site with a can of spray marker I had bought especially for the job—except it ran out halfway round and I had to finish the marking with flagging tape. The basement was to be L-shaped. The hole had to be dug about one and a half metres bigger all round than the building was going to be.

The digging operation was impressive. The bucket was as big as a bathtub but Henry was as accurate with it as an archeologist wielding a teaspoon. The soil was pale grey silt all the way. No hardpan, no water. Two huge mounds of dry, silvery earth began to grow on either side of the hole. Mike had borrowed a transit from Len so he could measure the exact depth. He stood in the

Digging the basement hole. Mike Witt is standing in the bottom.

hole and peered into the eyepiece. He held up a hand to Henry, with his fingers two centimetres apart. Henry put down the bucket and effortlessly picked up exactly two centimetres of dirt all along the bottom of the hole.

Some of the dirt was used to build up a road that would make a loop so that there would be a turnaround in the yard. I had cut the trees out during the winter. That took up the rest of Henry's day; the next was a Sunday and on the Monday he would work on the appalling mess that Gin's "escavator" had made. Until that was fixed, trucks delivering building supplies and cement would not be able to reach the site.

I had talked to the men about digging a drain field and a possible shallow well. If we struck water, they could dig the channel for that, too. Henry's boss, Len, said he could witch for water, but where he had built his new house they'd had to drill fifty-one metres! I was talking to Henry about it in one of the brief moments when he was not working. "I can do a bit of witching," he said. "I usually use two wires like straightened-out coat hangers with a right-angled handle at one end. They cross over if the water is there."

I'd never heard about that method of dowsing. In any case, wasn't witching something that only Other People could do? The only tool I had heard of was a forked willow stick and I'd tried that where Vodka attempted to dig for a well with his little "escavator" but had had no reaction. But of course, there was no water there.

I possessed only one coat hanger (which I guess is a good indication as to the status of my wardrobe), but of telegraph wire I had many kilometres—woven into fences, rolled onto two rotten drums, and simply discarded in tangled heaps. I picked up a hammer and a rock—the latter to use as an anvil—and flattened the wire until I could bend and break off two pieces. Each was a bit longer than my arm. I bent about fifteen centimetres at right angles at one end of each to use as handles. I held my hands in front of my chest, the wires pointing ahead like two pistols in a *High Noon* showdown. I was close to the cabin and I took a few steps away from the door. The wires started to waver toward each other. I was goggle-eyed. I took a few more steps and the wires swung apart again. I went back and forth and got an identical result every time I crossed the same place. This was fantastically exciting. But how to determine the depth?

About a year before, in the spring, I had made an amazing discovery. I had learned that it was possible to divine all manner of health issues with a pendulum. The only thing I had known about pendulums before that was that they hung at the bottom of clocks. I had never imagined that they could be used as dowsing tools.

Ever since I had been diagnosed with food sensitivities and fibromyalgia I had been cruising the net for possible solutions. I tried diets and supplements and self-hypnosis, and was still making periodic visits to a nutritionist. The first intimation I had that there something potentially helpful out there was due to an accident. During that preceding winter I had been working on the illustrations for *A Mountain Year* and I wanted to draw a picture of an immature salamander, which is called an eft. I googled it and the sites that came up could not have been further removed from baby amphibians. Their EFT was in capital letters and stood for Emotional Freedom Technique. The idea was to tap eyebrows and collar bones and other parts of your body in sequence, with your fingers, to get rid of inexplicable illnesses and stresses. Was this ever weird. However, I had thought the nutritionist had been just as peculiar when she had muscle-tested me for food by having me try to resist when she pulled on my leg, and her diagnoses had worked. The places that you tapped were actually acupuncture points. It was a technique, I learned later, that was used by a number of Energy Medicine practices and, because there were no needles involved, it was sometimes called acupressure. Within a short time I was hooked. I was convinced that all my aches and pains and food sensitivities were psychosomatic and if only I could find the right trigger, I would be cured. I religiously tapped my way through two months, often several times a day, with absolutely no effect whatsoever.

On one of the EFT sites, however, there was a reference to a Dr. Barbara Mallory who wrote about pendulum divining. I am not really sure why I looked at her website. Idleness, or perhaps serendipity—who can say? So many of these activities are touted by people who look as though they are straight off a Hollywood film set. I had no time for all these airy fairies, but on the pendulum page there was a picture of a rather grim woman, no longer young, who did not look at all airy fairy. For all that, she was doing some very strange things. She was holding the forefinger of one hand horizontally under her nose, like a moustache, while the forefinger of the other was stuffed in her belly button. It was apparently part of an acupressure routine to make sure your "batteries were in the right way round." Nothing ventured . . . I did as the woman instructed, and then made a pendulum out of a piece of string and a washer, which was the first suitable weight that came to hand. I held it in front of an apple, which I knew I could eat. The washer started to swing, apparently all by itself. I was dumfounded. I held it in front of a bottle of vinegar, which was something I could no longer eat because of the sulphites in it. Slowly the pendulum changed direction and was now swinging the other way. I could not believe that this was happening. I tried about thirty different foods. Most results were the same as had been determined by the nutritionist, but she was five hours' drive away from Ginty Creek and even harder to get to when I was up in the mountains. The pendulum was right in my hand. And it cost nothing!

I have now been using this amazing tool for four years. I never travel anywhere without it. I check every item in a supermarket, and every meal served in a restaurant. I get some funny looks—and even annoyance, as happened at one health food store when I refused to purchase a supplement the owner was recommending. He was even madder when I tried to convince another customer (whom I knew) that the supplement wasn't for her. (She took the store owner's advice: I realized I was going to have to be a bit more tactful about all this!)

Later, with the help of the pendulum, I made another huge discovery. It was in a book called *Energy Medicine* by Donna Eden and was an acupressure exercise to get rid of food sensitivities. Using the Yes/No answers the pendulum gave me, I was able to go successfully through the routine. Now I can eat anything except chemicals, particularly preservatives: basically, this means absolutely no processed food—which is actually quite difficult to avoid. I had thought I was eating healthily before, but I now realize that the quantity of chemicals that I had been consuming on a regular basis was mind blowing. Some of the preservatives are even found in organic food.

"Ginty was into that sort of thing," said Leslie Lamb while I was using the pendulum to check out the lunch she gave me. "What do you mean?" I asked. "She read tea leaves and stuff." Tea leaves, surely, were hardly in the same class as pendulums—or were they? (Tea leaf-reading is still something that I have never explored.)

I wondered if the pendulum could help determine the depth of the water that the witching rods had found in front of the cabin. I stood on the most likely spot and asked the pendulum if it knew how deep the water was. Slowly it began to describe a clockwise circle, which for me meant Yes. Was it more than three metres? An anticlockwise circle indicated No. Was it more than one metre? Yes. By narrowing the distances I determined it was about one and a half metres below ground level. Then I thought to ask if it was good water. No. That was a surprise. Was it contaminated? No. Did it have too much iron? Yes. (This is a common problem on the Chilcotin.) I tried another spot near the Packrat Palace. The depth was apparently two and a half metres but the supply was also too full of iron. As I walked the half kilometre up the field to the building site I was getting all sorts of readings. I realized that the wires must be very sensitive and be picking up every little trickle. It was spring, too: even allowing for the snowless winter and very dry spring, the soil would be as wet as it would get at any time of the year.

I started to get quite a strong reading close to the new basement and I asked Henry if he could have a go to confirm my findings. He walked over the spot and the wires moved for him. "There's something there," he said cautiously. When Henry had gone, I walked back and forth all over the knoll. I traced a seeming flow of water several paces wide that appeared to run right under the knoll and split on the slope leading toward the pond. The larger branch looked the most promising. The underground stream (if that's what it was) ran directly below the basement hole and, according to the way I read the pendulum, it was only two and a half metres down at that point. A well in the basement would mean that it wouldn't freeze, but if we dug down and it was a gusher we might end up with a swimming pool. I had phoned a well driller in Williams Lake and it seemed that I did not just need water; I needed something called hydrostatic pressure. This would enable the water to rise partway up the pipe and it has to do that otherwise it would be impossible to pump it.

Maybe the pendulum could give me some answers. It said there was no hydrostatic pressure in the basement but there was some at the bottom of the mound near the pond. "Is there any hardpan?" I asked. Yes. By asking, "Is it more than five metres?" "More than three metres?" and so on, I determined it was four metres below me. Is the water running on top of the hardpan? Yes.

I walked up early on the Monday morning to find that Mike had just pulled into the yard. Right along the new loop road, on top of the Caterpillar tracks that laced the silvery grey silt, was a set of large grizzly paw prints. "See that big toe?" said Mike, who was a bear hunter as well as a carpenter. "That shows it's a big old boar." The grizzly had walked up the road past the trailer, across the knoll where the kitchen window would be and then down toward the pond.

Henry's excavator could reach down six metres. It would take him only a few minutes to dig a trial hole four metres deep at the spot I had chosen. This was tremendously exciting. If I could predict the depth of water accurately, I could make a fortune! Henry clanked his machine around to the bottom of the mound (I had cut out a rough road down there to give access to an area I had cleared for a garden). Mike and I stood and watched with bated breath. Shovel by shovel, the hole deepened. Exactly four metres down, as predicted, the bucket grated against a layer of hardpan—the soil was dustbowl dry. Of water there was not even a hint. It was a long time later that someone suggested there might be two layers of hardpan. I tried to remember the exact wording of my questions. Had I in fact asked about the depth of the water or the first layer of hardpan? The opportunity to try the questions again has not come up. When I had the time, the ground was saturated with heavy rains. Anyway, I wouldn't be able to afford the well driller and all the pumps and pipes and pressure tanks until I had sold the mountain business. The idea of having a well would have to be deferred.

Henry next tackled my new road, widening it and rebuilding the ditches. The existing culvert worked fine, but another area would obviously need some kind of drainage. "I'll just put in a log culvert for now," Henry said. He dug a channel across the road, cut down several dead pines and laid them in it, then shovelled the dirt back on top. It was in a shady spot and the soil was still full of ice crystals—this was May 7. These thawed and made a horrible soupy mess for a day or two, but now at last the road could be used by heavier vehicles. The first was courtesy of Beeline—one of the freight companies that ply the Chilcotin—who brought the plywood and lumber I had ordered from the builders' supply store when I was last in town. The driver had also brought a couple of things I hadn't ordered, and had missed out on a couple of things I had. This is one of the joys of living out on the Chilcotin. The other joy is the freight costs. Beeline charged $600 for their delivery (but nothing for the returned, unwanted items: they would bill the supply yard for that). The polystyrene blocks were next. Bev and Ward were wonderful. Even though they were on the far side of Williams Lake, they charged only $400 to bring them to the door.

The first wwoofer I had that spring was a waste of time. He had been ambivalent about coming and I decided I could afford it and offered to pay him $100 a day plus keep. He had billed himself as a machinist who was good with tools and who was cruising around looking for a career change. When I met him I could not understand why he had come to the Chilcotin. He was a city boy with city aspirations who arrived in a city car. He pulled out cigarettes and I asked him to please not smoke inside anywhere and to be extra careful as everything was so dry. "That's okay," he replied. "I'm almost out of cigarettes anyway." I told him it was a forty-minute drive to the nearest store. "Oh," he said airily, "I can manage perfectly well without them." I set him to work ripping some of the timber out of the barn I had pulled down earlier that spring, and he accomplished a lot on his first day. On the second he asked for the afternoon off. He needed to go to the store. He came back with cigarettes and junk food. I feed the volunteers well, but I refuse to buy junk food. On day three I would have had him continue with the barn but, as the blocks were due to arrive, a good job to start while we waited at the building site was walling-in the outhouse. Kelsey and I had built the frame and a scrap metal roof in the fall, and the heavy green tarp had been draped around the walls in case a lot of snow drifted into the hole. This new wwoofer might have been a good machinist, but his skills did not run to hand-held carpentry tools. I had to redo most of what he attempted. He was useless at driving the monster Chevy pickup truck, too. He had no clue as to how to back it. (He'd probably never driven a standard before.) He was also, I was beginning to suspect, one of those males who had a hard time accepting that a woman could do those kinds of things better than he could.

Ward Haskins arrived with the huge piles of polystyrene blocks and the rebar. The wwoofer helped him unload them with a sour expression on his face. The next day was the Monday when Henry dug the well. The wwoofer knew this was going to happen and he knew of my great excitement; he never even bothered to come out of the trailer. How could anybody not be interested in digging for a well? After the non-event, I went over to the trailer and told the wwoofer I didn't like his attitude and he might as well leave. He was stunned that I would criticize him. He was gone within an hour. On the whole I have been lucky with my wwoofers: this one was an exception.

In this account I have organized the building stages into a narrative that flows logically, but of course it wasn't like that. I would learn a bit about one thing, order whatever was necessary, then learn something else about another stage entirely, which necessitated changing the first order. The phone was in the cabin, a ten-minute walk each way from the building site. I was constantly going back and forth. Some people could be called first thing in the morning, others could not be reached until the business day started. Still others were best contacted at night. Most people had answering machines, but I did not. "Best times to get me are between six and eight, morning or evening," I told everyone, but few bothered to return my calls. I felt like one of those jugglers with spinning plates on poles. One would be just about ready to fall off and I would have to run and set it spinning again. Meanwhile another was about to collapse.

The problem that made all this so complicated was the timing. We had not been able to do the digging and road work until the ice went out of the ground. I wanted to be in the mountains by the end of May, but Mike had even less time. He was due to guide a ten-day bear hunt in Vanderhoof and was leaving on May 17, which was in less than two weeks' time. He would be ready to work again on June 4 but for me that would be too late. I could delay my return to the mountains a little, but I was expecting people by the middle of June and it would take at least a week to clean the resort properly. All the mattress covers and blankets had to be washed (by hand); floors, ceilings and shelves needed to be scrubbed (in three cabins); and there were usually mice. Before Mike left he had to build the footings, let them set up, and then erect the walls, supports and scaffolding. And there was the small matter of buying concrete.

This proved to be the biggest headache of all. I now found out that I had to deal with something else: road restrictions. I had seen the notices occasionally on the highway but thought nothing of them. Now I learned they were put on every spring until the ice was properly out of the ground. Before they were lifted, heavy vehicles could carry only a partial load. I phoned the road services. They didn't know when the restrictions would be taken off: June sometime, they figured. I phoned a concrete company in Williams Lake. "It's usually in June sometime," they confirmed.

A local man had recently started a business to supply concrete. Mike seemed to think his product would be great for the footings but not fine enough for the walls. I phoned the local man several times before I spoke to him (I'd left messages on his answering machine but he didn't call back). He wasn't going to get his concrete truck on the road until after the restrictions were lifted. I would have to use the company in town. Their concrete price per yard was the same as the local man's, but they charged an extra $800 road time. For each truck. There ended up being four of them altogether. The road time cost more than the concrete.

Some people apparently pour the walls and footings of these insulated block walls at the same time, but the risk of blowout was increased. The first—useless—wwoofer had gone and the second had not yet arrived, so Mike brought along his girlfriend Leslie and her long-time buddy Aileen (pronounced Eileen) to help. I knew both girls slightly: I first met Aileen when she was about eight and living at the Precipice. Her dad is a logger; the family used to spend the summers in the trailer I had bought. When I met them, they were caretaking the Precipice ranch for the winter. Aileen had two younger siblings and another on the way. The two eldest children, both girls, were going to school in Anahim. They would stay with friends for the week and be fetched home for the weekend. I visited Dave and Rosemary that Christmas and got a ride back home with the kids. Their dad had built a sled with two seats that he could tow behind the snowmobile. He had welded skimpy pipe walls on either side. The contraption had no shocks and was flung about with abandon. It was a crashing, forty-minute ride to get down to the bottom of the valley. I was sure the sled was going to flip a number of times. I hung on for dear life and was bruised black and blue when I got to the bottom. The two little girls made this trip quite stoically twice a week.

For Christmas, Aileen received a sort of Barbie horse. It was pink plastic with glitter in its white mane and tail. It had accessories such as saddles that you could put on and take off. Aileen is in her twenties now and she is still horse mad. She is short, but one tough little body. She is always smiling and an incredibly hard worker. Leslie is much quieter. Her parents are guide outfitters and operate horseback tours in the Rainbows, one of the volcanic ranges north of the highway. Both girls wrangle for them in the summer.

The concrete truck operator who was to pour the footings put together a chute and was able to put most of the concrete where it was wanted. Some had to be moved with a wheelbarrow. It was Leslie who told me to pat the top of the cement to make it smooth; simply trying to smear it around was not enough. Patting it brought the water to the surface. The Harkises had lent us a re-bar bender. Mike cut short pieces and bent them at right angles; one part lay horizontally in the wet concrete, the other stuck upright; it would help tie the standing wall to the footings.

It would be a couple of days before the footings were firm enough to do the next stage so I asked Mike if he wanted paying up to date. He drove me round to the cabin. I had always walked back and forth along the trail up the fields, and no one had used the road for several days. There had been the merest skiff of rain, just a sprinkle that was now completely dry, but it had left a surface on the road as clean as a blank page. A mamma black bear had walked along one vehicle rut, two second-year cubs along the

other. Their prints were perfectly fresh and formed in every detail. The cubs had trotted back and forth a bit but Mamma had
plodded steadily on. We followed the tracks through the open
gate. We drove closer and closer to the cabin and I wondered if
we would see the bears at the building, but at the last moment the
road turns right and the bear tracks continued straight on: they
were heading toward the remains of the bull.

After a couple of days, Mike started to put the blocks together.
A young volunteer named Katrina had arrived by then. She had
planned on staying a while but had received a job offer she could
not refuse so would be able to work for only a few days. This was
a pity; she was not all that skilled but she learned fast and she
was a hard worker. The blocks looked startlingly white in the
sunshine; Mike was forced to wear his shades. The design of the
blocks was quite intriguing. Not only did they slot together neat-
ly, but crosspieces inside held snaps for rebar. Everything had to
be tied together with the kind of plastic ties that are ridged on
one side, which you can wrench tight but cannot undo. That was
my job. Mike lent me a pair of pliers to yank on them. One time
the pliers slipped and the handle whanged into my forehead and
gave me a huge knot above the eye. It didn't hurt too much after
the initial shock but must have been quite impressive because I
could see Mike stealing a glance at it once in a while. I was lucky
I didn't break my glasses; I was also lucky I didn't drop the pliers
into the wall. It was several layers deep at that point. What with
the crosspieces, the rebar and the ties, there was a spider's web
of structure inside and it would have been impossible to fish
anything out.

The next thing to concern us was the weather. All winter and
spring it had been dry, dry, dry, but the little sprinkle of rain a
few days before had turned the new part of the road to grease. A

heavy downpour would be a disaster. Heavy rain was the forecast for pouring day.

While we were finishing off the blocks, Mike casually mentioned we would need the pumper truck. I was under the impression that we wouldn't. I had visualized us all standing on the scaffolding with long poles shoving the concrete down into the walls. The chute was not going to reach to every corner of the walls and it would be a nightmare trying to wheelbarrow it on planks two metres above the ground. I wasn't entirely sure what a pumper truck was. Nor had I any idea if we would be able to get one at such short notice. I ran down to the phone. The woman in the office of the concrete business would not be able to tell me until the evening. I explained the phone situation and the kind lady gave me her home number so I wouldn't have to rush down again before they closed. It was suppertime when I called her: the pumper truck would indeed be available. They, too, were concerned about

The pumper truck.

the forecast and my potentially sloppy road. I was to phone and give a weather report at 8:00 a.m.

It was clear and windy out here but dumping rain in Williams Lake the following morning. It would take them four hours to drive the distance (they would be slower than a car because of the long hills out of Williams Lake). Would the weather hold? Mike brought Leslie, Aileen and a friend of Mike's from Tatla Lake, Doug McMann. Doug was a builder and carpenter who had quite a lot of experience in pouring concrete.

When the pumper truck was set up for business, it looked like some weird extraterrestrial vehicle. It extended two great insect legs, one on either side, and then sent up an enormously long elephant's trunk way up above the trees and down toward the walls. A cement truck was latched on, like a mating aphid; everything was controlled by a boxful of knobs that was slung around the operator's neck so that he could walk about and push the buttons at the level of his waist. He and Doug and Mike got onto

Pouring the concrete into the polystyrene blocks.

the scaffold, the clip was taken off the elephant's trunk, and grey aggregate coursed into the walls. Mike had me and Katrina bang the outsides of the walls with a hammer cushioned by a piece of two-by-four to make sure the concrete settled. At the last, Mike popped in the anchor bolts, leaving several centimetres sticking out of the top of the wall.

There was a yard of concrete left over. "Where do you want it?" the pumper truck driver asked. I had prepared a spot in the garden for just this eventuality: I had plans to build an outdoor stone bread oven, and any leftover concrete would provide a useful base. I had built a wooden frame out of old scraps of lumber and rebar. Even the long elephant's trunk could not reach that far, however, and the pumper truck would not be able to drive down my steep rough road. I had cleaned the pickup box of dirt and woodchips and asked if they could dump it there. The driver laughed. "If we put all that concrete in that truck," he said, "you'll never move it again." I remembered when the drum that revolves on the back of a concrete truck fell off along Highway 20 years ago. The concrete set in it before anyone could move it and then it was then too heavy to shift. It was there for half a decade. Someone had written Sputnik 1 on it in large black letters, and indeed it did look very like the kind of early space capsules that used to be parachuted into the sea.

I had no desire to have a rock-solid green Chevy truck as a yard ornament. "Make up your mind," said the driver. "Every minute of this delay is costing you money." I threw down a tarp and got him to dump the cement onto it. He kindly put in a bit more retardant first and stirred it around. The men and Leslie left, and Aileen, Katrina and I shovelled that stuff into the wheelbarrow and the pickup and took it load by load down to the garden. It was monstrously heavy and I did not think we would be able to move it all before it set but we did—just. It was stiffening up dramatically as we shovelled the last of it into the wooden frame.

And the next day, the promised rain came. It absolutely poured. I sank to my ankles in the silt on the new road. I had to put down planks just so that I could walk to the outhouse. It was the first substantial precipitation we had received since the previous fall. Talk about timing. It would have been several days before the road would have been fit for the heavy vehicle to use, and Mike would have been away on his bear-hunting trip by then.

Len, the owner of the digger, said I would need to wait for at least ten days before they could do the backfill. Even with the bracing inside, the concrete would not be strong enough until then to tolerate the weight of the dirt. In the meantime I should also get the floor joists up as they would help to strengthen the walls.

First, Kristina and I fastened on the plates. We laid a foam damp course, then drilled holes in the two-by-eights and slipped them over the anchor bolts. We now had a wooden sill to which we could attach the building. When time permitted between the other jobs, I had been preparing floor joists out of a mixture of logs and rafters salvaged from the barn. Using several short logs as rollers, I pulled them to the site. Kristina helped for one day but then she had to leave and I continued to work alone. It was a bit of a fiddle getting the joists across the wide ditch around the walls. The weather stayed gloomy and one morning wet snow fell. This was already the beginning of June. The building site was filthy with mud and extremely slippery, even when I had the scaffold to stand on, and that was rarely in the right place so I was constantly climbing up and down. The fibromyalgia was dragging me down. Everything ached. I really did not have the physical capability to do this kind of thing any more.

Then my chainsaw wiped out. I had finished the joists but

not yet put the plywood on. Len and Henry came back to do the backfill and dig a drain field. (We had remembered to put pipes through the basement walls where the plumbing, if it ever happened, was to take place.) It wasn't a very big drain field, as it was for grey water only. I would eventually have a compost toilet so no sewage would be involved. Pipes outside the building had to be buried two metres deep to be sure of avoiding the frost. "How long do you think a drain field like that will last?" I asked. Henry gave me a little grin. "If you don't have a water supply, it'll last a very long time," he said.

Finally the remains of the two heaps of dirt were removed and used to fill a dip in the road. What a terrible mess everything looked. "It'll soon grow over," the men said. But it wouldn't, or at any rate, not in my lifetime. The dirt on the knoll by my cabin had been exposed twenty years ago and only scattered tufts of grass and pigweed grew on it. The soft, duffy pine needle carpet scattered with clumps of soopollalie and juniper was gone forever.

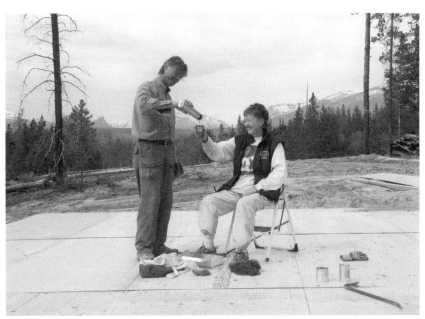

Dennis and Katie toasting the completion of the subfloor.

But the guys had done a good job at a reasonable price. The big Caterpillar excavator clanked away.

I was desperate to get into the mountains but I had to cover the hole before I left. If we had a wet summer, I would have a swimming pool by the end of it. Enter Katie and Dennis. They are the owners of the house I usually stay in when I visit the Bella Coola Valley. They had now officially retired and were planning on spending the whole summer at Stuie. Retired! Wouldn't it be lovely. Katie and Dennis were my age exactly. I was now working as hard as at any time in my life. Katie and Dennis camped for the night and helped me put the plywood on in the morning. We toasted our work with peppermint tea. A quick trip to Williams Lake followed, to get the saw fixed and buy supplies for the summer. I was staggering with exhaustion when I flew to my mountain resort.

CHAPTER 16

FIRE!

He [Ginty] had this goat named Wally. He was the stinkiest of all. "Why he stink so much?" I ask' her. She said it was the long horns made him stink. Some time later, this Wally died. She reeally upset.

When he [Ginty] got sick, he had to butcher all the goats. Fifty of them. The Indians [East Indians] buy them all. I make deer hides and I tried a couple of goats. Turned out quite good. You put them in water then take the hair off. Scrape with moose bone and stuff. Very hard work. Put them back in the water. Then when they dry, put oil on them. Used to use oolichan fish oil but can't get that any more. Now have to use any kind of oil from the store like for saddles and stuff.

One March time I went over there. You can walk anywhere [because the snow was frozen hard]. I was looking for moose. I come 'round her place. She standing in the corral. "Elaine, you help me," she said. "You help me." A goat is having babies and babies won't come. "You hold this rope reeeeally tight," she said. The rope was reeally slipp'ry with all that baby stuff. I just about got sick! "Keep pulling. Keep pulling," she said. And baby come out.

—Elaine Dester

That summer, the Chilcotin burned. There were fires everywhere. I had not expected to see Ginty Creek again until September but on the first of August I was evacuated from Nuk Tessli because of a fire a few kilometres upwind. Firefighters told me that it was almost certain to reach Nuk Tessli within two days; I and my clients would have to leave right away otherwise the smoke might prevent anyone from flying in to pick us up.

I drove to Ginty Creek through an atmosphere raw with smoke. It was late and a blood-red moon hung in the smoke-dark sky. When daylight emerged the following day, all the mountains were hidden. The sun glowed feebly behind its brown veil. There was no wind, and temperatures were in the thirties. The day after I arrived Highway 20 was closed in four places, two west of Ginty Creek, in the Bella Coola Valley, and two more between my property and Williams Lake. I was cut off in both directions. People were evacuated from Alexis Creek, about two hours east, and in two areas in the Bella Coola Valley. Katie and Dennis were at Stuie and they helped feed the firefighters at the Tweedsmuir Park Lodge next door. Fires were flaming on either side of them, high up near the rims of their valley.

A lot of effort was expended in fighting these fires, as Stuie is the location of the microwave tower that funnels all phone and electronic communication in and out of there. Helicopters battered overhead constantly, scooping water from the river, and Katie emailed that it sometimes seemed as though the choppers were going to dump their loads on everyone's heads. Stuie was also the marshalling point for traffic wishing to drive up The Hill. A major fire raged right at the top; at first the highway was closed completely but then people were allowed through early in the morning when the fire was less likely to be out of control. The powers that be were trying to discourage anyone from going into the valley but, in a video Katie emailed, the lineup waiting to leave looked like the ferry yard at Horseshoe Bay. There was some concern at first as to whether the weekly produce trucks would get through, but they made it; in any case, people can grow things in the valley. There would always be something to eat down there.

I was in constant touch with the fire boss in Williams Lake and the local fire coordinator. (How I blessed the phone: I did not have one in the mountains. It was so much more immediate than the internet.) The local coordinator was a man from Saskatchewan so he did not know the area and could only report what he was told, and that made for some confusion. He was not the only outsider: firefighters were shipped in from all over Canada (east of the Rockies it was pouring rain) and also from Sweden and even Australia. I was told that sprinklers were put around Nuk Tessli and they were closely monitoring my private little fire. It was so remote that it wasn't affecting anyone else and in any other circumstances they would have ignored it. I could not fault the fire service as far as my situation was concerned. No one minded if I kept bugging them on the phone even though there were much bigger problems in other areas.

When things get busy, the forestry, highways and wildfire websites are always out of date. In any event they record only the bigger fires. I discovered a satellite heat sensor website put out by the American Forest Service. It recorded every fire throughout the whole of North America since January 1 of that year. Yellow dots and blobs showed fires that were either cool or extinguished, orange indicated more activity, and red was out of control. Major problem areas were north of Kelowna and all around Clinton. My little fire showed red quite often, but it did not spread as much as everyone had feared.

There must have been sixty conflagrations on the Chilcotin alone. Most would be left to their own devices. Two were within twenty kilometres of Ginty Creek. Both of these were on the rise of ground to the north; the stronger and most feared winds always came from the west and south, so those fires were fairly low risk for me. They were the ones, however, that were making all the smoke.

All of a sudden, a 5,000-hectare fire popped up on the satellite heat sensor website. I asked the fire chief about it when next I spoke to him. "Oh that's nothing," he said." It's three small fires joined together and it's contained by three rivers. It's just scrubby stuff: beetle-kill and such. It won't go anywhere." Famous last words. The next day, the wind freshened from the southwest. At Ginty Creek the air gradually cleared to a thin haze and the wind rattled the aspen leaves. The 5,000-hectare fire popped over its watery boundary and soon blobbed red and huge on the heat sensor website. The three rivers form the Brittany Triangle, famous for its free-roaming herds of wild horses. Later, the fire was dubbed the Lava Canyon Fire after the river valley that it followed north. It was still burning in late September, long after the fire season would normally be over. I could see the smoke from the road when I drove to Williams Lake on my first shopping trip after leaving Nuk Tessli for the year. Its eventual area was estimated to be 65,000 hectares, making it one of the largest fires the Chilcotin has ever known.

It was strange being at Ginty Creek in August. I had lived in the area for nearly thirty years but had rarely visited the Chilcotin in summer. The wind, when it blew, sang an unfamiliar song in the aspens now that they were in full leaf. Most of the time I had seen them, their branches had been bare; at Nuk Tessli deciduous trees don't grow, and the wind makes a different sound when it interacts with pine needles. The aspen leaf miners were particularly bad that year at Ginty Creek. Circuit-board bugs, I call them, as that is what their track looks like. It starts tiny, where the egg hatches, then gradually widens as the larvae zigzag back and forth between the two skins of the leaf. The surfaces remain intact but the interior is totally devoured and the track is translucent, like the intestinal wall that is used for old-fashioned sausage skins. This year, every single leaf was affected and the trees had a silvery, insubstantial cast in the brown-hazed air.

Neither pond had much water in it; around the edges tiny white asters grew. Yellow rattle and northern bedstraw lay scattered along the trail between the cabin and the house. Foxtail barley lined the road in silvery, feathery clumps. Other grasses were faded in the open areas but along the riverbank they were still green. There they were full of large, tired dandelion leaves; geums; yarrow; a scruffy, purple-flowered aster; and the stunted, browning clusters of goldenrod going to seed. The skin and bones of the bull were still in the same area; one night the dogs barked a lot and the next morning fresh bear poop lay around the remains. Everything was tinted by the orange-brown light of the smoke-filtered sun. A few awkward fireweed plants grew out of a chunk of bank that lay half in the river. The colour of their smoke-dulled purple flowers was extraordinarily beautiful against the veiled sun's brassy reflection on the water.

It seemed that the fire in the mountains might not reach Nuk Tessli after all. A fairly insignificant creek was holding it in check. The weather was a little cooler and rain was forecast (it never materialized), and it looked as though I would be able to fly up there in a few days. It was at that point that Sarah came back into my life. She was the white-blonde nineteen-year-old who had wwoofed for me nearly two years before at Ginty Creek. She had expressed a desire to come into the mountains and I was only too pleased to accommodate her. Her parents brought her and another girl, a wwoofer from Germany, to Ginty Creek. Sarah uncoiled herself from their small car. She had grown up! Since

I last saw her she had been a dog musher for several months in Inuvik, wwoofed in New Zealand, stayed with her father's family in Denmark, and gained a lot of confidence. Her one-time long, silky hair was now a tangle of dreadlocks interspersed with tiny coloured beads. In the two days while we waited for the all-clear to fly into the mountains, Sarah and Anne-Katrin collected and split most of the winter's wood for the Ginty Creek cabin. We flew in to Nuk Tessli on August 9. I am not a good multi-tasker. I find it difficult to concentrate on more than one thing at once. The fire had consumed all my energy; I had done nothing at all toward the building of my new house.

CHAPTER 17

JAN PETRIE'S SAWMILL

I also blasted the C.O. at the Comox Airbase for having jets fly low over this place. Last year they did
that but the C.O. wrote and apologized. This present
jackass didn't, so I wrote to the minister of defence
and complained and then told him why I thought no
Libs were elected in BC or the west. . . . He hasn't
replied.

—Extract from a letter
from Ginty to Hilda Thomas

*She used to phone Comox and complain about the low fly-
ing fighter planes* [from Puntzi Mountain Air Base, an hour's
drive east of Ginty Creek]. *After that, they flew even lower to
annoy her. She used to employ Ed Cahoose to do some chainsaw work for her. He was good at climbing trees and cutting
branches off. Once he was working on a high ladder and one of
those fighters came over at tree top level. You can't hear them
coming when they are low like that. There is just a sudden
mind-shattering roar, and just as quickly they are gone. Ed
thought his chainsaw was exploding and he fell off the ladder.*

I was visiting Mr. Paul once. His cabin isn't there any more and the trees have grown up, but you used to be able to look down on the river. One day, while I was having tea with Mr. Paul, the planes came along the river and they were so low we were looking down on them. They just did it to annoy her.

—Jan Petrie

I called on Jan Petrie on the day I flew out of the mountains at the end of that summer, even before I drove home. He lives beside Highway 20 and his property is marked by a sporadic display of such items as small sheds, dog kennels, a gate of twisted pieces of wood and a sign advertising "Clearwater Lake Lumber." Every year or two a roofless log cabin stands a little back from the highway; he builds these for sale. In a sprawling dusty yard behind these quite attractive objects is a junkyard of wrecked machinery, rusted vehicles, decaying trailers and several small, battered frame buildings in various stages of being reclaimed by the forest that spawned them. Roofs that caved in during the big snow year of 2006 lie at the angles at which they came to rest. And yet, Jan is quite a handy guy. Pride of place in the yard is held by a long weathered-log frame, open to the sky, in the middle of which a circular saw blade bares its iron teeth. At one end of this construction sits a bit of battered roofing metal giving rough shelter to an ancient diesel motor from an old truck. Copper pipes wobble from the motor into an oil-stained, lopsided gas can. Electrical wires wander about in a tangled code clear only to the originator and operator of this eclectic collection of machinery.

Originally, Jan had been going to supply the wall timbers for the first cabin at Ginty Creek. He and his friend had recently bought the blades to make four-by-sixes with a double tongue and groove. They were all excited about it. My cabin was to be their first major building in this style; they would deliver the materials and erect the cabin for free. The blades were stored in a shed behind the Nimpo Lake store. Next door was a large motel. The motel burned to the ground overnight; the store was saved, but the shed, holding the precious blades, was destroyed. The shed kit that I ended up buying had to come all the way from the Lower Mainland.

Now I wanted timbers for my new house. I was going to use a style that was a sort of cross between piece-and-piece and timber frame. I'd erected a couple of the cabins in the mountains like this; an upright log was placed at the corners and vertically every two metres along the walls (more or less) and the spaces were filled with lighter material. In the mountains I had used half logs for the infill; here I would have the luxury of being able to obtain milled lumber. Most of that I would buy from Cameron Linde, who had supplied me with building materials several times already. His

Jan Petrie's sawmill.

mills could provide a much greater variety of lumber and in much greater quantity, but Jan could make the basic supports. I needed sixteen 1.75-metre uprights and two longer ones for the king posts. These would be raised at either end of the building to support the ridge pole and would form the gable ends. I would chainsaw the uprights to my own design (the profile would be a sort of T shape) but it would be very helpful to have a slab taken off one side. Jan had a bunch of solid, dry beetle-kill pine lying around. They were wider than most of the spindly trees on my place. He would bring them round in a couple of days, he said, in his van. (Van? I couldn't see anything resembling a van in the yard. And it seemed an odd choice of vehicle to use to haul a bunch of logs.)

It was a funny fall. After that one deluge in early June there had been no rain all summer. It was still very hot and the ponds were completely dry. By all accounts this was the first time in living memory that Nedra Creek had ceased to flow. I was desperate to get on with the building but I stole a couple of hours to walk along the bottoms of the ponds in case I never got a chance to do it again. The peaty earth of the lower one was greened over for the most part with tangles of yellow water crowfoot that were blooming merrily. Little spotted frogs hopped everywhere: all that I found I threw close to the soupy bathtub-sized puddle of water near the outlet. The dogs were hot and they plunged in to cool off—and emerged dripping with foul black mud. I didn't care much, as they lived outside in summer, but they had to do without their expected pats until they dried off.

The upper pond was mostly covered in thigh-high, golden tussocky sedges that were difficult to stumble through. The edges were laced with wild peppermint and its sharp tang was released as I brushed against them.

On the north side there was a table-sized patch of open peat and on it was a treasure—several snail shells, mostly of a kind that

I had never seen before. One was from the common ram's-horn snail; the others were long, elegant spirals a little larger than a finger joint. They were very fragile. As they touched one another in my hands they gave tiny mellow tinkling sounds quite unlike anything I could name. Delicious little fairy chimes. I found out later they were giant pond snails. This was the kind of exploration I loved—examining and discovering all the tiny evidences of life. While working in the spring I'd had occasional glimpses of birds; a yellow-rumped warbler doing its flycatcher acrobatics in a beam of sun between the pines; a bunch of cedar waxwings silhouetted against the sky like apples upon a tree. I longed for the time when I could pursue this wealth of rich natural detail at my leisure.

I also paid a visit to the much larger sawmill that lies between Nimpo and Anahim Lake. Its yard covers a huge area, for all the lumber it processed was air dried for two years. It produced sizes specifically for the building trade: two-by-fours and two-by-sixes, all seven and a half feet long. Nothing else. The mill had had a checkered career; it was now owned jointly by a sawmill in Prince George, the First Nations reserve at Anahim and a group of local people. But it was not operating. All the usable trees had to be accessed through aboriginal land and the First Nations wanted too much for the logs in this time of depressed lumber prices. However, lumber that had already been sawn was still being sold. Most was being hauled long distance to the States but locals could buy slings of two-by-fours and two-by-sixes. I arranged to pick some up in a few days' time.

The Lava Canyon fire was puffing smoke close to the highway and the air was murky for kilometres on either side when I went to town for my first shopping trip of the fall. A huge firefighting camp was still in operation at Bull Canyon near Alexis Creek. Just before going down the hill into Williams Lake, I drove the extra thirty kilometres south on the Dog Creek Road to the Linde Brothers Mill. I spent a couple of hours with Cameron and ordered heavy fir beams for ceiling joists, one-by-twelve rough-cut spruce for the walls, and two layers of lumber for the ceiling (insulation would be placed in between). Cameron would also pick up the three-quarter-inch plywood for the floor, roofing metal and bales of rockwool insulation that I ordered in town on the same trip. He would bring everything as soon as the roofing metal arrived in Williams Lake, which would take about a week.

The man who engineered the roofing order lives at Alexis Creek, which is about halfway between my place and Williams Lake. He makes part of his living selling steel buildings but he also has a ranch and has recently won an environmental farming award. He visited Ginty once. The goats, he said, were everywhere—on the hood of his truck, in the back, on top of the cab. He had to close the windows to make sure they did not get inside.

In town I also bought chimney parts, nails and tools, and a huge pile of organic vegetables from a market garden—what a treat after such a barren summer; I salivate even now, thinking about them. If I ever sold the ecotourism business, I would be able to grow a garden.

I was very much hoping I could construct a roofed shell over the basement hole before I left for my annual book tour in six weeks' time, but I would not have time to do it myself. I checked out available labour. Mike Witt, the carpenter who had organized the basement, was away hunting until November: that would be too late for me. Aileen was also away hunting with another outfitter. After that her dad needed her to help with fencing contracts but she might be free for a few days here and there. Aileen and Henry (the excavator driver) were now a couple. When I had last seen her in the spring she was arranging to partner Henry in the annual Nimpo Lake canoe race. They had known each other for a while but were not together then. Neither had much experience with canoes, but for this race it didn't matter. Brute force counted for much more than finesse. The race runs for several kilometres along the Dean River. There are twenty-two beaver dams to hop over, and one of the prime objectives is to tip your opponents into the water. Aileen and Henry were doing well until they hit a rock. They had to haul out and mend the hole in their canoe with duct tape. They came in last. Then they moved in together. I guess there are stranger courtships.

It had been a van at one time. The roof, sides and floor extended only as far as the back of the drivers' seat; the rest had been cut away to the chassis. A few battered old boards provided a rough deck and the shorter logs that Jan Petrie had cut were piled on it. Behind was another chassis on wheels with no deck at all; it was carrying the two long logs. Jan had been using hybrid vehicles since long before the words were becoming established in society. He drove around the yard and backed the trailer to unload the logs. He wouldn't let me help, just flung them off, puffing and panting, then lit a much battered home-rolled cigarette and drew on it to help him get his breath back. He moved his "van" a little and switched off the motor. "Those ponds didn't used to be there. It's all dammed. Ginty spent thousands of dollars on the excavating. I drove a Cat for her for a while," he told me. I had already found a lot of the old excavations. Under the scrubby willows and new pine forest were literally kilometres of banks and ditches. No water ran in any of them now; the country had the look of a medieval barrow.

"Oh well, I'd better let you get on," said Jan, squashing the stub of his cigarette into his vehicle's ashtray. The sun had dipped behind Noghwon already. Jan climbed back into the van and turned the key. A couple of tired groans: the battery wasn't going to make it. I thought I might have to fetch my van and the jumper cables, but Jan wasn't fazed. I saw now why he had parked the vehicle just so. It was at the top of the slope leading down to the dip in the road where the culvert lay. Jan let in the clutch and was soon flying down the road, the trailer leaping behind. With a clattering bellow and a black cloud of exhaust, the motor fired and he was away.

CHAPTER 18

BRITTA

She had her quirks. She would see someone reading and bust into laughter.

As I got older, I wondered why she lived the way she did. I asked my family but no one talked about things like that then and I got no answers. I think she was very lonely. She was always inviting people to come over and visit.

She helped Mum [Elaine Dester] a lot. When we were going to school in Tatla, Ginty was teaching in Tatlayoko and she would drop us off. Sometimes Mum would give a little money to Ginty who would go to town and use it to buy Christmas presents for us. Ginty was always there for people like Mum.

—Rhonda Nygaard

A young German woman called Britta had written to me wondering if I could use her as a wwoofer. She was "training to be a carpenter," she stated in her email. Just before she arrived she asked if she could bring her best friend who was also wwoofing in Canada at that time. The more the merrier as far as I was concerned.

Their first job was shovelling. I had pulled the tarp off the foundations and had been appalled at the dampness in the basement. And it had been such a dry year! Every joist was covered in grey mould. Most of the dampness must have come from the drying concrete, as the floor was pure dust. I had been advised to use the tarp to prevent rain from filling the basement, but in retrospect it would have been better to leave it off. Of course, no one had any idea how dry the summer was going to be. The ventilators I had designed in the tops of the walls were covered in dirt, and this had exacerbated the problem. Henry had piled the dirt high because he said it was going to sink a lot, but so far it had not, so our first job was to not only free the tops of the walls but also to channel the earth away from the house so that if it did rain, the water would not run down against the walls. We soon had a depressingly large pile of dirt and we had moved only a fraction of what was going to have to eventually be taken away.

The second job was to rip the strapping off the Packrat Palace. The rancher from the Precipice had taken most of the metal away during the summer (with my blessing). I figured the packrats would not have been able to mark the strapping with their scent and other treacly excretions. It was incredibly hot: 29°C, which for the latter half of September was insane. I used the monster green pickup to haul the strapping round to the site. That afternoon we went to the Anahim Mill to pick up a sling of two-by-fours. We had to use the van for that as the pickup was not insured. A hot, wild wind was blowing through the yard, and whirlwinds of dust slammed into our faces. We had been warned that we would not be able to get the whole sling into the van but it looked to me as if there would be plenty of room. We were busy loading away when the lady in the office came bustling out. "You really ought to check out your suspension," she advised. Sure enough, the poor little van was nearly flat on the ground. We hurriedly unloaded half; even so, the van had a serious tilt toward the rear and drove as if a tire was flat. I was extremely careful on the bumps and potholes of the telegraph road. The two women went back to fetch the second part of the load.

Britta's friend quit after that. It wasn't the work, and I would have been very happy for her to stay on, but she was incredibly homesick for a boyfriend she had left behind in Revelstoke. It was the boyfriend's car that had brought the wwoofers; it departed with the friend. Britta, however, was easily worth two people. Tall, strong, cheerful and attractive, she was, like so many of my wonderful wwoofers, worth her weight in platinum. A carpenter, however, she was not. She couldn't use a chainsaw and I was surprised to find that she was not very good at banging in nails. The mistake was a language error: she was not studying to be a carpenter but a fine furniture maker, what is known as a cabinetmaker in Europe. "We don't use nails on the kind of things I make," she said. She showed me samples on the computer: her joinery was exquisite. My father was a European cabinetmaker so I grew up with furniture like that.

Cameron was due with the lumber I had ordered from him so we had to move the heap of dirt we had made when we had cleared the top of the basement walls. The pickup truck wouldn't start so I used the van with a tarp spread in the back and Britta used the wheelbarrow, and we spent several hours shovelling and depositing the soil into holes that had already formed on the road. Even though we levelled the ground, a large area was still grey with silt and every gust of wind swirled it into our faces. We were going to have to do something to protect us while we worked. I spread out the big tarp that had covered the foundations. We weighed it down with scrap lumber. When Cameron arrived, he drove right onto it and winched off his load in the middle. He uses a manual lever to turn the roller that slides the load off. He could hardly shift the lever. Cameron is a small man, "150 pounds soaking wet!" he said. Britta must have had at least 30 kilograms on him but although she jumped right off the ground to hang onto the lever she could not shift it at all. Cameron managed it in the end. He drove away and we cut the banding apart and sorted the load into piles. One-by-twelve rough-cut spruce for the outer walls in one place, insulation in another; one-by-four tongue and groove for the ceiling in another pile; long two-by-sixes for the rafters beside the insulation; plywood and the roofing metal in their own separate heaps.

I hate chainsawing, and ripping the sections out of the logs that Jan Petrie had brought was very tedious work, even with the slab taken off one side. It took me several days. Britta might not have been good with a chainsaw but she was an excellent peeler. The bark on the dry beetle-kill was really tough to get off. Jan had

Cameron Linde with the load of lumber.

Britta peeling the uprights.

lent us a great tool welded from a truck spring, so that helped; the commercial peelers were too feeble. Finally, about a week after Britta had arrived, we put up the first corner post. What a milestone! Six other uprights followed in quick succession. Suddenly, as we walked up from the cabin, there was an alien presence on the knoll. It came into view just as we approached the stile that crossed the fence, the point where I had climbed it hundreds, maybe thousands, of times already and seen nothing but an uninhabited knoll. The newly peeled logs thrust into the sky like rockets on a launching pad. Next we raised a king post. We first had to build a scaffold to support it, both on its way up and after it was raised, but it went up smoothly, courtesy of the come-along I had "borrowed" to erect my very first cabin in the mountains. I had never returned it—it is one of the most useful tools I have had. Jan Petrie came by that night with some more timbers and he was suitably impressed that two women had done this without heavy machinery. (This time he was driving a pickup. Its battery was okay but it had no key. He started it by pulling off the end of the steering column and shoving in a flattened bit of metal. We all have our own skills!)

The heat continued and then the temperature suddenly crashed to -10°C and it snowed. We received only a few wet flakes followed by spits of rain, but the next morning something shiny caught my eye in the direction of the lower pond. A thin sheet of water was beginning to creep across the dry bottom. Within a few days the pond was full again; it must have rained quite a bit more in the hills. Two mallards sat on it, but the next day it was frozen and it never thawed again that year so I did not see much of the fall migrating waterfowl. The deciduous trees seemed to have been caught on the hop by this very peculiar weather. A few turned golden and dropped their leaves in the normal manner at the end of September, but the rest stayed green. In the middle of October it turned really cold. The leaves blackened over night; many remained on the trees all winter. Fall colours are a result of the tree shutting its systems down to prepare itself for the cold. What would happen to those that had failed to do so?

When I was still in the mountains I had received an email with the message line: "Wendy Wong: Wishing to Meet You." My first thought was "Prostitute." It wouldn't have been the first time I have had such solicitations—one of the perils of having a business website and an androgynous name. I had already moved my fingers to dump the message when I noticed a line at the bottom of the screen to the effect that the writer had read one of my books.

What good luck that I kept the message! Wendy aspired to having a cabin in the wilderness. She was already negotiating with one of the resorts at Nimpo that was trying to sell a remote cabin and she wanted to learn various aspects of living in the bush. Could I give her some information about building? "If you come right away," I replied, "you can have some hands-on experience." Wendy was going to a trapping course in Prince George over Thanksgiving weekend. She would be able to come for a few days beforehand. I had managed to track down Aileen as well. Henry was getting ready to ship his steers to market. Helping him would be her first priority and after Thanksgiving she would be fencing again but she would be able to spare us a day or two. Britta and I had all the key uprights for half of the building in place. They were held in position by temporary diagonals nailed to the tops of the basement walls. We built a scaffold to stand on and we were now ready to raise the first lot of ceiling joists.

Round logs roll up easily. The timbers I had bought from Cameron Linde were square, which would make the rolling a little more difficult, and they were made of fir, which is much

From left: Britta, Aileen and Wendy raising the ceiling joists.

heavier than pine. Still, by using skids and wrapping the rope twice around the log, we managed to haul them up one after another. Wendy was a city woman and not at all strong but she had really good ideas about how to do things. Britta and Aileen were the muscle people. Wendy was the gopher on the ground at first but soon graduated to the scaffold while I took pictures. Britta and I were somewhat untidy workers and we could never find anything when we were working by ourselves. Wendy had a tidying mania—and we could never find anything after she had organized everything, either—but we worked well together and had fun. The joists were long enough for only half the building, and we covered the living area first. It was necessary to spend a lot of time trying to get the spacing right and the tops of the joists exactly level. We needed to raise the second king post before we could do the next lot: everything took an agonizing amount of time but otherwise went well. The second king

Aileen trimming the ceiling joists.

post was raised in the morning and we sat on a lumber pile to have lunch, admiring the golden column stretched against the dark-blue sky. A Brewer's blackbird landed on it and surveyed the scene. "Someone approves of my post," I laughed.

The second lot of joists received a baptism of snow—it fell while we were working. Aileen walked back and forth along them brushing her way clear as she went, like a Jain monk sweeping the ground just ahead. Aileen was also very skilled with a chainsaw and was a lot more limber than me so she did most of the awkward trimming high off the ground.

We started on the ridgepole on the Saturday of Thanksgiving weekend. Wendy had left for her trapping course so there were just the three of us. We tacked several pieces of plywood onto the ceiling joists to give us something to stand on. The ridgepole was a real brute. It was a tree I had fallen from what would eventually be the garden; it must have tapped underground water because it

From left: Aileen and Britta levering the ridgepole to the skids.

was a really good size for this neighbourhood. I managed to get a thirteen-metre log out of it. It had been lying in a sunny spot, peeled, for two years but still seemed far heavier than it should have been. I had dragged it up to the working site with the van and had taken a slab off the side—the flat part would go on top to hold the rafters. However, I had been unable to keep the saw cut accurate (the log was far too long for Jan's mill, even if we'd had any kind of way to get it there) so I had fastened two-by-sixes on the top and shimmed them to make a level surface. I figured that this job would be much easier to do on the ground than when the pole was up in the air, but it was not helping our efforts to roll it. Using lengths of thin trees as levers, we coerced it over the ground to the bottom of the skids. Then we climbed onto our temporary plywood platform. Aileen and Britta hauled on a rope at either end and I used the come-along in the middle. The come-along's cable was wound twice around the log just like the ropes. Centimetre by centimetre, the log came off the ground. It had been dull all day and was -11°C, even in the afternoon, with a bitter wind blowing. I had not realized how late it was until a vague gleam of yellow appeared in the cloud near the mountains. Aileen ran to check her car clock. It was 6:00 p.m. Time sure flies when you are having fun. Aileen had promised Henry she would be home early to help butcher a cow. We put supports under the half-raised log and tied it firmly to the skids in case a curious moose or bear rubbed itself against the structure and undid all our work.

Aileen was occupied elsewhere the following day, so the partially raised log stayed tied to the skids. It was Thanksgiving Sunday, and Britta and I spent it erecting a scaffold to raise the ridgepole on top of the king posts. We needed three platforms attached to three upright poles taller than the king posts; these last would be used to anchor the ropes and come-along. They took all day to build. They seemed such a waste of time and effort when they would all have to come down again. I was also in an agony of suspense because a fall of several centimetres of snow was forecast. We would not be able to work up there if it snowed; it would be far too slippery to be safe. I had managed to cajole Aileen into coming back on the Monday morning but that was absolutely the last time she would be free for quite a while. If we didn't get that ridgepole up on the Monday we would be skunked. The day produced a bitter wind and -16°C temperatures, but it stayed dry and we got that log into place. It was by far the most difficult ridgepole that I have ever raised. Only when it was finished did Britta tell us how scared she had been all the time up there. She was terrified of heights. How brave and unselfish of her to keep this to herself until we had completed the job.

Once again we had timed it by the skin of our teeth. The following day snow fell to the tops of my hiking boots. Britta's only shoes were a pair of falling-apart runners and her feet were freezing. She was able to get into a pair of my gumboots, but there was

From left: Britta and Aileen high-fiving the ridgepole raising.

no room for spare socks and her feet were still cold. There was no point in buying footwear for her because she would be starting her journey back to Germany in a couple of days. I squeezed more work out of her first, though. We shovelled the floor—I did not want all that snow melting into the basement—and then we went to fetch a sling of two-by-sixes from the mill. No dust blowing now, only the wet snow to freeze our hands as we loaded the timber. The next day the temperature shot up to plus 14°C and it dumped rain.

CHAPTER 19

THE ROOF

My wife was called Betty. One time she was complaining that she couldn't get the kids together at Christmas. Her birthday was August 10th, so the family decided to have a surprise Christmas party for her then. A tree and Christmas lights and everything. We were still at the ranch at Anahim Lake at the time. Betty and I went with Ginty to the Graham Inn for a meal and Ginty said she had a present for her. When we got back to her place, Ginty gave Betty a baby angora goat. It was dark when we got home and I went to the barn to settle the goat and started the light plant so we could have Christmas lights. The kids had set everything up while we were away.

My son and I worked [on the Packrat Palace] *for most of two summers and part of one fall. The basement was already there. That next winter she came to buy hay from my ranch. She accused me of stealing fibreglass insulation off her place. We didn't part on very good terms from that encounter and I never went back.*

—Lloyd Norton

Enter Sarah once again. While in the mountains she had expressed an interest in dogsitting for me while I was to be away on the book tour. Her carpentry skills would be invaluable now and I offered her a small wage if she could come two weeks earlier than we had originally arranged. She arrived with Timber, another white husky from the Arctic Chalet looking for a home. He and Harry had a few scraps at first but they soon settled down. Sarah's dreadlocks had gone; now she wore her white-blonde hair close-cropped, with a pink streak down the front.

We stripped down the scaffolding and nailed the tongue and groove onto the joists to make a ceiling for the downstairs room and, finally, a decent platform for us to stand on while we built the roof. I had hoped to do this before we raised the ridgepole, but there had not been time. I wanted to make a sort of mansard roof, one with a hip joint in the sides. It would give me a lot more room in the attic—the house would in effect have two storeys

Sarah nailing on the ceiling boards.

The rafters.

above ground. I had never built one before and it took a bit of fiddling around before I figured out how to do it. I knew that if I did not get the ends absolutely square we should have all sorts of problems when it came to placing the metal. I thought that using Cameron's machine-cut lumber for the rafters, instead of logs as I had always done before, would make the construction easier, but it seemed just as difficult to get it right. I fretted monstrously at the delays. There were less than two weeks to go before I had to leave for the book tour.

When Sarah arrived it was mild and damp. There were a couple of nights when it did not even freeze, but then the frosts started. As surfaces were now constantly covered with rain or snow, we might have to wait for some time until the ice thawed enough to make it safe to work on the roof. Then the winds came back. They were strong and bitter and it seemed so much more difficult to balance on ladders or roof parts when we were also fighting the buffeting cold.

When it was too icy to work we did bits and pieces downstairs. I'd had a cookstove for a couple of years—a small enamel one that had been a friend's grandmother's. It was rusted in places and the top was cracked and buckled (my friend had cooled it by flinging cold water onto it) but the firebox was not in too bad a shape. It had been stored all this while in the porch of the little cabin. First Sarah and I went along the highway to where cliffs had broken into sharp-edged stones. We piled these in the long-suffering van and used them to form a support for the stove. On a day when the frost was not too bad we cemented them together. I had bought a bag of ready-mixed concrete. I found out too late that it was full of large pebbles and was not at all suitable but we used it anyway. I would have to finish the job properly later.

Even with all the plates and tops and doors removed, the stove was monstrously heavy. I backed the van to the door of the cabin. Using a couple of planks as a ramp we wriggled the stove inside. When the cement was hard we eased the stove onto the rock base. It had to be positioned exactly right to allow the stovepipe to pass safely between the ceiling joists.

It had been difficult to calculate exactly the number of pieces of stovepipe that I would need—how many standard and how many insulated—and I ended up having not quite enough. I had to get a section shipped on Beeline, one of the local freight companies that ply the Chilcotin. This allowed the chimney to poke out of the roof above the rafters. We tied it with rope so the wind would not blow it over. The next morning I baked bread. This turned into quite the celebration. During the winter I had often baked on top of the heater in the cabin but that was a slow process as the fire had to be carefully monitored and only a very small loaf could be baked at one time. I had not wanted to lose precious building time doing that, so when I had helpers we had been existing on bannock and store-bought bread. The latter was locally made in a bakery at Nimpo and is certainly far better than anything that comes on the produce truck, but I found it quite insipid. My bread is a meal in itself. In any case, we were not in a position to run down to the bakery very often, so bannock, which can be made in a frying pan, had become the staple. Homemade bread was going to be a real treat.

I had mixed the dough with cold water the night before and instructed Sarah (who was staying in the trailer near the house) to light the fire in the little cookstove at about 8:00 am. In the morning I shaped the dough into loaves and drove them up in the van—they would not have travelled well in a backpack. The gauge on the oven door did not work very well but it soon felt hot enough when I waved my hand inside, and in went the bread. We ate it the minute it came out—lunch was at around 10:30 that morning! The next time we baked, Sarah threw in a batch of

The cookstove.

cookies. The house had no roof or walls but we had a stove with an oven and it felt like a home.

Not for the first time I thanked my lucky stars that timid little Sarah had come off the bus at 100 Mile and into my life. In the two years since I had first met her she had become a very able carpenter. She had not used a chainsaw until she came to me this time, but within a couple of days she was cutting complicated carpentry joints. She had a lot more patience than I in making them fit properly. She orchestrated pretty much all of the strapping.

The roof was starting to take shape. Once we started on the metal we had the wind to work around, as well as ice. The wind usually got up just about the time that the frost melted. If a gust were to come at the wrong time it could damage the metal and would certainly be very dangerous for us. We would start one job,

Sarah nailing on the strapping in the bitter wind.

then be driven to do something else, then snatch some time at the first when the weather allowed. Time dribbled away.

One afternoon a man drove into the yard. He was building a truck for his nephew, and Vodka, who had still not moved the wrecks out of the lower meadow, had told the man to see if there was anything he could use. He said he had done a lot of carpentry work and would love to help. I told him I had run out of money. He eyed the Chevy pickup, which was sitting where it had died. (I had never got around to putting the new battery in it: the pickup was such a brute to start, it seemed easier to use the van.) The visitor said he would be happy to trade the Chevy for work. This might be a good solution. I could not see how we would finish the roof before I left and I did not want Sarah working up there on her own.

That weekend, toward the end of October, was the opening for moose hunting. For the first time in years there was no draw, and the country was alive with the sound of four-wheelers. It snowed a little again (the first lot had melted) and I found fresh wheel tracks right to my cabin (which is half a kilometre from the building site). I started locking the door for a while. I don't feel I need to at any other time, but yahoos on four-wheelers with guns give me the creeps. No one seemed to kill anything within ear-shot: the only firearms we heard were across the river. The owners were still away, but their son and grandson were up for the week. Four-wheelers were driven round and round the field for a while and there were sporadic shots at some hapless target.

Jan phoned me on the Saturday night at the beginning of the moose hunt. He had a tale of woe. Had I picked up a chainsaw along the road? He had been going to get some logs up behind my place and there'd been a small tree across the road (I had no-ticed it and had simply driven over it). He had decided to cut it out. For some reason he had left the saw on the ground when he climbed back into his truck. He remembered soon after but by the time he went back the saw was gone. Most days no one at all would be driving that road, and if they did they would know who to ask and be able to find the owner of the saw. Jan was just unfortunate enough to pick hunting weekend. "And," he wailed, "it wasn't even my saw. I borrowed it off this guy. Now what am I going to do?" I told him that I had a bunch of Husqvarna parts if he wanted to try and cobble one together. It would be the kind of thing that Jan could do. When he came over I also gave him the old Stihl I had bought from Ken Jansen as a spare. It was a monstrous brute that I had to stand on so I could pull-start it with both hands and I would not be likely to use it again. If I did have a chainsaw emergency I could simply borrow it back. (In fact Jan's saw did eventually turn up. The person who found it returned it after a week or so.)

From left: Aileen and Sarah putting metal on the roof.

Aileen hanging from a rope finishing the roof.

Five days to go. Aileen was free again for a short while but the first days she came it was either too icy or windy to do much up top. She worked downstairs putting up wall pieces but I really didn't have the money to pay her for that. Money, weather, time: it went round and round in circles. Fitting the metal around the chimney was agonizingly time consuming, but then the weather was kinder and things started to go faster. The day before I had to leave saw more than three-quarters of the roof done. The women would have to finish it on their own. The last two pieces of metal would be the tricky ones as there would be no strapping left to stand on and the ladder was not long enough to reach the higher portions of the roof. They emailed me pictures of them putting in the last screws. They had rigged up harnesses of ropes and hung there like climbers on a north face while they finished the job.

It had taken five women (some of whom were there only for a few days) five weeks to build a weatherproof shell for an eighty-square-metre house using no heavy machinery. We were all quite proud of ourselves.

CHAPTER 20

WINDOWS AND WIRING

[The initials of the locals have been changed. It is unknown who M— and B— were, so their names have not been included either.]

Dear M... and B...

Thank you so much for all the nice things you did for me. I'm so glad you both seem so well and happy . . .

The truck has a few minor rattles--the glove compartment catch fell apart and the hazard light wouldn't turn off. Luckily, Jim from Towdystan was here working on the Datsun and fixed both temporarily. . . . The glove compartment fell off previously and the book of directions was locked in.

The cat population is getting up there again. Sylvia has three greys and a minute black. Annie had her kittens under the barn then hauled them onto my bed. So far I have homes for three or four older cats and three kittens.

The caretaker did boom all except fiddle about. A real do your own thing hippie turned Jesus

freak--along with A... and D... God in his wisdom saw
fit to make A... impotent so now he is pious rather
than lecherous . . .

    F... underbid S... for doing the garbage dumps.
I'm sure F... will make it pay. He has no machine in
working order to do the job! Now only F... boozes. The
rest are all "Born Agains."

    I'll write anon.

Love, Ginty.

—Extract from a letter to unknown people.
It was found inside a magazine at Ginty's house, so pre-
sumably was never sent

We had a reasonable amount of snow that winter; most of it fell while I was away on my book tour. Sarah emailed me that she was quite happy being snowed in. I arranged to have the road ploughed at the end of November but more snow fell before I arrived home on December 5. It was a little slithery driving on the road and I wasn't sure how Sarah's car with no winter tires or all-wheel drive would handle it. It was -27°C and dark when she wanted to leave. I had to jump-start her car and I drove with her to the highway but she made it okay and had no trouble with the rest of her journey.

The book tour was a disaster. When I don't have a new book I often travel to locations further afield, and I had arranged a trip east to Banff and then south to the Nelson area before going to the Lower Mainland. In the past, libraries would obtain grants from the BC government to pay speakers and often contributed toward travel expenses as well. Premier Gordon Campbell, in his wisdom, had cracked down on all the arts' support grants. I did not know this until after I had arranged the trip, and when so many people had worked hard on my behalf I didn't like to cancel. Speakers' fees and travel grants were therefore virtually non-existent. I had been counting on grossing the usual $3,000 or $4,000 by the end of the tour to pay my regular fall bills, but I made a quarter of that. I was on the road for five exhausting weeks; I would have been better off staying home and doing something constructive. The immediate bills—land office fees for the mountain business mostly—amounted to $3,300. I begged a $1,000 loan off my publisher while down at the coast but that disappeared almost at once because my van wouldn't start (it never did like wet coastal weather) and had to be towed; the garage replaced all the electronics (without telling me they were going to do it) and charged $800. "Ouch," said my publisher. "Pity it didn't happen over here [Sunshine Coast]. We have a great mechanic and all the van probably needed was a $1.50 wire." But there was nothing I could do about it.

I'd had a few enquiries re the sale of the mountain business but none of these had come to anything. Katie from the Bella Coola Valley lent me a couple of thousand. I had never been in that kind of debt before. The publisher would get his money back when the royalties came out in June but I did not know when I would be able to pay Katie. In the meantime the government was threatening to close the lease on the mountain resort if I didn't come up with the rent. There was no work locally and for me to try and find something elsewhere was not practical. Firstly, I would need somewhere to live; secondly, I had two large dogs to deal with. They were not apartment material. A low-wage job in town, even if it was available, would not be enough to pay living expenses. So I hunkered down at home and drove for mail, water, occasional groceries and to the library as little as possible. I did not feel I could afford any other social life.

Recreational asthma was now added to my health concerns. This had been plaguing me for years but only in a minor way. Now it had become a major problem. Just walking from the cabin to the upper property was enough to set it off. Sometimes it was so bad that after the shortest spell of activity I would be gasping for hours. Not only was I not getting enough exercise, I was also suffering mentally. Walking and observing nature is my raison d'être. To have to restrict it was driving me crazy. I knew the asthma's upsurge was most likely a response to my financial woes but no amount of acceptance of this seemed to make any difference. I began to think I was going to be like Ginty—start a big dream and then have to give up long before it was finished due to ill health. Ginty was only a few years ahead of me when she died. On the internet I came across a site that recommended wearing a scarf over one's mouth to moderate the effects of asthma, and that helped a lot.

I also suffered dreadfully from a lack of fresh vegetables. I grew sprouts: alfalfa, sunflower, lentils, radish, fenugreek, clover, and broccoli if it didn't rot, but somehow they weren't enough. I craved bok choy, kale, chard and other leafy greens. The local stores supplied none of these; when I asked about them the storekeeper said I would have to order stuff like that by the case as no one else would buy it. I didn't have a fridge or a freezer—my small solar power system would not run the electric fridges available at that time, and propane fridges were incredibly expensive. The storage place I had built to stop the produce freezing when I went away was not a lot of use at keeping things cool. I had coolers and blankets but, even using these, the porch was usually too cold and the inside of the cabin too warm so fresh food did not last long. I spent a lot of energy dragging the coolers out for a short time during the day and bringing them back inside at night but buying case lots of vegetables was not going to work. Besides, anything acquired locally was riddled with chemicals. I could not wait for my life to get less complicated so that I could grow a garden and process my own food.

I researched the possibility of having organic produce brought up from the coast but this would involve two freight trucks—one north to Williams Lake and the other west onto the Chilcotin. Both trucks would have to be refrigerated. For a ten-kilogram box, each truck wanted payment; together that totalled $60. A ten-kilogram box of produce would probably cost less than half of that in the first place. So I put up with rubber broccoli, ancient green peppers speckled with soft depressions of rot, and spring onions covered with slime. During the first part of the winter I worked on *A Wilderness Dweller's Cookbook*. It was more a dissertation on the difficulty of getting food into the wilderness than a collection of recipes, and I wanted to call it *The Hundred Mile Diet, Ha Ha Ha*, but although the title was used for a chapter inside, the publisher wouldn't go for it on the cover.

As the bones of the book took shape I was able to put it aside periodically and start to work on the house. Sarah had not been idle while I had been away. She had finished the wall fillers, framed what I hoped was going to be a bathroom, insulated the whole floor and covered it with plywood, and fitted the first layer of studs for the wall insulation. (I had a chuckle when I found a couple of timbers decorated with splodges of dried blood: Sarah must have given herself a few good whacks with the hammer!)

As I had done with the cabins in the mountains, I wanted to make two layers of insulation in the walls. Part of the reason was to cover the first row of studs, which would reduce leakage of heat, but placing one of the layers on the diagonal would also make the structure much stronger. Sarah had put the diagonals in, nailing them not only to the uprights and the floor but also to the wall boards. It would take a major earthquake to shift the building now. I would fit the insulation between the diagonals and put a second layer of studs vertically on top. They would not only contain the extra insulation but would also provide a structure to support the pine tongue and groove I was going to use for the interior walls.

Before tackling the insulation, however, I fitted the window that faced the mountains. I had already bought the double-glazed units; all I had to do was make a frame for them. Because the window holes were all boarded up it was very dark inside the house. It was also cold; letting sunlight into the room through glass would help make the temperature more comfortable to work in. I picked an afternoon that wasn't too chilly and wrenched the plywood off the big window hole facing the mountains: light flooded in. The design of the window was a triptych; double-glazed units are heavy and I could not have lifted a picture window unaided. Besides, I thought the smaller panes more practical; if one of them broke, it would be less expensive to replace. The afternoon sun lay in slabs along the floor and cheered the place up considerably.

The first round of insulation was next, and then I started the other main window. This would look out over the pond. Once more I was going to go through the monstrous frustration of building a bay window. Each one I have built faces the sunrise

The first window in the new house.

The beginnings of the bay window in the new house.

and I can sit and read or lie in bed and watch the morning come into the world. This bay window, which looked over the pond, took weeks to construct. I would do part of it and then have to be involved with something else for a while. For a time it was open, then I blocked it with tarps, but the rain and snow still blew in at times. The last of the glass wasn't fitted until the fall.

It was an extremely gloomy winter. It was mostly quite mild, although the temperature did stay below freezing most of the time. But day after day a lid of freezing fog clamped down on our world. This extended over most of central BC. In Williams Lake and 100 Mile House the conditions were similar except the ground temperature was higher and they soon had no snow at all. Such conditions had not been seen in 100 Mile in living memory. The gloom was exacerbated as the shortage of power meant I was condemned to candlelight during the dark hours. I am like the solar panels: I need sun to keep my batteries charged. In a city I would be a SAD sufferer for sure. I am often asked why I don't use the wind to create electricity. The setup is cheaper to set up than solar but windmills wear out quickly and sometimes break; also, I hate the noise. When they are operating, they whirr or whine. If they are attached to the house the whole building hums. The main reason I don't have them, however, is the weather. In between storms, winters are usually calm. It is heat that generates air movement in the sky. In summers there are few days without some kind of breeze but then I have all the power I can possibly use. During the six-week spell of ice fog that we had that year, the air was absolutely motionless and a wind-powered turbine would not have been any use at all.

Sometimes the fog layer would allow a blurry gleam or two of sun and I could work a little longer on the computer. The laptop doesn't take much power so once I had finished my email I would disconnect the satellite internet while I worked on the manuscript. The publisher rejected the first draft of the cookbook; I rewrote a chunk but he liked that even less. We eventually agreed on content that we could both live with. The cookbook would be published in the fall.

I put up the vertical studs but did not finish the second layer of insulation because the house was to be wired. Even if I never used hydro, I wanted the wiring to be done properly. Enter Sarah again, but this time with her parents. It so turned out that her dad was an electrician. When he had brought Sarah up during the summer his eye had fallen on the hideous green Chevy, which, as we had needed no extra help to finish the roof, was still sitting there. A lot of people wanted that truck: I could have traded it for a trailer or for help to construct the roof, and now Bert was salivating over it. I couldn't imagine a more ugly vehicle; presumably it was a man thing. Bert's wife, Yvonne, also looked at it askance. "I have another just like it at home," Bert enthused. The upshot was, he agreed to do the wiring in return for the truck and some time at my mountain resort. This was a huge bonus for me, not only regarding the cost but because it was almost impossible to persuade an electrician to work this far away from Williams Lake.

Bert and Yvonne did the work over Easter weekend, which was at the beginning of April that year. I ordered a bunch of veggies from Williams Lake; the Gregersens would pick them up on their way through. As an afterthought, I asked the store for an Easter lily. Poor Sarah! I had not realized that the Gregersens were going to be travelling in a small car. None of them are small people and the car was already stuffed full of tools and electrical gear. The veggies were packed into two apple boxes and the Easter lily was huge. Sarah had to sit with it on her lap the whole three and a bit hours from Williams Lake.

Sarah helping her dad with the wiring.

It was bitterly cold. The wind whistled through the doorless door holes and the unfinished parts of the windows. Bert and Sarah (who was working toward her electrician's ticket) wired, I gophered and Yvonne hugged the cookstove, which was going full bore but provided little comfort. At the end of it I had a bunch of sockets that could be powered by the generator—in other words, I could run heavy machinery if I wanted to—and a separate wiring system for the lights that would be attached to the solar power storage batteries once I had moved the system over. I would now be able to complete the insulation and the inner walls. Bert and Yvonne would come back a month later to put in the switch plates, light sockets and smoke alarms.

On their second visit they also brought a 550-metre extension line for the phone. These kinds of cables are apparently used on construction sites: they can be laid on the ground and, although they are not designed to be driven over, they can withstand a lot of abuse. Having a phone up at the new house was a godsend as I could now deal with phone business without having to run back and forth all the time. The original extension running along the top of the fence to the cabin would be moved once I had finished living there, but for the moment I had two phones. I had put my sleeping bag on a foamy in the bay window of the new house and given Bert and Yvonne the cabin to sleep in as the mattress down there was bigger. I was reminded of Sarah during her first visit when she had said she would phone me from the trailer if there were any bears and I had laughed at her. Bert and Yvonne were able to call me when they were ready to come up for breakfast.

Later that month, Chilcotin Freight dropped off two wwoofers at the end of my road. Etienne and Cyrille were twin brothers from Germany. They had a very individual way of looking at the world. They arrived with piles of stuff—a huge backpack and travel bag each plus a couple of smaller items of luggage. They had wintered on a farm in Northern Manitoba so had a lot of heavy clothes. It did not occur to me that they would not have sleeping bags.

I put them in the trailer. I slept down at the cabin; it was not very restful in the new house as the opaque builder's plastic that covered most of the glass-less bay window flapped and creaked with the slightest of breezes. On their first morning the brothers were late for breakfast. Part of the reason was that they got lost trying to find the trail between the two places but also they were not sure of the time. Etienne arrived clutching his cell phone. Could he please charge it up? He knew he could not use it as a phone but it was the only clock the brothers had. They had managed to light the little tin stove the evening before but of course it could not stay warm for long and in a couple of hours, without sleeping bags, they were freezing. They lit the stove again and the trailer warmed at once; thereafter they vowed to set the alarm to wake them every two hours so they could relight the fire. The battery

Cyrille and Etienne nailing battens over the gaps between the boards.

did not last the night. Even after I had found them all the spare bedding I had, it wasn't enough and they continued with this routine for the rest of their stay. The day they left they checked into a motel; Cyrille said later that it was the first proper sleep he had experienced in three weeks.

They were hopeless at splitting wood (I ended up doing most of that), they were incredibly slow at anything they tackled, and they ate huge amounts. Basically, I was feeding four and getting the kind of work I would expect from one person. Their saving grace, however, was that they had a penchant for carpentry work where, although they worked slowly, they did a really good job. They first nailed bits of strapping over the gaps between the wall boards, then insulated and laid about half of the floor in the attic. After they had gone, a young man called Gabe helped me for a few days. He did most of the rest of the attic floor; we could not complete it as I had to design the steps up there first and I couldn't do those until the basement steps were made. So far, we had been accessing the attic with a ladder.

I put the inner wall up in the large porch-cum-workshop and built three doors. Most of the two-by-six tongue and groove fir I had bought to make the doors had warped terribly but I could not afford to replace it. Neither did I have the time, and the doors had become a priority. Firstly, it was still miserably cold working on the interior with the wind whistling through all the openings, and secondly, the hummingbirds were constantly getting inside and freezing or starving to death. Both rufous and calliope breed here, and each species is incredibly aggressive. Hummingbirds are programmed to love red. The flowers that they pollinate are usually red for that reason. The feisty bundles of feathers do not distinguish between organic and non-organic substances, however, and they are equally attracted to gas cans, chainsaws and the red heads of woodpeckers. The shade they liked best, unfortunately, was on the plastic covers of the rockwool batts. We now had copious amounts of these lying about the place and the hummingbirds fought fanatically over them. I had the twins bale the plastic up so we could take it to the dump, and I stuffed the bales inside so the wind would not blow them away. This drew even more hummingbirds indoors. If the birds were in overnight and the morning was frosty, they died. I rescued dozens, grabbing them against the windows and encasing them in my large, rough hands before releasing them with a bumblebee zing back out into the sunshine. Three of them succumbed, however, before the doors were all hung.

One thing I was determined to do before I went into the mountains for the summer was install the skylight over the bay window. Most of the vertical sections where the glass would go were still covered with plywood but I would be able to do those alone and they could wait until the fall. I had never added a skylight to the bay windows I had built before but was always frustrated when I could not see the moon or stars while lying in bed. I visualized a much more elaborate design but with my limited carpentry skills it ended up being quite basic. I used a single long piece of double-paned glass supported in several places underneath. I would never have been able to lift it if Gabe had not been there. While we were up on the ladders we could hear cows bawling. The rancher at Kleena Kleene was driving his livestock along the highway to their summer pasture. In days gone by, all the ranchers used to move their cows on foot, many of them taking weeks to get to summer pastures or the stockyards in Williams Lake. This cattle drive is the last one to be conducted on a public highway in the Chilcotin. The sound was yet another reminder of the turning of the seasons; once again it was time for me to leave for the mountains.

CHAPTER 21

FROM FIRE TO FLOOD

Ginty had the knowledge of writing letters, and also a phone. Mum [Elaine Dester] *can read and write but my dad* [Mack Dester] *was illiterate so if there was anything official to do from the government, anybody who needed help could go over and Ginty would sort out the problem. She was very good that way.*

Now I am quite confused about this next thing. I had a great aunt in England called Isobel and Ginty used to phone her and have me and my sister talk to her. My cousin researched this later and found out that Great Aunt Isobel must have died long before. But in my memory we were talking to her. Whoever she was, she sent books and magazines from England, even clothes. One time we got blue jeans. We thought jeans were only for boys then, so we gave them to my brothers.

Ginty was a difficult person sometimes. When we went to Williams Lake she would ask us to pick up stuff for her. We'd have to go to all the stores. Trouble was, she wanted every little service for nothing. She said we were going to town any-

way so it wouldn't be a bother. That's why people didn't like her.

I left the Chilcotin twenty years ago because I wanted to further my education and get a better schooling for my children.

—Karen Dester

The spring flood, which usually peaks a few days before I go into the mountains for the summer, was late. The weather stayed unseasonably cool. The water eventually came up but it made a pretty feeble show compared with the spring floods of previous years. It never even covered the largest gravel bar. We thought we had received a reasonable amount of snow but it disappeared in a flash. Everyone was commenting on how quickly it had vanished. The swamps and meadows that usually carry water for weeks were instantly dry. It can't have been the lack of frost, as some people speculated, because Gabe dug a hole to ground the electrical system. It was in the shade by the door and Bert had been unable to finish the job while he had visited because the soil had still been like concrete. It was the last thing Gabe did before he left at the end of May. He would dig a bit then wait for the next part to thaw. He kept hitting frozen soil all the way to the bottom of the hole, which was sixty centimetres deep.

During the summer, Highway 20 was closed again due to fires. Forest fires that disrupted our lives so much were rarities when I first came to the Chilcotin but now it seemed as though they were becoming a way of life. This time most of the activity occurred at the east end of the Chilcotin around Alexis Creek, where the blockades happened several times. Williams Lake, being downwind, was plagued by smoke. A great many people were evacuated, but for health reasons rather than because they were directly affected by the flames. Toward the end of summer another fire blocked the top of The Hill into Bella Coola so once again the central Chilcotin was cut off. Anahim Lake was only thirty kilometres downwind from the Hill fire, and the community was told to evacuate. Rosemary and Dave at the Precipice prepared to go out, too; they deemed it safe enough where they were but if the fire had reached Anahim their way out would have been compromised. In the end they stayed put. Nuk Tessli is quite a way south of the highway and I could see that I would not be affected; even the smoke had not been too bad there compared with a lot of places. The fire season finished dramatically at the end of August with a heavy rainstorm. Very often a violent storm builds up at the end of summer and this was very welcome. More puzzling were three more deluges throughout September, which usually has long fine spells. This year gloom and wet prevailed throughout that month. Usually, when it dumps like that in the fall, the lake in front of the mountain cabins will rise as much as fifteen centimetres, but when this September's downpours happened, the water level stayed low. There was fresh snow on the mountains but it didn't look to be a huge amount from my vantage point.

On my last morning at Nuk Tessli, I had an inkling that powerful things were happening. I was supposed to fly out the day before—Saturday, the 25th—but we had yet another twenty-four hours of torrential rain and the pilot could not see well enough to find his way through the mountains.

Sunday, September 26 was hazily sunny and calm, and I started to carry the outgoing freight down to the wharf. Sid would obviously have no trouble flying in, but when I saw the wharf, I was astonished to find that the lake had risen over seventy centimetres overnight. This was unprecedented. It was almost at spring flood level, but at that time of year it would take weeks to peak. The last twenty-four-hour deluge would not do that on its own. What must have been a great deal more snow than had been apparent from the cabins had obviously melted at the same time. I immediately thought of Bella Coola. My lake ultimately drains into that valley. The Hill had already been closed for a couple of days due to slides. What would this extra volume of water do down there? Most of the people in the area live on the flood plain—there is not a lot of choice in that narrow, steep-walled valley. They are always in terror of floods.

The pilot was delayed—apparently it had been foggy on the Chilcotin—so we arrived at Nimpo late morning and I spent an hour or so visiting with him and his wife, all of us winding down at the end of the tourist season. I had left an empty water container in the van and I went to the post office to fill it and pick up mail. I then called in at the bakery to buy a couple of loaves of bread. I planned to drive to Williams Lake first thing in the morning. After four months in the mountains there would not be a lot of food at Ginty Creek and I would have to do a major shop. I would not have time to bake.

The husband of the baker runs a mechanic shop next door. "Did you just drive from your place?" he asked me curiously. "No, I have just flown out of the mountains," I told him. "Well I heard the road was closed near your turnoff," he said. He could not give me any more details. Maybe the closure was on the other side. Maybe it was just a bit of extra water on the road that would soon go down now that the rain had stopped. Maybe it was just a rumour.

It was warm and pleasantly sunny as I drove along. The surface of the road was dry; everything seemed orderly and peaceful. Then, round a bend, I encountered a vehicle parked sideways across the road. It was an SUV belonging to the RCMP. A few metres beyond was a hole in the road. Not just a pothole but a five-metre-deep Olympic-sized swimming pool completely cutting the road in half. The cop pointed to two orange cones in the middle of the road. "Half an hour ago," she said, "there were five."

I still could not grasp what was happening. I went to the edge of the river. It used to be hidden by trees at that point but now a wave of brown water was smashing head-on into where the highway had been. Every few moments more soil would avalanche in with a hiss of falling stones and gravel. The soil was mostly glacial silt, easy meat for the pounding water. Despite all the rain that had fallen, the soil a few centimetres below the surface was dry and as it fell it gave off a scent that immediately transported me to my childhood when I had a summer job harvesting potatoes. What weird things one thinks of at times like these.

It was the noise that was so extraordinary. Not just the roar of water and the whooshing rattle as more stones fell in but the booming and bumping of big rocks and logs, invisible under the brown soup, being bowled along by the flood. Worst of all were

The big fall flood of 2010 destroyed Highway 20 in many places.

huge cracks and detonations as trees were broken by the wild water's force.

By now several people were beginning to congregate—all locals in their town clothes on their way to Williams Lake. One of these was Len Lamothe who owned the earth-moving equipment that had dug my basement. He would obviously get a good chunk of work out of this. There was a big smile on his face.

Some of us eyed the side of the road, which was a shallow ditch that might have been driveable in a pinch, but more stuff was falling into the hole all the time and the ditch probably wouldn't last long. My turnoff was perhaps five kilometres further on; the cabin was a further four kilometres and I thought I could probably walk home. The cop, however, would not let me leave my vehicle anywhere near there. I didn't know what to do. Then two distant figures appeared on the steep bank above the washout. They were Ken and Sylvia Dyck; Ken is the foreman for the Tatla Lake division of Interior Roads. If they could come across, I reasoned, I could go back with them.

One of the locals said they would take my van back to Nimpo. What should I take with me? The van had quite a lot of food in it but there was not going to be much that I could carry. I grabbed a few things, a bit of dog food, some edibles for myself (including the two loaves of bread), the smaller daypack containing the computer and modems, the mail, and the few vegetables I had flown out with me in a small cooler. Sylvia said they would help to carry them. The items in the van had been packed for the plane. Space had been the priority for the flight so odd things had been crammed into corners of unrelated boxes and trying to remember where things were and imagine what I would need was not easy.

We had just started up the bank when a yellow Interior Roads helicopter landed on the highway. Ken turned back to consult with them and that delayed us a little more but finally we climbed above the flood. The steep bank was saturated and extremely slippery. I wondered if the whole lot would slide in while we were up there. If anyone had tried to drive in the ditch they would have been instantly bogged. I carried the backpack and hung onto the rope I was using for the dogs' leads: I didn't want to let them loose in case they took off on some adventure of their own. Sylvia wore the little daypack with the computer in it, and Ken took the cooler.

I thought that we had only this washout to worry about but around the next bend about half a kilometre of the highway was under violently rushing water. Trees had already been dumped onto the tarmac. Ken's yellow pickup could be seen on the far side. We bush-bashed through forest and swamp and eventually drew level with the truck but in between us and the highway was a raging ditch. Ken and Sylvia had crossed it easily when coming the other way but that had been a couple of hours before. The ditch was no more than two or three paces across but extremely swift. The water was brown with silt and we could not see the bottom.

I doubt we would have made it without the long rope I had been using as a dog lead. A few small aspens grew on our side of the torrent. I let the dogs loose; time was of the essence and the situation was sufficiently serious that they would have to fend for themselves. I fastened one end of the rope to a tree. Ken took the other and then waded uncertainly into the water; just then the helicopter, which had been rattling at treetop level above our heads, landed beside his truck. The men had come to tell Ken that another washout was happening further east and if he did not move his truck soon it would be stranded. Their arrival was timely because one of the men could take hold of the other end of the rope and pull it tight. Ken got over okay; I waded in next. The water was crotch deep. At the last moment my feet were swept from under me. As the man holding the rope grabbed my arm, the rope was slackened a little so I went over backwards. I landed on my backpack which hit the edge of the highway so I was not seriously wet above the waist; the camera that was slung over my shoulder was not so lucky. Fortunately Sylvia managed to stay upright. If my computer had gone in the water that would have been a disaster.

The dogs were yelling and yipping and running up and down on the other side but I could not ask Ken to hang around. I knew the dogs were good swimmers but they obviously recognized that this was not their normal water element. First Harry and then Badger plunged in and both emerged looking pretty scared and half drowned but none the worse for their ducking.

We piled into the truck. Ken and Sylvia had offered to drive me right to the cabin but it would have taken an extra half-hour to take me there and back so I told them to let me off beside the highway. I did not want to risk having the washout cut them off. I had two backpacks and a cooler, and four kilometres to walk to get them home. The sky had dulled over and it was beginning to look like it would rain again so I took the computer first. I figured I could use the wheelbarrow to fetch the cooler and the backpack. The road curves away from the river and the thunder and boom and crack of water that had filled my ears for so long gradually diminished until I approached the cabin. The river noise swelled to a roar again and I wondered if the building would still be there. It was a fair distance from the river but the soil that supported it was just the same loose, fine silt that had succumbed so easily along the highway. Trees grew between the cabin and the river on the upstream side but I had no idea if they would be able to hold the bank in place. The roof came into view first: it seemed to be at the right angle. When I got to where I could see the river, it looked no worse than the top of a high spring flood. For the moment, the cabin was safe.

It was already late afternoon and I thought it better to fetch water before I collected the rest of my possessions, as it would be dark when I came back. I thought briefly about the twenty litres I had collected from the post office, which was still sitting in the van. I took a couple of empty milk jugs and started to go toward the river, but I realized that the water had the consistency of chocolate porridge; I probably would not be able to filter it well enough to make it drinkable. So I went to Nedra Creek, to the place where Ginty's ashes had been scattered after she had died. This was the stream that Ginty had used for her irrigation projects—and the water that Health Canada had rejected so adamantly as a drinking supply. It ran in a small groove in the land just past the Packrat Palace. The water would have to be well boiled before it was safe to drink but it was only slightly cloudy and I figured that most of the silt would settle out once the jugs had sat awhile.

It was amazingly hard work pushing an empty wheelbarrow up the hills and back to the highway. I couldn't help but remember the similar rescue of produce at the beginning of my second winter at Ginty Creek. Before I loaded the backpack and cooler into the wheelbarrow, I walked along the highway to see the washout that the helicopter guys had warned Ken and Sylvia about.

About half a kilometre from the end of my driveway is a large, sprawling house. A sign by the road advertises it as "Moose Head Ranch," but there is no vestige of a farm of any kind, not even a summer garden. Instead, the straggling yard is full of machinery and wrecked vehicles; I seem to be the only local person who wants to get rid of wrecks instead of collecting them. The owners are usually away during the winter and not there much in the summer as far as I can make out. They did not seem to be home now.

The house had been built right next to the river. The view

from the living area is stunning; water rolls along in front of the window barely three metres away. In normal times it is fascinating and mesmerizing to watch. Beyond is a wet spruce riparian strip that is wonderful shelter for wildlife. Just upstream from the house is a sharp bend in the river. The water was now pounding against the bank and being flung around the bend in front of the house. It was driven with such force that there was an obvious slope to the surface of the river, both to the side as well as downstream. I was surprised to see that the bank was still holding its own, but if this kept up it would surely not last long.

Somewhere upstream of my turnoff the river had split into two. There was now a raging current on the far side of the highway as well as in the normal riverbed. Just past the driveway into Moose Head Ranch's yard, the new branch of the river was in the process of cutting a ditch across the road in its efforts to rejoin the main stream. This was the washout Ken had been warned about. A ten-metre-wide waterfall was cascading into the yard before boiling in a brown roaring snake through the cottonwoods. Unbelievably it just missed the house on the downstream side. The building was now marooned on its own tiny island. I did not see how it could possibly survive.

The night was eerily pale as there was a moon above the clouds, and it was wild with noise. Not only was the water roaring but there were strange whooshing and tinkling sounds, rather like icicles falling off a roof. Periodically there were more cannon shots. The dogs kept barking at every strange sound; they didn't know what was happening either.

In the morning, the river had dropped enough to show a bit of a gravel bar. I was to determine later that it had peaked between three and four in the morning. The sun shone at first, but accompanied by strong, warm winds and racing rags of cloud; the break in the weather would not last long.

I ventured out toward the river where it was hidden from me by the belt of trees. The tops of the closer ones were still visible but instead of a slope running down through them followed by a band of flat grass wide enough to drive along, there was now a three-metre-high cliff. Half the trees and a huge swath of fence had been swept away. The river had gouged out a new bay—right where the trailer used to stand before it was moved to the upper property. I estimated probably a third of a hectare was in the river. That was all the hissing and crashing and snapping I had heard during the night. The cabin was safe for now, but a couple more floods like that and it would be in a precarious position.

The Bella Coola Valley was receiving major news coverage all over Canada. It was declared a disaster area. I emailed Katie and Dennis down at Stuie, in the upper part of the valley, to find out how they were faring. They replied:

The road is gone in both directions in several places. The airport is flooded and closed. The water-powered hydro plant went, so the valley is back on diesel generation—but they have only a couple days of fuel because the fuel truck is out of the valley for maintenance, so no way to deliver it to the plant. We have stranded people staying here (thank goodness we got cabins cleaned out). Luckily we didn't lose power for long but the river has done major re-routings and taken out large chunks of Highway 20 and several bridges. Still have phone and internet thanks to the microwave tower being close by here. We've been asked to take stock of how much food, medications etc. we've got for everyone here—they don't know how long we will be isolated—could be a few days or weeks. Sounds like they are going to put on extra ferries to bring in supplies and equipment and hopefully take people out that way. If so we may get out to Rupert as planned but we don't know yet when, and if, we'll be able to get down the valley to Bella Coola to catch a ferry. Certainly the highway between here and The Hill is gone big time so getting out of the valley that way will not be feasible for a while.

First the damn fires, now floods. What will happen next? More heavy rain forecast for tomorrow on top of the "saturation point" we've got already. Today we tried riding our bikes up the road to where we would have to hike to see some of the damage, but we ended up having bears in front and behind us on the highway—they have nowhere else to go, I guess—so our neighbour escorted us back home, with a bear on one side of their car and us riding on the other whenever we passed them. It is quite crazy. What an amazing change a day can make. One day everything is quite normal then you wake up and find everything in chaos, bears confused and wandering through the yard trying to find a way through water where it has never been before, looking for food that is so important for them at this pre-hibernation time.

The following day was sunny. Waves of sound wafted along on the wind from the direction of the washouts: the mutter of trucks; the heavy drone of a big backhoe. In the afternoon I walked down to the highway to see what was going on. There was a new small washout right at the end of my road. The water on the upstream side was already a metre lower and I don't remember thinking it a threat when I wheelbarrowed my supplies home but this was an indication of how much higher the water had gone before it peaked. The Nimpo side of the highway was good for about a kilometre but a new river ran across the road there. I could not see the bottom and had no idea if any of the surface of the road had been damaged but it was swift enough to deter any further exploration in that direction.

Going east, I didn't even reach Moose Head Ranch this time. The highway was badly gouged on either side. What was left of the tarred surface hung over the remaining core like a mushroom. I had no idea what had been washed away underneath so did not dare go further. I called the dogs and put them on the lead; I did not want them breaking through and possibly getting washed into a narrow space and drowning.

Where the waterfall had cascaded off the edge of the road on the evening of the 26th there was now a large, jagged-edged ditch three metres deep cutting the road in half. On the far side of the ditch was a flatdeck, indicating the highway was driveable on that side, and in the yard was a Cat working although I could not see it. Unbelievably, the house was still standing. It now had a large bund of boulders where the river had been smashing into the bank. Although the water was much lower, the current was still very powerful. A huge logjam of shattered trees had built up at the point of the turn. I found out later that the owners of the house had been in Kamloops. They had received word of the flood late in the evening and driven straight home, arriving about 4:00 a.m. That would have been at the flood's peak. There had been seventy centimetres of water in the yard. It had leaked inside the house and made the floors wet, and also washed away the steps of the porch, but otherwise there was no damage. The husband "borrowed" a neighbour's Cat (knowing he would not have minded under the circumstances) and never got off it for forty-eight hours. Jan Petrie from the sawmill a little further down the highway was commandeered to help and he operated a backhoe until it was obvious that the house would be saved.

CHAPTER 22

'EVACUATION

She was an ugly person. At least, that was my first impression. I am three years older than my sister [Karen Dester] *and I was in grade two when Ginty taught at Kleena Kleene. Being a First Nations person I had this idea that all white people were pretty and well-groomed. In first grade I went to Tatla Lake school and the teacher we had there, Mildred Klaus, fit the picture perfectly. But Ginty wore cargo pants— I don't think they were called that then, but they were mannish and had big pockets on the sides. She also wore a big floppy man's shirt. Her hair was just whacked off as if she had put it in a pony tail and cut it like that. It lay at all at different lengths about shoulder level.*

I did not have good memories of her. That year the school had maybe twelve kids. She was very strict about making you do handwriting correctly. She had her favourites, and anyone she liked she spent a lot of time with and always gave them 100 percent marks. The rest of us were treated badly. She had a problem with one of the boys, and his older sister, who would have been about ten, threw a chair across the room. There was a big stink about that. But most of us were

*ignored. We would sit on the floor and play cards. We suf-
fered for the lack of attention because it carried over to the
following year.*

*Ginty lived in the teacherage. The school was one half
of a long building and the teacherage was the other. Ginty
didn't like to do dishes and one of the other students would
go over and help.*

*When I grew older, I appreciated her more and could
see that she was a good person, really. But when you are a
small child things look different. I am just telling you the
way it was.*

—Rhonda Nygaard

When I had elected to walk home I had assumed that the
flood situation would be resolved in a day or two, but this
was obviously not going to be the case. I was well and truly cut off
on both sides. My van was at Nimpo. The food I had brought with
me would soon run out. The planned shopping trip to Williams
Lake was now out of the question. Already I was cooking millet
and rice for the dogs but I didn't have a good supply of those items
either. I had no vegetables, not even sprouts seeds—some were in
my van and I had planned to buy more in Williams Lake. I had no
yoghurt starter and no powdered milk. Drinking water was also a
concern. I continued to haul it from the creek that Health Canada
had condemned so roundly. I boiled it for about half an hour and
used the pendulum to tell me when it was safe to ingest. I was
careful to use the boiled water for everything that went into my
mouth, even cleaning my teeth, but it tasted horrible—swampy
and foul. The creek had been high, but not excessively so; all the
flooding had come from the rivers that had headwaters high in
the mountains. My river was still thick with mud. While it was
raining I parked the wheelbarrow under the eaves. Whether it was

stuff on the roof (but surely the roof would be well washed with all that rain) or residues in the wheelbarrow I don't know but that water did not taste good either. Even after it had been boiled, the pendulum liked it even less than the creek water.

The West Chilcotin Tourism Association was keeping us informed of events by email. It was estimated that about six kilometres of highway had been compromised by flooding on either side of my turnoff. The communities of Anahim and Nimpo Lakes could go neither east nor west; nor could any trucks carrying fuel or produce get in. Urgent medication and mail was being flown to the Anahim airport.

There seemed to be some kind of infrastructure set up for people who were stranded in the Bella Coola Valley. As soon as someone was in the office on September 29, I contacted the Anahim Lake RCMP and asked what provisions were in place for flood victims in our area. "Do you know of anyone short of food, ma'am?" said the lady sergeant in what I could only describe as a nasal "You don't know what you are talking about, why are you wasting my time?" kind of voice. "Yes," I replied. "Me."

She took some convincing. Anahim Lake has five RCMP officers but most of them are rookies who move on as fast as they can. None of them knows much about the geography of the area. "We can do one of two things," the lady sergeant informed me when I had managed to convince her of my plight. "We can either make a grocery order from one of the stores and fly it in by helicopter or bring you out to Nimpo."

I did not want to go to Nimpo. I was desperate to move into the new house. I knew it wouldn't be finished but I had counted on being there for the winter. I had only five weeks before the start of the book tour for *A Wilderness Dweller's Cookbook*. It was not just a matter of building shelves and installing the heater stove, moving pots and pans and clothes and food, and finishing the woodshed and filling it full of firewood; the solar power system and satellite internet would have to be moved, too. The latter needed a skilled technician and all this needed to be arranged. Already I had lost several days of this short fall window. Moving things from one place to the other could not be done without my van but if I was home I could at least start on the construction work.

The other alternative—ordering groceries from the store—was not an option that would work for me either. There was almost nothing in the local stores that I could eat. I am sensitive to preservatives of all kinds, even those found in organic food, so I could not buy processed food of any sort—no cans, no packaged goods, no juices, nothing. And of vegetables and fruit there were none because the supply trucks had not got through. There was quite a bit of food in my van and the sergeant even offered to try and find it but because of the way it was packed I would need to be there to sort it out. I also wanted my chainsaw, some paperwork and certain reference books, and I would have to buy dog food and so on.

"Couldn't I come to Nimpo, organize what I need, then fly back?" I asked. The sergeant informed me that I could have one flight only; they were not running a taxi service for people. Fair enough. So I planned to walk out. I figured the trip to beyond the farthest washout would take three to four hours. I found a driver who would come from Anahim to pick me up. I got permission for him to go through the barrier that had been erected on the Nimpo side (that alone required three phone calls), and by the end of the day I had it all organized. I would hike out, get my stuff together, spend the night at Anahim and use my single helicopter ride to fly back the following day. In the morning I presented this solution to the sergeant. It was already 9:00 a.m.: no one seems to be in the office very early there. I would need to set off at the crack of dawn to make my plan work, so could not initiate it until the following day.

"That's not going to be possible," the sergeant droned in her monotone. "The helicopter will be available only today. You are not going to have time to do all that before they leave the area." (Do they teach them to speak that way in police school?) "The helicopter is leaving Bella Coola and going back to the island." "But there are all kinds of helicopters going back and forth all the time," I said. "This one is an RCMP helicopter. I am not authorized to commandeer any of the other helicopters that are flying back and forth. You can phone the emergency services in Williams Lake if you like and see what they say but the chopper will be through in an hour or two and if you don't make use of it you will have forfeited your ride." Drone drone.

It was foggy. They would not fly until the fog dissipated. Maybe I would have time to organize a solution that was more acceptable to me. I frantically left messages with the emergency services and when I was eventually contacted by a human tried to persuade them to see it my way. But they preferred to fly me out to Nimpo and pay for a cabin at the motel and give me a food allowance. Surely that would cost more than a single helicopter ride. "At least you'll be safe," said the woman at the other end of the phone in a soothing voice. But I'm perfectly safe, I wanted to scream. I just want some food. But there was nothing I could do.

The fog cleared quite soon after that at Ginty Creek but apparently it was still thick at the top of The Hill. I had to stay by the phone. Then I got a call telling me the dogs would have to be crated. I had only one crate—the one that Harry had arrived in at the Anahim airport. Both dogs are very used to small aircraft and completely blasé about flying, but crates are RCMP regulations. (As a matter of fact I had been rescued from a mountain hike by an RCMP helicopter once and the dogs had not been crated then.) There was a search for another crate but then they decided there would be no room for two in the chopper anyway. They would probably have to make two trips.

At about 2:00 p.m. the helicopter landed in a field near the cabin. There was another officer there as well as the pilot. (Why? Did they think I would need restraining?) When the crate was manhandled into the chopper there was not even enough room for the other passenger. They decided that one dog and some gear would come on the first trip with me; the other dog and the passenger would go on the second trip. "The dogs are very good friends," I said. "We might be able to jam them both in the one crate. They will be very squashed but how long will the flight take—ten minutes? They can probably handle that."

Now the plan was to take me and the dogs first, and the gear and the other officer second. (See? If they had let me walk out and fly in with, say, the Interior Roads helicopter, it would have been much cheaper.) The dogs were eager enough to climb in.

I am evacuated by helicopter.

Harry popped up first; he is much more limber. Badger always needs a boost. He jumped up willingly but suddenly saw that the entrance to the crate was blocked by Harry's rear end. We shoved, he lunged inside, then immediately tried to turn around but we slammed and wired the door. Poor guy; his body was bent like a pretzel.

We lifted off. I don't like flying in small planes but I quite enjoy helicopter rides. At least, I thought, I would be able to get a good look at what was happening to the highway, but the pilot made a big swing to the south. Unbelievably he was going to fly well away from the river. Was he so insensitive that he couldn't understand how desperate I was to see what was going on? I asked him to fly over the washouts but by the time we were over the highway, my turnoff and Moose Head Ranch were behind us. All I could see were the areas I had walked past with Ken and Sylvia. The new, wide riverbed, littered with broken trees, ran where the highway had been as much as in the bush. Gravel bars had now emerged

An aerial view of a small part of the big fall flood of 2010.

and the brown water snaked between them, glittering in the sun. The steep bank where Ken and Sylvia and I had stumbled around the first washout was long gone into the river. A huge cliff stood there now.

The fall colours, as we flew over the land, were splendid. This was another frustration for me: the trees had obviously survived their lack of proper shutdown the year before and were making up for the non-event of the previous year. I was going to miss the show. Soon we were over the south end of Nimpo Lake. Cabins lined the waterfront. From ground level, or the water, they would all appear tidy and attractive but from the air, at this low elevation, we could see all the junk piled in the back corners of the properties. (To give people their due, a lot of this would not have been visible a year or two earlier, but the pine bark beetle has devastated the Nimpo/Anahim area and the tree cover has had to be removed.)

I was given a billet at the Waterfront Motel in a not-quite-waterfront cabin. It had been professionally built by a big log-building firm in Williams Lake and was very luxurious. Lots of running hot water, a shower, flush toilet and propane heating. The water was drinkable out of the tap. It was from a well so had no chlorine in it. The weather was finally gorgeous and the fall colours were beautiful. A lot of people would pay good money to be in a place like this.

I found the cabin depressing, however. Frustration because I didn't want to be there was a part of it, of course, but the design of the place was ridiculous. A fake woodstove (heated by propane) was placed partially in front of the picture window so it was not possible to sit there and enjoy the view or the small sun allowance that filtered through the trees in the afternoon. A dining table and chairs filled most of the room. The only comfortable place to sit was on the double bed at the back—and it was so dark there that to read I had to switch on the light even during the brightest part of the day.

There was a phone but I had to go to the store and buy a phone card with my $22.50 a day food allowance to use it. (Fortunately, I was able to find enough non-chemical food for me from the supplies in my van, and the store still had a couple of bags of dog food for sale.) Nimpo Lake can access a high-speed internet tower but I could not pick up a signal in the cabin. Instead, every day, I would walk up to the coffee shop at the post office, Bean Out West, and plug my laptop in there. At Ginty Creek I had unearthed an old camera. The zoom did not work properly but I could still take snapshots with it and I spent a lot of time uploading flood photo journals on my website and exchanging news with others. Facebook displayed hundreds of pictures of the devastation in the Bella Coola Valley. Many people had been evacuated. The ferries were running daily but their capacity was limited. Katie and Dennis were still stuck up the valley at Stuie, about seventy kilometres from Bella Coola itself: their departure date was getting crucial as Dennis was due to have an operation on his hand.

Plans were afoot to link the West Chilcotin with the outside world. There was apparently a fairly decent logging road that ran from Tatla Lake more or less parallel to the highway several kilometres north of Ginty Creek. From my excursions on top of the bluffs above the river I had seen clear-cuts on the low hills in that direction and wondered where the access was. Len Lamothe and Henry, and anyone else who had any kind of digging machine or dump truck, were working on a feeder road to join the logging road to Highway 20. Progress was slow as none of the machinery was that big and nothing from outside could get in although there was an army of machinery on the other side. They worked around the clock. Six days after the flood (so much had happened, it seemed much longer) the first vehicle from outside drove in front of the Bean Out West. All of us (mostly other strandees doing their internet, like me) jumped up to look at it and cheered. It was a big flatdeck carrying an enormous bulldozer. But it was not heading back toward my area: it disappeared in the direction of The Hill. The switchbacks were not in fact damaged all that much. It was the rivers that had made all the mess. Young Creek crosses about a third of the way down The Hill. The bridge was still standing but the road had been completely swept away on both sides. The same happened with what had been a comparatively minor creek above Katie and Dennis's home and with several other rivers further down. I had supposed the violent destruction by my turnoff had been due to a jam somewhere that had blown out but it seemed as though all the rivers had been as explosive.

The bypass was open to the public the day after the flatdeck

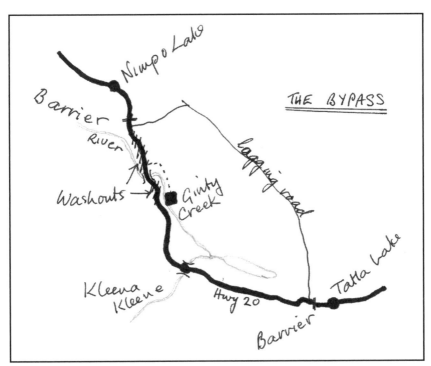

A sketch map of the bypass.

came through. It did not help me get home to Ginty Creek, but at least I could go to Williams Lake and get some decent food. It was Saturday, though: I needed a brake job on the van so there was no point in going to town until after the weekend when the mechanic would be working. In any case there would probably be glitches on the bypass to iron out first. It was apparently very rough—the equivalent of a forty-minute drive on the highway was taking most people a couple of hours. On the first pass a vehicle got swallowed by a boghole and they had to do some emergency repairs on that stretch. It was not just the rocks and heaps of dirt and bogholes that slowed people up but the necessity of dodging all the heavy machinery. Because of that we needed a pilot car. They were leaving every two hours on the hour. There would be no allowance for latecomers. If you missed the car you waited two hours for the next one.

A friend of mine in Anahim, Mort Grass, needed to go to the hospital in Williams Lake for tests. Mort is another ex-resident of the Precipice. After he had come west, he gave up his driver's licence and surrounded himself with horses, including a beautiful matched team of Morgans. They were blond with white manes and tails and those wonderful hairy fetlocks that heavy horses have. Mort is a pleasure to know. Still elegant and quite the lady's man at eighty-six, he was a tennis pro in one part of his life and a chef in another. His eyes are good, he is not deaf, and he is extremely well read. He is well informed about current events (much more than I am) and a delight to talk to. In latter years his health has not been good and he has had to give up most of his animals and his life in the bush. He lives in a not very clean, rundown log house next to the police station.

Because of the bypass and all the stuff that needed to be done, we would have to spend the night in town. I told Mort I want-ed to try and get most of my shopping done on the first day so would like to be in town early. Two hours on the bypass, two and a half more hours to Williams Lake—to reach town at a reasonable time we would have to catch the 6:00 a.m. pilot car. At 4:30 a.m. I phoned Mort to make sure he was out of bed and drove to Anahim to pick him up. We reached the barrier with fifteen minutes to spare.

It was pitch dark. There were no power poles on this stretch of the highway and a generator had been employed to run a powerful arc light. A small sandwich board was propped beneath it bearing the single word Flood. We were quite a distance from the washouts, however, so I had no idea what was going on there. A car was parked near the light; a person was employed round the clock to monitor the checkpoint. At least some people were getting a bit of work out of the situation.

We were the fifth vehicle in line and quite a number had driven in behind us. We plunged onto the new road, which was mostly pure dust. All that rain, and now I could hardly see in front of me for billowing clouds of silt. It was like driving through a bag of

Driving in convoy on the bypass to Tatla Lake.

flour. Periodically, enormous machines loomed out of the dust-cloud dark like primeval monsters. They had to pull to one side and idle to allow us to squeeze past. We did not have too many bogholes.

Once we hit the main logging road the surface was a little better, although we now encountered a lot more rock. As we reached the eastern end, daylight emerged. As I suspected, we had been climbing quite a lot. I had been told by the garage not to use my brakes more than necessary but even in low gear I could not slow down enough without them on the long ride down to Tatla Lake. The road came out by the log church a couple of kilometres west of the settlement.

I would stay with Patricia in 108 Mile overnight and be at the mechanic's in Williams Lake at eight the following morning. Mort's appointment was then and he would get his tests done while the brakes were being fixed on my car. Mort stayed in town; his host would take him to the hospital. The plan was that I would pick him up from there once the van was repaired—Mort should be all done and ready to go by then. But when I arrived at the hospital late morning, Mort still had not been examined. He knew he was not to have anything to eat or drink, but he had forgotten and had ingested a cup of coffee. They told him his procedure would have to be delayed for a couple of hours; in the meantime some dire emergency was announced and all the doctors disappeared. I went back into town and did a couple of other small jobs. Early afternoon I returned and Mort was still waiting. "He should be in there in a few minutes. Give him an hour after that and he will be ready to go," said the nurse. I came back an hour later: different nurse. "He should be in there in about ten minutes. You can pick him up an hour after that." I eyed the clock. We were going to miss the 4:00 p.m. pilot car as it was. Would we make it in time for the 6:00 p.m. shuttle? I tried to pin the nurse down more specifically and explained my concerns. "What pilot car?" she said. The nurse had no idea the highway had been closed. People in Williams Lake rarely take any notice of that huge hinterland they generally refer to as "out west." She thought she'd heard something about the Bella Coola floods, but that was a long time ago, wasn't it? We made it to the barrier with time to spare for the 8:00 p.m. pilot car. It was 10:30 when I dropped Mort off at his gate.

Heavy machinery had been brought in to work on The Hill from the top down, and more equipment had been carried in by ferry to start at the bottom of the valley and work up. Katie and Dennis were at last able to drive down to Bella Coola and fly out to their destination. A woman strandee who was frequently hooked up to the internet at the same time I was in the Bean Out West told me her story. She lives in the valley and had been on vacation with her two kids (whom she was home-schooling) and had been on her way home. The Hill had been blocked so she had stayed in a friend's vacation cabin at Nimpo, thinking she would have to wait no more than a couple of days. In the meantime the rivers went on the rampage so she was stuck. She had heard from her neighbour in the valley that her house was all right, just surrounded by mud and debris. The neighbour had sheep and goats; the sheep had drowned but the goats survived by climbing into the attic. Many cows were drowned; the bears were eating them instead of their usual diet of rotten fish because the floods had swept the rivers clean. People feared that if the bears got a taste of the dead cows they would turn to live ones, so they were being shot out of hand.

Now that the bypass was open, my new friend could go home. Normally it would have taken her a little over two hours to drive down The Hill to get to her house. Now she would have to drive east to Williams Lake, north to Prince George, west to Prince Rupert, and then catch a ferry to Bella Bella and another to Bella

Coola. The ferries would be paid for by the emergency services; the whole journey would take three days.

Another friend emailed me from the Bella Coola Valley:

> Most people we know had water up to their windows along grant road and in hagensborg. thankfully the water receded quickly and homes were largely water free within one-two days. the mess people are dealing with is mostly the mud left behind. one person lost his home entirely on walker island (it floated away) and even more unfortunate for him he is american and his house here isn't his "principal residence" so he doesn't get a dime from the flood relief. the flood relief is actually very disappointing for most people since it covers NO expenses/losses in someone's basement (including ruined washer/dryer/ hot water tanks/furnaces, or structural costs). i feel really bad for these people . . . everyone is trying their best to help out their neighbours—it's really uplifting to see. the road is a mess still, they're working on it furiously . . . the river has drastically changed and has found new channels almost everywhere we've looked. supplies came in yesterday by boat so there are milk and eggs again. luckily most people in bella coola are crazy for canning, smoking, freezing pretty much anything they can get their hands on and there hasn't been any really hardships encountered yet. even the restaurants are running still. the only hardships being encountered right now due to lack of food are for the animals. there are no fish in the river right now so the bears are VERY hungry and many have been shot this week because they're killing livestock and approaching humans (two sows were just killed leaving four cubs to be

260

shipped and rehabbed in smithers). the cougars are getting very bold and twice they've attempted attack on humans in one particular area in hagensborg. a mother cougar was just killed because she was after some livestock and she left behind three small kittens (unfortunately they don't have rehab for kittens and they were put down).

CHAPTER 23

GETTING HOME

Beside Ginty's cabin was a lean-to like a carport. It was piled with papers and magazines. Must have been years' worth. I'm quite a collector of things and I thought some of the magazines might be of interest to a museum and I told that to Ginty. But you know what she did? She let the pigs in there. What a mess! I had grabbed a few things and out of them fell the postcards and letters I sent you.

The last time I visited was with my husband, Rick. There was a big dead horse right in the middle of the driveway. Why she left it there, I don't know. While we were visiting, Rick walked down to the river. There were all these clothes in there, weighted down with rocks. Rick came up and asked about them. "Oh, I forgot my laundry!" Ginty said.

—Rhonda Nygaard

There were rumours that there was some kind of a back way into Ginty Creek. I knew that the telegraph road went through Edgar's property and came out somewhere near a ranch. Parts of the road were apparently in very poor shape, being nothing but bogholes through beaver dams, but the rancher and Hattie came to Ginty Creek on four-wheelers every fall looking for their cows. Only Hattie was home when I phoned. "Of course you can come through our place," she said. "But my partner is down at the coast and Edgar has his gates locked, and I don't have a key. There is a four-wheeler route that I could show you to get around his property but it's too steep to drag a trailer so you wouldn't be able to get much stuff in." I figured Edgar would be amenable to letting me go through his property under the circumstances and decided to call him. He would not be able to deliver a key—his main home is in the Bella Coola Valley and he was stuck down there—but maybe he could mail it.

Our single Chilcotin phone line was in a very precarious state. Somewhere along the ruined highway, when the water was at its height, a pole was apparently hanging free with its bottom floating round in a whirlpool. It was still attached to the line but was in a position where no one could get to it and we had been warned that we could lose the phone at any moment. It crackled and echoed and often cut out for short periods without warning, but it kept going.

Edgar answered the phone civilly enough, although he had plenty of grumbles about his trapped situation, but as soon as I mentioned the rancher's name, Edgar got into a snit. Edgar and the rancher have a powerful hate for one another. Edgar worked himself up into such a rage that I could practically feel the saliva spitting at me down the line. I couldn't get a word in edgeways. I was just wondering how to end the call when there was a piercing whine and the phone cut off all by itself. It was just a temporary break, but the timing was perfect. It was obvious, however, that I was not going to be able to get home that way.

There was also talk about mushroom-pickers' routes. These were mostly First Nations people hunting for pine mushrooms. One of the informants mentioned Henry. His parents used to drive cows along that way somewhere. Henry, of course, was doing twelve-hour shifts on the highway, but Aileen was home. She said she would ask Henry when she next saw him and with his advice she thought she might be able to find the way. She had an old Volkswagen pickup that had a very high clearance. I had bought a good three weeks' supplies in Williams Lake, including gas for the chainsaw (I couldn't remember what I had at home.)

On Thursday, October 7 we loaded my two dogs, Aileen's two dogs, the twenty-litre water jug rescued from my van and now full of potable water, and all the supplies into the back of the pickup. Aileen added a come-along, ropes and an extra chainsaw. We drove past the barrier onto the closed part of the highway and tried a couple of likely bush roads. Some were quite wide but full of windfalls. We cut them out but the roads kept fizzling out in old cutblocks. Some were barely traces of roads at all. We lurched along them over roots and through bogs in the pickup. They seemed to be heading in the right direction but, even if they went anywhere useful, there was no possible way I would ever get my van along them. We tried every likely track, but it eventually became obvious that nothing close to the highway was going to work.

Back at the barrier we happened to encounter a First Nations friend of Aileen's. He knew the mushroom-picker's route. It ended, he said, by an abandoned one-ton along Edgar's road. I knew where that was. It was quite close to home—I had walked past it a number of times. Aileen's friend told us we would have to go onto the bypass then turn off it about two-thirds of the way along, before the road started the long drop to Tatla.

We pulled into the line at the barrier and started off once more with the dusty convoy. We found the turnoff without problem. The first part of this logging road was quite good. We were very high up, travelling through clear-cuts, and after a while could see way down into the valley along which the highway ran. It was a rather dreary, hazy day but I could pick out Finger Peak and the lake that lay in front of it. We were congratulating ourselves as to how easy it was when the road suddenly ended. We backtracked. Off to one side, through a partially grown-up clear-cut, was a thin, winding trail. We would have dismissed it but it had been used fairly recently by four-wheelers. It didn't look wide enough for the pickup but Aileen thought we'd give it a go. We plunged down. As we descended through the logging block we could see the thin sandy ribbon of the trail twisting along an uncut forest floor below. Once in the trees our vision was limited and there was now no sun to give us any idea of direction. We came to a T junction. Which way to go? Soon there were more forks and a whole network of trails. Wherever possible, we headed down. Then we encountered barriers in the form of banks and ditches, the kind of blockage that the forestry put up to deactivate their

The spruce bog: the last obstacle between me and my house.

roads. "I heard that some old guy had complained that the mush-room-pickers were abusing his place and got the forestry to put these barriers in," Aileen said. It was easy enough to guess who that old guy would have been. The four-wheeler tracks skirted round but there was no room for the pickup to do that. Aileen simply drove over the top. The drop was more vertical than horizontal. That truck was an amazing vehicle. More forks in the road. We had twisted so much that I had no idea where we were heading but the country was flattening out. The forest was a little taller, still scruffy, but somehow it looked right for Ginty Creek.

We came to a spruce bog. Aileen stopped the van and walked through. She disappeared and came back grinning. Right around the bend was the one-ton. The bog was spongy but Aileen thought she could manage it. We lurched through—and we were on Edgar's road. A splash through a beaver dam, a couple of twists and turns, and we were home.

As I was planning to move into the new house, it made sense to unload all my supplies at the upper property. I had expected to get the place a bit better organized first but who knew when I would be able to use my own vehicle. Aileen offered to drive down to the cabin and help me carry some items that I would need from it, and that was another big help, but she could not stay long as it was already getting late. I wondered if she would be able to find her way home through that maze of ATV trails. I made sure she had some food and gave her the gas I had brought in—I had checked my store and found enough for my immediate use and Aileen wasn't quite sure if she had enough to get home as the gauge on the truck wasn't working. I asked her to phone me when she got back and she called a couple of hours later. She had been able to follow her own tracks through the network of trails; the steep barrier had not presented a problem and the bypass was a breeze as she snuck through without benefit of the convoy.

I had been away for ten days. The first day I revelled in getting myself organized; inevitably there were a number of items I had not thought of when Aileen had her pickup here and I went back and forth with the wheelbarrow a few times. The river below the cabin had dropped a lot and it had completely changed course again. The main channel was slightly more central but the ditch underneath my bank, which usually had some water in it, was completely filled with silt and gravel. It sloped almost to the top of the bank. The big logjam made by the cottonwood trees that had fallen in from the point had completely gone although oddly enough the point had not lost any more trees. Scattered along the river were other huge piles of debris; one bristled with the poles from the snake fence that had edged my property where the trailer had once stood.

The next day I walked down to the highway to see what was going on. The wind blew steadily from the west and the drone of heavy machinery was a constant accompaniment as I tramped along the road. A big Cat was working on the washout on the far side of Moose Head Ranch. The house seemed to be unoccupied

The buried station wagon at Moose Head Ranch.

again. The highway still mushroomed out at the edges but I followed muddy machinery tracks, figuring the road had to be safe where the vehicles had driven. The neighbours' yard was a metre deep in sand and gravel. The wrecked vehicles were half buried and there were drifts of shattered glass where some windows had been stored but the owners had made some sort of order in the living area. A station wagon that appeared to have been a roadworthy vehicle sat in a sea of sand to the tops of its wheels. The back window had been broken and the interior was full of the river's leavings.

A dump truck brought gravel to the washout; its load looked like a teaspoonful when it was dumped into the hole. There must have been countless numbers of teaspoonfuls because to my great surprise a pickup truck slowly drove right through the washout. It dipped down low enough so that the top of the cab was level with the highway, but the driver didn't seem to be having any problem climbing out the other side. I walked over to hole. The sides now sloped at quite a shallow angle. I asked the Cat operator when he thought I could bring my van in. He looked at the dip and shrugged his shoulders. "Any time you want," he said. Why had nobody told me? Instead of engaging Aileen I could have waited for a couple of days and then gone through the barrier to Tatla Lake and driven in from that way myself.

Now I had to figure out how to reconnect with my van. I didn't like to ask Aileen to pick me up again: the round trip would take her most of a day and with a ranch to run and Henry working long shifts she had enough to do.

Presumably I would be able to hitchhike from the end of my road to one of the barriers—either east or west, it didn't really matter. Once there I would be able to ask people who were lined up to give me a ride. I would have my dogs with me but there would most likely be at least one pickup in the queue.

It was not quite light when I set off. It was two and a half weeks since the flood. Along with my lunch and a few emergency supplies in case I got stranded, I carried three twenty-litre water jugs strapped on to my backpack frame. I would have taken more but couldn't figure out how to tie them on. It was a dull morning with a nip of frost. Cooler was good: cold temperatures usually mean more stable weather. I hiked down to the highway. I figured it might be slightly easier to get a ride going east because there were one or two residents in that direction but then I would have up to two hours' wait and the long journey back over the bypass. Going west I should have only a few kilometres to hike around the flooded area before I hit the open road. There was bound to be traffic going back and forth between the work area and Nimpo. And if I went that way I could get a good look at what was happening.

Smaller holes had been filled in and a rough pickup trail wound around the worst of the damage that was at my end of the washout. On either side of the road most of the forest was still standing, but it was drowned in debris: mud, boulders, monstrous tangles of roots. The water had obviously reached much higher levels than when Ken and Sylvia had driven me along the highway. I could see heavy machinery up ahead. The men, none of whom were local, stared at me in surprise as I walked past. Here was this past-middle-aged woman hiking along the road in the middle of what to them would be "nowhere," with two large scruffy dogs on bale-string leads, carrying a backpack bulging with water jugs.

The rough pickup road did not seem too bad at first. Maybe I would be able to drive home this way. But then I came to the part where the half kilometre of river had run over the road. To my left a bit of the tarmac still remained. To my right was a whole new riverbed several metres deep. It had washed away the far side of the road to make a silt cliff. And here was the fabled telephone

Where Highway 20 used to be.

pole that had swirled around in the whirlpool. Now it was high and dry, but still hanging suspended from the wire. No one had been able to get to it yet to fix it. A little further on, another pole had been washed away at the bottom. Here the ground was flatter and the pole hung at a forty-five-degree angle. The extraordinary thing was that there was a tangle of roots caught at the top of the pole. The water could not possibly have been that high: the pole itself must somehow have been dragged down and then released back up once the water pressure had eased. And yet we still had a phone. That must be one tough line.

Round the next bend was the washout that the Dyks and I had walked high on the slippery bank to get around. The vehicle road suddenly went straight up. Nope, don't think I could get my van up there! It was all I could do to scramble up the almost vertical Cat tracks on foot.

From the top I had a good view of a backhoe placing huge

boulders along the edge of the river. As I watched, a dump truck brought more rocks. There was a quarry near the Nimpo end of the bypass; the dump truck must have come from there. If it was going back it could take me right to the barrier. It parked but kept the motor running and I hastened down. It was a very big dump truck and I reached as high as I could and rapped on the bottom of the door with my stick. A startled woman driver stuck her head out. Sorry, she said, she was not leaving the area until 7:00 p.m.; nor was anyone else. Everyone was working twelve-hour shifts.

So there was nothing for it but to keep on walking. Not far along was a place where the river had grabbed at the edge of the road but not gone across it. Even when I had driven from Nimpo on the day the flood started the river had been hidden by trees at that point; now we had a huge vista of a wide swath of gravel bars littered with debris. Behind was a new, raw cliff. Rip-rap had already been placed along this bank.

I walked and I walked. The drone of the machinery grew less. Occasionally the sound would swell on the wind and I would think that something was coming but the road remained empty. I kept the dogs on the lead as I didn't want them to be off in the bush somewhere if anyone did come by. They plodded on beside me. I find it very difficult to walk on a flat, hard surface. I am soon in a lot of pain. A cattle trail meandered near the edge of the road and it was easier for me to walk on the softer, more uneven ground, but there the dogs found all sorts of delicious smells and they pulled and yanked in all directions. I was too exhausted to cope so went back to walking on the highway.

I walked for hours. I had almost reached the barrier when a pickup came by and took me to the checkpoint. The driver was a kind of gopher who went back and forth between all the working areas to make sure everything was okay (phone and radio signals do not always work well in the mountains). Unfortunately he was not going to Nimpo. But then there was a stroke of luck. The convoy of traffic was just arriving from Tatla Lake. Except it wasn't much of a convoy; there was only one vehicle behind the pilot car. But it was a pickup. I flagged it down. Two men sat inside. "There's no room," said the driver. What? I thought. I have to wait two more hours? "I'll get in the back with the dogs," I said. "There's no room," the driver repeated, but I was already round the back and opening the tailgate. And he was right—there was no room. The back of the truck was stuffed with tools. I shoved the dogs in; there was no space for them to stand without balancing precariously on the equipment. Just inside the tailgate was a generator and I could sit on this. I did not feel very safe but the generator had handles on either side and I could hang onto those. The driver was obviously angry. He didn't know where Nimpo Lake was so he was clearly not a local. Fortunately we did not meet any cops. It was a cold and windy ride as I was sitting high up at the back unprotected by the cab, but anything was better than walking at that point.

So I picked up my van, some mail and water, and drove back to the barrier and over the bypass to Tatla Lake, then west again to the flooded area. It was dark when I arrived. A roadblock had been erected but I ignored the warnings and wriggled by. There were more minor washouts; these were marked by flashing lights. A generator system had been set up to operate these. A backhoe was piling dirt opposite Moose Head Ranch. The driver gave me a dirty look. The dip in the washout was now only minor and I drove through with ease. I had lost two and a half weeks due to this flood; I had only two and a half weeks left to organize my house for the winter.

CHAPTER 24

MOVING IN

Pa fell and had to go to Williams Lake to the hospital. He'd chipped a bit of bone off his fused elbow. On the way in, Father Coffin who was taking him in didn't figure he'd make it so called the ambulance. He [Ginty's father] doesn't remember this. He was suffering from shock. He is okay now.

Ma figures I should look after her. She's phoned twice--offers me her house etc. . . . Just thinking about her and all the unpleasantness make my neck glands swell up. If I'd been a teenager in this day and age she'd have been hauled into court for child abuse. So I declined her "things" with thanks. After being told for years she never wanted me in the first place it is rather comical that I don't want her in the last place. She suggested I put Paw in the military hospital and look after her! We should just put her in Essondale where she should have been years ago . . .

When Paw goes, I'm going to avoid my brother, too. I just can't see bothering with them . . .

```
     Coyotes got over forty of my chooks including five
broody hens. Eglet, the matriarch of the flock, was
one. She, Cacklia & Noirene hatched about the same
time. Noirene got snatched one morning--her thirteen
chicks were peeping mournfully so Eglet came cluck-
ing and took over the orphans along with her eleven.
The next day Cacklia's ten were orphans so Eglet took
over those too. She was really busy clucking, scratch-
ing, spreading herself to cover "her" chicks and then
she got done in. Now eleven are left. Even Zaza got
eaten.
```

—Extracts from letters
from Ginty to Hilda Thomas

There was plywood on some of the windows, which made the living room dark, and the plastic that covered it flapped in the wind. No matter how short of money I was, I could not stand living with that for much longer. If I had known what the flood would do to me I could have measured the windows during the brief time I had been at home before I was helicoptered out and then bought them when I went to town with Mort. Once I knew I had to go to Nimpo, however, I had not been able to leave the phone even for the ten-minute walk up to the upper place. Now I was able to make the measurements and order the rest of the living area windows. I used up a precious day to go to Williams Lake to pick them up. What a joy it was to install them and finally have the bay window complete. The outer room still had plywood on two of the three windows and the upstairs was completely boarded in but at least downstairs I could now enjoy the sun and the moon and the view.

Once again I was living in a mess. Piles of lumber filled the floor space, and sawdust and shavings littered the rough plywood floor no matter how much it was swept at the end of the day. The back door was half a metre above ground and I leaned an old plank against it so I could wheelbarrow firewood right inside. I constructed a make-do plywood kitchen bench with shelves to put dishes on, and dog food and other supplies were stored in what I hoped would eventually be a bathroom. I built kennels and a temporary workbench in the outer room.

A priority was to contact the techs who would move the satellite internet dish. I had the phone in the new house but had to go down to the cabin every day to use the internet. The people from Williams Lake who had installed the dish in the first place did not usually come out this way any more. A man who lived in Anahim Lake now performed this service. He was not answering his phone, however; besides, with the long drive around the barrier to Tatla and back again, his road time would be just as much as for anyone coming from Williams Lake. When I could not raise the local man I phoned to town again. They had certainly heard of the flooding and were pleased to garner my news. They took pity on me and said they would try and come in about ten days' time. I already had the equipment so there would be no charge for that but the installation would be $250 and road time would be $500. A couple of days before they were supposed to come, the local man called: he had been out of the province visiting sick relatives. He balked a bit at the thought of the bypass but agreed to come. Unbelievably, the highway was suddenly opened the day before he was due. Single lane traffic would be controlled with a pilot car for quite a while but what a difference it made to me. Not only would I have to pay much less for the satellite installer but now I could go to Nimpo for water. I had found a source in Tatla Lake, an outside tap behind the trailer that the pastor of the church lived in, and it looked fine—until I put it in a white mug or clear glass. Then you could see all the little brown floaters. They looked like shreds of moss. I immediately started boiling the water for internal use but this seemed to precipitate the floaters and they looked much worse. The pendulum insisted the water was safe, and it tasted not too bad, but drinking it required some fortitude.

I had two volunteers by the time the satellite was installed. They were a couple from England. I did not find them easy people to like. They did not smile when I greeted them as they drove into the yard in their beater of a car but gave off an air of superiority, as if whatever I presented to them would be beneath their dignity. The were both extremely tall. Their hairstyles were identical— long tangles of felted lumps that were not what I had come to expect from dreadlocks but that simply stuck out in a matted mess. The male volunteer could be distinguished by his beard.

They moved around in a languid manner and were usually slow to get started but I have to say they worked well enough when they decided to make the effort. The man told me he could use a chainsaw and I noticed that he spent a lot of time taking it apart and cleaning it, but when I wanted to use it the teeth were so blunt I wondered if he had got the chain in the wrong way round. When I snapped at him about it he turned soulful eyes toward me and said he didn't know how to sharpen it. In Europe, it seems, no one maintains their saws themselves; they all take them along to a sharpener. But why did he not tell me he couldn't do it? I was frantic to get stuff done before I went away and had no patience with this kind of idiocy. Tools would be left out at night to get rained on or frosted and I had to explain jobs in every detail: they did not have a good notion of how things worked. For instance, they did not at first fill the woodshed to the top as they thought I might not be able to reach. Had they never heard of a ladder? Did they really think I had designed a space that was not going to be filled? I had originally hoped that they would look after my dogs when I was away but I now wondered if that was going to work.

For all that, they were a help. They moved the ugly, heavy heater stove from the cabin to the house, sawed stovepipe lengths to fit, swept the chimney, walled in the woodshed, hauled vanloads of cut wood from where it had been stacked near the pond, and filled the woodshed. They placed insulation between the joists at the tops of the walls in the basement and built a pretty decent set of steps down there. And they helped move the solar power system from one place to the other.

The only artifact of any interest that I have found on either property is a set of heavy wagon wheels attached to a solid tongue. They had apparently been built extra sturdily because they were designed for hauling logs. They were sitting in a grove of small aspens; several had grown up through the open spaces in the tongue. Old rotten grass was axle high and I wasn't sure if the wheels would hang together when I cut the grass away. But I chopped out a couple of trees, hacked the wheels free and, amazingly, the whole thing rolled forward with ease. Ben and Nathaniel were working with me then and I still had the old green pickup. We manhandled the heavy wheels onto it and drove them to the upper place. I thought they would make an ideal stand for my two solar panels.

When I first had solar power, all I needed, it seemed, were batteries, panels, an inverter and the wires that joined them. Several advisors had recommended adding a charge monitor to make sure the batteries were not overcharged and a battery status monitor that was supposed to tell me how much power the batteries had, and these had been installed in the cabin. They were attached to fuses and shunts (don't ask me what they are; I left them joined to their various bits). I drew a diagram and carefully took apart the equipment in the cabin. I also drew little sketches of the backs of the solar panels and the way the wires joined them. Each panel was a different make and had a different attachment for the wires.

While the volunteers constructed the frame that would support the solar panels on the wagon wheels I reassembled the various components inside. I was pretty sure I had got them right. Then I unrolled the new cable to the panels—and found that, in the move, a little junction box had been pulled off one of them. Without it, the sketch I had drawn relating to that particular panel was useless. If the panels were linked the wrong way round, the whole system might blow. I searched the van and scoured the ground near the cabin where the panels had stood but there was no sign of it. I wired the panel I knew to be correct; for many years I had used only one panel anyway. The batteries had been fully charged before I moved them and the battery status monitor continued to read "Full" so I assumed that everything must be working properly. I had been warned never to let the battery level on the monitor go below 65 percent.

That night we used the new, low-power, twelve-volt lights that Bert the electrician had installed. There were still piles of lumber and half-built projects all over the place but the dull yellow glow at the flick of a switch made it seem as though the house was beginning to come together. The next day the lights had not been on long before they dimmed. The weather had been dull but the monitor still read "Full." The inverter lights, two little domes one on top of the other, indicated subnormal power. Both should be green but the top one was flickering to orange.

The satellite internet installer came—that at least went without a hitch—so I was able to google the company that made the panel I was having problems with and found that some of their panels had the positive link on the left and some had them on the right. There were apparently + and - signs on the wires. I searched and searched: there were absolutely no marks of any kind. They must have been on the gizmo that had been lost. I wired everything together and hoped for the best. I checked the battery status monitor: it registered "Full." I was a little bit surprised as the weather had been dull and I would have expected a small re- duction by now.

And that night the lights died again. The power input light on the inverter wavered to red. I rechecked my wiring. Everything seemed to be in the proper place. I phoned and emailed Dave Neads in the Precipice, Bert the electrician and the man who had sold me the equipment in the first place. The solar power guru said I must have blown the whole system when I moved it over. He gave me some tips and I tried them all out, but the lights would die out within a few minutes. We were back to candles and flashlights—a real nuisance when trying to find anything in the muddle of building supplies and boxes.

During the day, as long as the sun gleamed a bit on the panels, the inverter lights would stay green. After dark the system would quickly die. The battery status monitor continued to register "Full." All I could think of was that the batteries were no longer holding a charge. They were only four years old: they are suppos- ed to last eight or nine years. I had suspected for a while that one of them was not operating properly as the liquid level would be below the top of the plates after I had left it for four months while going into the mountains. The other three were always fine and the mountain batteries were happy to sit for eight months with- out attention, even during the winter cold.

I could have got batteries from Williams Lake but I would have had to go into town to fetch them as not many carriers will handle them. I didn't want to waste the time. The volunteers, fortunately, enjoyed candles. They would have used them even if electricity had been available. I would be leaving them my old laptop so they could do email but I told them that they probably wouldn't be able to use it unless the sun was shining on the pan- els. This wouldn't bother them as they were late risers (I like to check my email in the dark in the morning so I don't cut into the working hours of the day). Failing all else, they had the phone or could drive to Bean Out West at Nimpo Lake and use the wireless internet there. The frustrating thing was not really knowing what was wrong. And all this extra messing about was taking so much time.

Then I got a message from Moose Head Ranch. The owners were back again and were worried about the trees in their yard that were buried in sand. Could my volunteers come down and give them a hand? They would pay them a small wage. On the one hand I was frantic to get work done and felt I could ill afford to let them go. On the other I was glad to have some time away from them. Personally, I thought that the Moose Heads' trees, which were mostly cottonwoods and inured to flooding, would survive pretty well, but the volunteers would no doubt be glad of a bit of extra cash.

The volunteers had moved from the trailer into the cabin. I didn't begrudge them the accommodation while they were working elsewhere. They had their own vehicle so could drive to work. I was a bit put out, though, when they came looking for food. I did not see why, when I was so desperately busy and the volunteers were working for somebody else and earning money, I should have to cook for them. I was surprised that the Moose Heads did not feed them. That is what is usually done in a sparsely populated place like this. I let them take what food they wanted down to the cabin but I was not going to do the extra work of preparing it.

I made a mail and water run to Nimpo. I was expecting boxes of books to come to the post office, and they arrived just a couple of days before I had to leave for the book tour. I called into the Moose Heads' yard on my way back. The volunteers were hand-digging out around the trees, gently brushing the dirt away until they could see dark soil or grass. The rest of the yard was bedlam.

Jan Petrie, from the little sawmill, was as happy as Larry sitting on one Cat, the owner of the place on another. The roar of machinery was deafening. They were digging up to a metre of sand out of the yard, putting it in a dump truck and taking it up to the highway. By a stroke of luck, the material was of a perfect consistency for road repair, so the Moose Heads were selling it to Interior Roads who were using it to fill in the holes that the river had made. What goes around comes around. At least the Moose Heads were able to glean some money to pay for the tremendous damage to their yard.

I heard at Nimpo that Interior Roads were "putting the river back where it belonged." I was pretty skeptical about that. True, the edges of the river were now lined with big boulders, which would be much harder to wash away than the original silt and gravel, but the river had completely changed course in the bush and would have all sorts of new forces when next it flooded. The first indication that those thousands of expensive machinery hours to "fix" the road had been ill planned came during the first week in December.

With some misgivings I left the volunteers with my dogs and set off to promote *A Wilderness Dweller's Cookbook*. I phoned the volunteers several times while I was away to make sure they had not burned my house down (I never had this concern with my other housesitters) but everything was always fine. Toward the end of my tour they told me they had the opportunity of a cheap flight to England and wanted to leave a few days before I could get home. We arranged to meet in 108 Mile House where they could bring me the dogs.

I tried calling the volunteers the night before I was due to meet them. There was no answer. Perhaps they were out for a farewell dinner with the Moose Heads, who were difficult to reach by phone, always providing they were home in the first place. I called my own number again the following morning, long before the volunteers were likely to get out of bed, but still no reply. Why had they not called me? Then I found out that I had given them the wrong phone number for Patricia's house. Amid the frantic preparations for leaving, I had left them an old office number of hers. I had told them to meet me at the 108 gas station. Nobody was there. I drove across the road to the supermarket and there was their car, and nearby were my two scruffy dogs on their ropes. The volunteers, it appeared, had bailed out of Ginty Creek a day earlier than expected. Jan Petrie had called them and told them that the highway was flooding again. It had been mild and, although the ground was covered with snow, the river had come up a bit and was piling against the flimsy barrier constructed on the highway opposite Moose Head Ranch. So little rain and already the road was flooding. Machines were brought along and an extra bit of bank was piled beside the river but it didn't look as though it would hold during a real flood. It would be interesting to see what would happen during the spring runoff.

A decent root cellar in my basement had been high on the to-do list for the fall but because of the floods there had been no time. I was not quite sure if the temperature in the basement would stay above freezing. I was a little concerned that, if the house was empty for very long, the organic potatoes (from the Precipice) and a few home-canned goods I had managed to put up might freeze. I figured that if the volunteers put them on the mattress and wrapped them in the down comforter and blankets they might survive.

There had not been enough snow to warrant ploughing the road and I arrived home before dark. The volunteers had piled various items on one of the mattresses and dutifully covered them with the bedding, but the home-canned fruit and potatoes were sitting unprotected in the room. The items they had deemed important were the electronics: the computer, the modems and the inverter. These freeze on a regular basis and they have never given me any bother. I just make sure they are thoroughly warmed up to get rid of any condensation before I use them. Fortunately, it had been comparatively mild (about -12°C outside) and daily sunshine had meant that the interior of the house had stayed above freezing.

The place was filthy. True, it was not the easiest place to clean, having rough plywood counters and floor, but soot and candle grease were caked on everything. Pots had never been washed on the outside—some had food caked on the inside as well. But the dogs were happy and healthy and it had been a lot easier for both me and them to have someone look after them at home.

The building mess was depressing, and I was to make a lot more before I could live with it, even though I was resigned to virtually camping in the unfinished house until I could sell the mountain business, whenever that might be. An advantage of moving into a home at this stage, however, is that it is easy to change one's mind. So I dropped the computer table a few centimetres, made the seat under the southwest window narrower, and so on. I had bought four new batteries while down at the coast, taking a gamble that they would solve my power problem, and they did. The battery monitor still read "Full" no matter what was in them but I had now learned to look at the second figure that comes up on the screen, which represented the volts stored in the battery. Ideally it should be 12.6 or more; sometimes it was over 14. I must never let it go below 11.6. I wished I had understood enough to check this figure before.

On December 20 I drove along the highway and picked out a small spruce growing below the phone line. Brushers were scheduled to cut all the vegetation out of there in the spring so I felt no guilt at taking the tree. I set it up in the corner of my new house and decorated it with all the bits and pieces I have collected over the years. It was a special solstice celebration for me: not only was I now living in the absolute last house I will ever build but also it was the night of a full moon, with a full eclipse to boot. That has not happened on the winter solstice for five hundred years.

The weather stayed dreary, as it had done since September. In many places it was too cloudy to see anything at all but at Ginty Creek the blurry outline of the moon shone dimly through the overcast. Unlike my friends who stayed up to try and see this once-in-a-half-millennium event, which peaked at around two in the morning, I did not have to keep dragging on a coat and trudging outside. I lay in my toasty warm bed and watched the moon change shape as it slowly moved across the skylight in my bay window.

I move into my new house.

CHAPTER 25

GINTY

PAUL, Nedra Jane (Ginty)
Late of Hodgeson Rd., Williams Lake, B.C. for-
merly of Kleena Kleene, passed away at the
Cariboo Memorial Hospital on April 24, 1990
in her 70th year. Cremation at the Crematorium,
Prince George. No funeral or memorial service by
request, but if friends so desire, donations may be
made to the Williams Lake Hospice Society in her
memory. Ginty will be sorely missed by her many,
many friends in the Cariboo & Chilcotin and
throughout B.C.

—*Williams Lake Tribune*

The following timeline was among the material given to me by
the late Mildred Baines.

*c.1920. Nedra Jane Paul born on Vancouver Island, prob-
ably Victoria, daughter of William Adrian Beviss Paul
and Ruby Thomas.*
1937. Age 16, King Edward High School, Vancouver.

1938. Age 17. Lord Byng High School, Vancouver.

1954. Age 33. After receiving a BA at UBC, she received Secondary School Teacher's Permanent Certificate (UBC), and certificate from BC Summer School of Theatre (UBC).

1964. Began tape-recording interviews with First Nations people. She continued this until 1966.

1975. Age 54, had moved to Kleena Kleene to live with her father.

1986. Age 66. Ginty was in a car accident near Williams Lake and sustained a basal skull fracture. She recuperated for a time at the home of Phil and Hilda Thomas and family in Vancouver. One of their daughters is now Mildred J. Baines.

1990. Age 70. Ginty died at the Cariboo Memorial Hospital; cremation was at the Crematorium in Prince George. There was no funeral or memorial service by request. The ashes were scattered at Kleena Kleene.

2001. Ginty's tapes were donated to the Northern BC Archives at UNBC.

Ginty was a lot of fun. My husband, Jack, was a pupil of hers, oh that would be grade nine or ten perhaps, when she was teaching in Williams Lake. This would be right at the beginning of her teaching career. He liked her. She was different. She didn't always stick to the standard school rules and the kids learned all sorts of things.

She herself was well educated. She went to art school in France. I always likened her to Emily Carr although I never saw any of her artwork.

She didn't have an easy childhood. While she was at

school, her dad would have her with him during the summer when he worked as a linesman.

My mother's sister taught her in Crofton House. Ginty didn't like my aunt. My aunt was a real stickler for rules. Ginty taught in Williams Lake for a number of years. She was young then, in her twenties. She would come over to our house often. She was lively and cheerful.

When her father died, Ginty gave me his egg collection. They were displayed in a cabinet. He would take all the eggs from a nest. People did that then: it's illegal now, of course. Some of the eggs were from England. They had all been beautifully blown but the mice had got into the collection and destroyed most of it. I still have the little cabinet, though.

I used to visit out there sometimes. I had a little VW with a pull-down top. The goats were everywhere, on top of the car and everything the minute you stopped. I was worried about the canvas top so drove the car into a corral but there were so many stumps in the corral I did some serious damage to the underneath.

When she had that accident in Williams Lake and rolled her truck I got a call from the hospital because she had a neighbour's dog in the back and it had got thrown out. She was so upset about the dog she asked me to go and look for it. It was Christmas Day and I was in the middle of cooking a turkey, but I went out there and found the dog. It was a great big thing, a Great Dane or something. I took it right into the hospital so that she would know not to worry about it. She was amazing. Her head was twice normal size and she was having the stitches put in while she was talking to me but all she was concerned about was the dog.

My son Ted and I went out there [Ginty Creek] when

her ashes were scattered by the little creek that runs through there. There used to be a little cross near one of the log cabins.

You had to admire her. She was cantankerous and always feuding with neighbours but she was always cheerful and loved animals. It would be nice to think that someone wrote something good about her.

—Libbie Abbott

ACKNOWLEDGEMENTS

Thanks as always to Rosemary and Dave Neads, my forever wilderness neighbours. It is a change to write about a place that is less remote than theirs!

Thanks also to John Macdonald who provided background information about the Dester family, and Sage Birchwater who suggested other contacts. The late Mildred Baines generously shared documents pertaining to Ginty, and some letters that Ginty had written to Mildred's family.

This book would not have been half so interesting without the wonderful reminiscences of Libbie Abbott, Joe Cortese, Elaine Dester, Karen Dester, Jeanie Fell, Jim Fell, Sandi Giovanelli, Ken Jansen, Deborah Kannegeiser, Joanne Kirby, Leslie Lamb, Louise Moxon, Lloyd Norton, Rhonda Nygaard, Jan Petrie, Lynne Rettburg and Hattie Thompson.

And last but not least, thanks to Alan and Elizabeth Bell for the use of their come-along—again.

ABOUT THE AUTHOR

Chris Czajkowski grew up in England, travelled the world with a backpack for a decade, and arrived in Canada in 1979. Three years later she was building her first off-road cabin in the wilderness, about 150 kilometres inland from Bella Coola. In 1988 she moved to a higher location on a fly-in lake where she built three more cabins and created the Nuk Tessli Alpine Experience, an ecotourism business catering to hikers and naturalists. She has written ten books about her nearly thirty years of wilderness living.

In 2006 Czajkowski bought a derelict homestead at Ginty Creek, not too far from the mountain resort but with rough road access. In 2012 she sold her Nuk Tessli business, making Ginty Creek her full-time residence.

Ginty Creek is still quite remote, being three and a half hours' drive from the nearest bank, traffic light, supermarket and cellphone tower. It is ideally located for Czajkowski to pursue her love of wilderness and the natural world. She has several more books in the works. For more information on her books and artwork, and an update of her adventures, visit her blog:

www.wildernessdweller.ca

Martin Weinhold photo

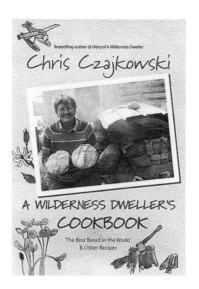

A MOUNTAIN YEAR
NATURE DIARY OF A WILDERNESS DWELLER

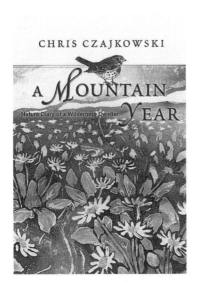

CHRIS CZAJKOWSKI

In 1988, Czajkowski walked into British Columbia's Central Coast Mountains to build a homestead, a business and a life. In this illustrated journal, Czajkowski intimately describes the splendour of seasonal transformation with her trademark expressiveness; each day brings new obstacles and surprising revelations.

ISBN 978-1-55017-441-0 / hardcover / colour art & illustrations / 6.5" x 9.5" / 184 pp / Oct. 2008

WILDFIRE IN THE WILDERNESS

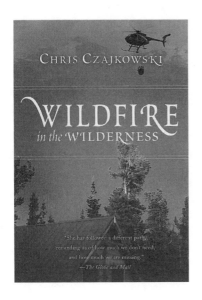

Czajkowski shares stories of shimmering mountain peaks, roaring snow-fed creeks, bears, eagles and monstrous storms; and tales of her dogs. The book culminates in a white-knuckle account of the all-too-close Lonesome Lake fire of 2004, from its infancy as a lightning strike reported in nearby Tweedsmuir Provincial Park, to Czajkowski's realization that her first wilderness cabin had been consumed by fire, and the dreaded moment when she was ordered by radiophone to evacuate everyone from the area.

ISBN 978-1-55017-375-8 / paperback / b&w illustrations / 6" x 9" / 224 pp / Aug. 2006

DIARY OF A WILDERNESS DWELLER

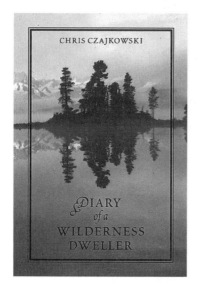

In the late 1980s, Czajkowski left her truck at the end of a logging road 300 kilometres north of Vancouver and hiked for two days on unmarked wilderness trails to the site of what would become her home. This is her account of building three log cabins, an eco-tourism business and a life beside an unnamed lake 5,000 feet high in the Coast Range mountains.

ISBN 978-1-55017-357-4 / paperback / b&w Illustrations / 6" x 9" / 209 pp / Sept. 2005

SNOWSHOES AND SPOTTED DICK
LETTERS FROM A WILDERNESS DWELLER

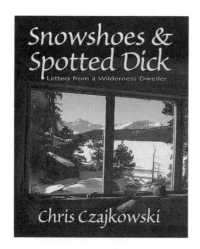

Czajkowski builds her fourth cabin in the wilderness with hand tools, two chainsaws, an Alaskan Mill and the help of Nick Berwain, a young German who corresponds with Czajkowski long after his return home. In her letters to Berwain, Czajkowski details how she breaks trails by snowshoe with her two pack dogs, encounters grizzly bears, builds a custom stone oven and learns how to use it to bake bread—and spotted dick, a traditional English steamed pudding. The letters also chronicle Czajkowski's challenges and triumphs as she tries to finish her cabin.

ISBN 978-1-55017-279-9 / paperback / b&w photos and illustrations / 6.5" x 8" / 304 pp / Mar. 2003